Critical Perspectives in American and African Literature

with Special Reference to Ayn Rand and Chinua Achebe

Critical Perspectives in American and African Literature

with Special Reference to Ayn Rand and Chinua Achebe

Hyacinth Pink

CWP

Central West Publishing

This edition has been published by Central West Publishing, Australia

For more information about the books published by Central West Publishing, please visit https://centralwestpublishing.com

A catalogue record for this book is available from the National Library of Australia

ISBN (print): 978-1-925823-20-2
ISBN (ebook): 978-1-925823-35-6

About the Author

Hyacinth Pink, a professor by day and a writer by night, presently heads the Department of English at the Kumaraguru College of Technology, Coimbatore, India. Hyacinth Pink carried out her research at the M.Phil. and doctoral level at Bharathidasan University, specializing in comparative literature. One of the global experts in English language and literature, she is multi-skilled and has more than three decades of teaching-learning experience in journalism and mass communication, ELT, women's studies, creative writing, etc. She is a poet with more than a hundred published poems to her credit. She is the author of 8 technical creative language books and a book on 'literary criticism'. Dr. Pink was awarded the prestigious Dr. Radhakrishnan Gold Medal on Teacher's Day in 2016, for her contribution to research and innovation.

Contents

Preface

The problem of human isolation can be studied in the abstract as philosophers do or with reference to the changing social and psychological climate as sociologists do. It is not my intention to make an in-depth study into philosophy, sociology or psychology. My objective is implied in the title of this book. It is a study of the theme of the individual versus society in the fiction of Ayn Rand, the American novelist and Chinua Achebe, the African novelist.

I have been honestly puzzled by the statement, assumptions and implications of what the individual versus society meant. I often wondered who was the more successful, the individual who set his own standards and ignored society or the conformist, who merely abided by the terms set down by a vague identity termed 'society.'

Down the ages, one observes that those who took steps down new roads were individuals. Prometheus stole fire from the Gods and was probably burnt at the stake he had taught his brothers to light. The first man who invented the wheel was probably torn at the rack he had taught his brothers to build. A Jesus Christ was crucified, a St. Joan burnt alive, a Mahatma assassinated. Their goals might have been different. But a common current flowed through all of them-that theirs was the first step, the road new, the vision unborrowed. It is the first man, the 'unsubmissive', who stands in the prologue of every legend mankind has recorded about its beginning. There was no such concept as a collective brain or stomach. Yet every man feared and lived in conscious awareness of this abstraction –society!

Deeply interested in this theme as a necessary subject for living on this earth, I decided to explore the argument:

Whether the sphere of moral and imaginative values by which an individual functions in society, is in fact autonomous or related to society.

And so I chose two authors who supported primarily the contrary concepts of the hypothesis: Ayn Rand, the American novelist-philosopher and champion of rugged individualism; and Chinua Achebe, the Nigerian novelist and champion of the collective consciousness.

The fiction of both acclaimed writers present man in a multiplicity of relationships with his fellow human beings. These writers reveal what happens when the cords that bind man with the realities external to himself are severed and he is set adrift. .In the case of Ayn Rand, individualism strengthens the protagonists and the parasitical society is made to realise its helplessness without these individual creators. The concept of individualism is depicted as ultimately triumphant. But in Chinua Achebe's works, the individuals who are seen emerging as autonomous individuals, meet with failure as this well-knit, peaceful Ibo community does not loosen its hold on the individual.

This perhaps justifies the present study which crosses all man made boundaries thus 'looking at Literature not in their separateness but in their inter-relatedness' as Dr. Chellapan observes in his article ' Literature Without Walls.' The comparison of these two literatures is done more on a contrastive basis , yet with an eye on 'the unity underlying the different ways under which the human spirit has sought expression creatively under different cultural patterns, The works are comparable because of their affinity in genre, theme and language.

The concept is analysed mainly from the point of view of the major protagonists, the chief strivers. Ayn Rand's individuals approach the heroic in their determination to go to it alone, like the Kira Argounovas, Howard Roark's and John Galts; Chinua Achebe's individuals wither away in silence in the beginning after having fought a losing battle like the Okonkwos and the Ezeulus, but gradually the individuals emerge leaving the clutches of a glorious past behind them and loose themselves in the Western world. While Rand's individuals bear the badge of triumph, Achebe's individuals to a certain extent suffer a taken of defeat. But unlike Rand, Achebe is the spokesman for a positive kind of individual creativity for a healthy society.

The book has been divided into three Phases. Each Phase has been serrated into three sections. The first section explores the argument from the Randian perspective, the second from the point of view of Chinua Achebe and in the third section, both Rand and Achebe's perspective on the theme is compared and contrasted, highlighting the growth and development of each phase.

Viewed as a whole, the writing of the two novelists falls into a pattern of search and discovery. There is a progression from the tortured realization to alienation to an acceptance of it; from the impotent striving of the autonomous individuals to the fruitful loneliness of the creator.

My goal is to contribute this book to research resources rather than engage in polemics. But I must admit there are bound to be certain lapses and limitations in this study because there has been a dearth of secondary sources on Ayn Rand. A review of the literature and criticism done so far reveals that most of the criticism that exists in on Rand's Philosophy - Objectivism; and so I had to argue most of the points stated in this book supported mostly by textual data.

I

Introduction

The fictional form itself as a literary genre has undergone considerable changes during the last two hundred years, replacing the classical world with a subjective and individualistic one. The rise of individualism as a global phenomenon and the awakening of communal and traditional relationships have in the course of history fostered the kind of private egocentric life one finds in the heroes of the eighteenth century novels. In Western Europe, the spreading of social cohesions was undermined by the individualistic pattern of thinking and life, and new modes of personal relationships eventually developed. Fictional narrative gradually evolved as the principal technique for capturing the intricacies of the individual consciousness. Thus, in The Rise of the Novel, Ian Watt argues, while the novel as a literary form took root, simultaneously private experience emerged as socially significant (Watt 1967:53). Gradually, the novel form itself reflected this development, moving from a neutral omniscient narrative to the point of view novel, and later to the much more subjectively centred "stream of consciousness novel" (Ibidem).

Bhalla, quoting Amarjit Singh in "Self-definition" as a moral concern in The Twentieth Century American Novel observes that the new society in America started taking shape in the beginning of this century, through a technological revolution, the seeds of which were sown from centuries ago in renaissant Europe. America, as a culture, has been part of the European Reneissance and until the advent of the twentieth century, it has always been on the receiving end (Bhalla 1981:iv). But the centre of gravity shifted in the beginning of this century, and during and before the First World War, America became the home of new technology, and her literature burst upon the world with tremendous force and energy. The American modernist writer broke away from the restraint of his own society and started articulating his own experience in terms of his own independent individuality. Young American writers became part of an international movement and many artists went away to live in Paris to imbibe the new culture and fight American puritanism. The new modernist writer tried to dispense with the old consciousness of absolute ideas and created new modernist works of art. This brought in its wake (as Ramachandra Rao observes in The American Fictional Hero), "an acute self-consciousness and a sense of terror born of uncertainty, and indignity of modern existence" (Rao 1979:vii), a condition created by the break-up of small village community and family. The anti-social organization, the aloneness and the concomitant boredom, are all aspects of modern life, which are portrayed by a modernist writer. The basic emotion is fear and the basic urge is escape. But the struggle of the modern writer is to find a way out of this contemporary confusion, and to achieve a psychic stability, by creating myths which can subsume new realities.

"The American novel was born", according to Richard Chase, Bhalla observes in The Twentieth Century American Novel "out of a culture of contradiction". Its genesis, according to him, lies in "the aesthetic possibilities of radical forms of alienation, contradiction and disorder (Bhalla 1981:ix). D. H. Lawrence discovers contradiction in the 'duplicacy' of the American literary mind because of a basic opposition between the 'puritan consciousness' and the 'native spirit of the place'. The spirit of the American continent (as Olga. W. Vickery observes in Language as Theme and Technique in Modern American Fiction) has been reckoned with by the American imagination as the terrifying and mysterious theme of the 'frontier' in American fiction. The guilt prone American self-underwent another baptism of terror realizing its limited capacity to cope with the physical and spiritual demands of his new homeland (Vickery 1970:179).

There is a sort of continuity in the tradition of the American novel though the context has changed, observes Frank Kermode in Continuities. The new technology, the mechanical world wars and the fear of survival has not only accentuated the old terror and made it a perpetual nightmare but also made it universal - a condition of existence for all men all over the globe in the twentieth century. The American novel has acquired a new immediacy and relevance not only for the American but also for all those who are interested in contemporary life and art (Kermode 1968:223-224).

The need for the transmutation of the American self was first realized by Henry James. Frank D. Mc Connel joins issues with this school of thought in his recent book, Four Post War American Novelists: Bellow, Mailer, Barth and Pynchon and asserts that with the advent of Hemingway, Fitzgerald and Faulkner, "the big three of the twenties" the American novel enters the modernist phase (Mc Connel 1977:xii-xiii). It is the war and its terror, as a reality and as a metaphor, outside and deep down in the human psyche, which provides the warp and woof to their novels. Hugh Kenner tells us in A Homemade World: The American Modernist Writers that in the thirties, the war assumes ideological and psychological shape and the novel becomes Marxian and naturalistic though Malcolm Cowley thinks that the hard realistic surface of the novels of the thirties should not obscure the idealistic core. According to him, the novelist creates Biblical myths in contemporary terms to find solutions to urgent social problems. The novelist of the twenties continues writing but the social conflict assumes greater importance now and as the clouds of another war darken the absurdity and surrealism, indicating another psychic shift (Kenner 1975:xii). The sense of insecurity and terror, disintegration and disillusionment now become accentuated still further, and survival assumes a more sophisticated and complex form. Man, in the contemporary world is now worried about achieving some sort of psychic steadiness in order to exist in a social set up. The old organic structure, which had already been undermined by the modernist novel, now gives way to a symbiotic, relativistic, open-ended and elastic form. Not that the symbolistic or dialectic patterns are not in vogue, but now the artist chooses whatever suits his theme more freely without caring for convention.

Ihab Hassan, in his book Contemporary American Literature rightly pinpoints the following as the most important features of the post-modern novel:

> *Survival appears indeed both the secret and paramount obsession of contemporary man.*

In America particularly where change changes at a dizzy rate, man rushes even faster, questions do not only concern the Doomsday Bomb but memories of holocausts from Auschwitz to Hiroshima, a succession of wars from Korea to Vietnam, the earth exploding in numbers, ravages to natural environment, renewed awareness of poverty in America, the discriminations of race and sex, political protests of every kind (Hassan 1973:2,3).

All these perpetuate a mood of crises that no writer can entirely ignore. Human privacy is invaded, as the media of control and of communication exchange their functions, as computers at once ease and complicate the pattern of social existence. Increasingly the public realm seems ruled by a variety of fantasies, instantaneous, comical and dreadful. For the individual, violence, nihilism, offer no genuine alternatives to the surrealism of mass society and the super state. This experience shared abroad, deepens the affinities between American and European literature, between nations witnessing the strange paradox of a world extensively homogenized yet intensely fragmented. Yet despite the culture of the post war era, curiously violent and hedonistic, angry and apathetic, the American writer makes a place for his imagination in it, which is the second pre-occupation of the artist.

The greatest problem of our time has been that war psychosis has outlived the war. It has become permanent and universal. American preeminence after the second world war created cold war abroad and conformism at home. This conformism threw up a counter culture in the 1950's. Philip Roth in his article, "Writing American Fiction" says that this leads us to the third most important preoccupation of the artist, his search for the authentic voice. All artists are now suspicious of the voice of the establishment, for invariably it seems to be opposed to the stirrings of the individual soul. The quest for authenticity is ultimately linguistic namely the search for the true word. This becomes a measure of the individual's affirmation of life in the face of a destructive and pervasive nihilism. The contemporary artist struggles to establish his own linguistic and stylistic dominion - his own artistic space (Roth 1977:35).

These three quests of the contemporary writer, that is, quest for survival, identity and authenticity are in line with intellectual movements in other fields of enquiry. The critics have interpreted the general drift of Western Culture in modern ways. According to Kermode, 'the early modernists like Eliot, Joyce, Yeats, Hemingway, Fitzgerald and Faulkner felt that the debacle of World War I has signalled an end of the self-assured creativity of the Western civilization" (Kermode 1968:223-224). They produced different visions and versions of the 'Wasteland' and found an antidote of universal decay in visions involving a retreat to myth and "traditional" faith. But the second generation of modernists represented by writers like Jean Jenet in France and William Burroughs in America represent a complete and even joyful acceptance of the fact of apocalypse. Kermode's argument is supported by other enthusiastic critics like Susan Sontag, George Steiner and Richard Poirier. Sontag calls the new approach "style of the radical will", Steilner calls it the "Pythagorean genre" in fiction and Piorier designates it as the art of "performing self" (Ibidem). But they more or less agree with the basic premise. They think that new fiction is moving towards a radical redefinition of human personality and human freedom. The old restrictions that society applies to blind an individual will, now vanish and man is liberated into a free, guiltless celebration of the life of the senses, of unselfconscious delight unencumbered by the weight of the rationalistic critical spirit.

It is difficult of place Ayn Rand into any specific school or tradition as she herself declares in her early notes, that she belongs to no tradition, but may perhaps stand at the beginning of one. Quoting Rand, Barbara Branden says in The Passion of Ayn Rand: "I know I am challenging the culture and tradition of two and a half thousand years" (Branden 1986:56). Rand's life was the material for her fiction. Rand began her novelistic career in the early thirties. Her first novel We The Living set in Soviet Russia was published in 1933, and her last novel Atlas shrugged in 1957. Rand, an emigrant from Russia had a Russian taste for long prophetic fiction. She was born on Feb. 2nd, 1905 as Alice Rosenbaun, to an affluent Jewish family in St. Petersburg, Russia. It was the time when the Revolution was sweeping the impoverished countryside. Life changed drastically for Rand when her father's business was nationalised by the Communist government. The spiritual construction of the Communist philosophy, that people should Live for the State, was worse than the material deprivations. The proper basis for government, according to Rand, was an individual's right to life, liberty and the pursuit of happiness. Since America was founded upon these principles, Rand decided to live in America, the only country where she could flourish as a writer and philosopher. Rand had always thought of America as the land of her dreams.

Rand was the natural resource of her fiction. In the "Introduction" to The Passion of Ayn Fand. Barbara Branden writes: Her person encompassed the grandeur of the heroes of her novels, their iron determination, their vast powers of intellect and imagination, their impassioned pursuit of their courage, their pride, and their impassioned pursuit of their courage, their pride, and their love of life-as well as the terrors, the self-doubts, the lack of emotional balance, the private agonies that are so alien to an Ayn Rand hero. Her virtues were larger than life – so were her short comings (Branden 1986:i).

Not many in this century have been so admired and so savagely attacked. She is viewed as goddess, as a seminal genius and an ominously dangerous corrupter of the young, as the mightiest of voices of reason, and the destroyer of traditional values, as the espouser of joy and the exponent of mindless greed, as the great defender of freedom and the introducer of malevolent values into the main stream of American thought (Ibidem:16).

Despite the furore her ideas have generated, despite the fact that they fill the pages of thirteen books, despite the fact that her philosophy has had a powerful and still accelerating influence on American culture, little is known about Ayn Rand, the human being; and still less about Ayn Rand, the woman. Her public and professional activities took place on a lighted stage; her private life was lived back stage, curtained from view. But Rand was one of the most remarkable and complex individuals of the time. Those who worship Rand and those who damn her, do her the same disservice; they make her unreal and they deny her humanity. But there was something infinitely more fascinating and infinitely more valuable than either goddess or sinner. She was a human being. She lived, she loved, she fought her battles, and she knew triumph and defeat. The scale was epic; the principle is inherent in human existence.

Rand was greatly influenced by her father, "a silent, self-made man with firm convictions, who considered ideas and the spread of ideas as the most important thing in life" (Ibidem:63). Franz Rosenbaun's strongest issue was individualism. He was committed to reason, but unfortunately not by stated conviction. Rand's relationship with her mother was of a pitched battle.

I disliked her quite a lot. We really didn't get along. She was my exact opposite. She was by principle and basic style, by sense of life, extremely social, she was not really interested in ideas, but in the social aspect. Our clashes in childhood were that I was anti-social (Ibidem:75).

Rand, in her later writings, was to exemplify this contempt for the social as a constantly recurrent theme. Lillian Rearden, the major female villain in Atlas Shrugged is characterized as someone whose emptiness of spirit is exemplified by her passion for social interaction, for parties, for being the centre of a crowd of people.

In the Rosenbaun's home, religion had little significance. While Franz Rosenbaum was non-religious, Anna Rosenbaum was religious in an emotional, tradition way, not out of conviction, more out of devotion to the religion of her own mother. She gave her children no religious training. Rand never denied she was Jewish, but in later years she declared herself to be a committed atheist for two reasons. Leonard Peikoff, quoting Rand, in The Early Ayn Rand: A Selection from her Unpublished Fiction, writes:

i) I decided to be an atheist. I had decided the concept of God is degrading to men. Since they say god is perfect, then man is low and imperfect and there is something about him which is wrong.

ii) …. Since no proof of the existence of God exists, the concept is rationally an untenable invention. It was all decided in one day (Peikoff 1984:36).

The essence of Rand's present belief is there. It focuses the issue of reason versus mysticism. She was not, a militant atheist. The belief in God, seemed to her so patiently irrational, that it did not deserve to be fought. It was not the concept of God that she would battle throughout her life, it was what she saw as its source, its wider meaning: the rejection of reason. It was to the battle of reason, the tool and the lorry of the heroic man that she would dedicate her life. Rand would contend throughout her life that man's mind, his reasoning faculty, his power to grasp logical connections is his basic tool of survival: and mysticism, the anti-rational, the anti-logical as the instrument of death. To Rand, the physical manifestation of the power of man's mind is Technology, a phenomenon which fascinated her even as a child.

Intelligence was the quality she most admired, and she responded to it with the greatest pleasure and respect. In her earliest childhood, her intellectual precocity was recognized and admired by those around. She asked the right questions and believed that a mind needs the stimulation of its equals. She placed on intelligence what can be termed a 'moral' value. Intelligence and virtue were to become inextricably linked in her mind and her emotions. There she saw no unusual intelligence, nor the capacity for dedicated productive work that she believed to be its consequence. She saw no value that meant anything to her in personal terms. This was the beginning of a series of value clashes with the people around her, that was to mark the whole of her life. Rand felt an angry defiance that was to characterize her attitude towards all of her values. "I know but they don't. This is mine. It's not theirs" (Ibidem:149). As a child and an adult, Rand worshipped joy. Rand believed that pain and suffering were meaningless aberrations, never a normal part of life, never to be considered important. Thus, man's happiness as the goal and purpose of his life, became a fundamental theme in her writings, and despite the pain and bitterness that her life contained, it became a theme she struggled to keep alive in her life contained, it became a theme she struggled to keep alive in her life contained, it became a theme she struggled to keep alive in her psychology. In Atlas Shrugged, Rand's last novel, the first words that Dagny Taggart, the novel's heroine speaks to John Galt, the man she has waited all her life to meet are: "We never had to take any of it (pain and suffering) seriously, did we?" "No, we never had to", answers Galt (AS, p.66).

Rand had a passionate concern for spiritual consistency. This was also a significant element in alienating Rand from people and the world around her. The battle between good and evil was the major element she saw in literature. It later drew her to such disparate literary figures as Victor Hugo and Mickey Spillane; it caused her to see the world as a giant battle field in which her personal god and devil were locked in endless conflict. There was good in the world and there was evil, one had to choose sides in the battle, and one had as writer and as human being, to enlist one's energies and one's life on the sides of the good. As Rand matured, the detective and the jewel thief became opposing philosophical ideas, but the principle remained the same.

Leafing through a boy's magazine of adventurous stories Rand came across one entitled, 'The Mysterious Valley' a heroic French detective in pursuit of a dangerous jewel thief. "It was a love affair for me from the first instalment. That expression which I carried thereafter of the detective who overcame all the obstacles in pursuit of his goal and in the end was triumphant began with the story" (Branden 1986:153). One can observe in all her novels that the spirit of Cyrus intelligence, independence, courage, the heroic became the spirit of all the fictional characters she would create. The name 'Kira' which she chose for her first novel We The Living is the Russian feminine of 'Cyrus' and so also Howard Roark in the Fountainhead, John Galt, Hank Rearden and Franciso D'Anconia in Atlas Shrugged. As an adult, she translated Cyrus's courage into intellectual terms, but the basic nature of the heroic terms was never to alter.

When one looks at the life of Ayn Rand, one must wonder if the dogmatic absolutism of her certainty, the blinding conviction of her own rectitude and her special place in the world, the callousness of her intolerance for opinions that were not hers, the unwavering assurance that she was alone to know the truth and that others must seek it from her, the savage innocence of her personality, was not the fuel required for the height of achievement she attained.

Just as when one looks at history's great achievers, one so often encounters the desperate loneliness and alienation which is perhaps the emotional price paid by men and women who see further than their brothers; so, one also encounters these qualities in Ayn Rand. And one must wonder if they are not precisely the qualities that make possible the courage and uncompromising dedication of those who forge new paths through the unknown, enduring and persevering, shouting defiance at the enormity of the opposition which follows them at every step of their lonely journey, and adding new glories to our world. A lesser conviction would never have made it possible.

In contrast to those who have seen in the economic crises of the twentieth century, the waste of Capitalism, Rand, obsessed with the fear of collectivist association, has seen universal salvation possible only through even more intensive laissez-faire Capitalism. While providing an ever-increasing audience with the soothing rationalization of self-primacy, all of Rand's works, expose the sharpness of the familiar line drawn between 'self' and other'; and thus, she challenges us to recognize that the society which does not encourage individualism invites a tyranny of bland mediocrity. To prove her case, Rand offers us an extreme individualist hero in auto fetishistic armour, but whose preoccupation, unlike that of Narcissus, actually strengthens him. Rand understandably fears centralized community, which robs the individual members of their independence and gives them, in exchange, rules, orders, and demands of conformity. Rand's personal experiences in Russia justifies her attack on dictatorial collectivism.

Any Rand writing in an age of crisis during the second world war finds (as Leonard Peikoff observes in The Ominous Parallels) that "America Reverses Direction". America, as conceived by the Founding Fathers, lasted only about a century. There were contradictions and government controls of various kinds from the beginning. Irving Kristol and other businessmen were social servants and should administer their 'social surpluses for the community. Henry Demarest Lloyd, a leader of the antitrust movement named, in his article, "The New Conscience" in the **North American Review**, the base of this new approach to government. "The principles of self-interest", he said "is one of the historic mistakes of humanity"; what America needs is a system" in which no man will have a right to do with his own what he will, but only a right to do what is right" (Lloyd 1888:342).

America's capitalistic system breaks down and Rand fears that collectivism will harmonize with the American myth of rugged individualism and her fiction assumed a prophetic air. Arthur A. Ekirch, Jr., in his book **Progressivism in America,** quotes Charles R. Van Hise, President of the University of Wisconsin and a spokesman of the Progressive Movement in 1910: "He who thinks not of himself primarily, but of his race, and of its future, is the new patriot" (Ekrich 1974:151). President John F. Kennedy in his inaugural address of Jan. 20th, 1961 said: "My fellow Americans, ask not what your country can do for you, ask what you can do for your country" (Kennedy:1961). Irving Kristol, a neoconservative intellectual, 1972, writes: "Self-government, the basic principle of this republic, is inexorably being eroded in favour of self-seeking, self-indulgence, and just plain aggressive selfishness" (Kristol 1972:33).

Culturally and politically, World War I was the turning point. It marked the end of the individualist era throughout the West. The Americans yearned in 1920 to go 'back to normalcy' i.e. a return to a civilized world which respected man's rights and its consequences: international harmony, lasting peace, a rising standard of living, unobstructed freedom, self-confidence and hope for the future. Arthur. A. Ekirch, Jr., in **Progressivism in America,** tells us that America faced "the aftermath of global breakdown, the mushrooming of European dictatorships, the growing fear that the selfless crusade of 1917 had been a senseless slaughter, the growing claims of men's duty to their neighbour and the newer claim of America's duty to the world" (Ekirch 1974:151). In 1919, quoting Herbert Hoover, a then capitalist, Arthur Ekirch observes that Hoover rejected laissez-faire in favour of the progressive middle way between socialism and anarchism. "We are passing" he said, "from a period of extremely individualistic action into a period of associational activities" (Ekirch 1974:258-59). The New Dealers were more explicit than the Reformist Movement. "Whether we like it or not", sociologist Henry Pratt Fairchild wrote "The Great Economic Paradox" in **Harper's magazine** that "modern life has become so highly integrated, so inextricably socialized, so definitely organic that the very concept of the individual is becoming obsolete" (Fairchild 1932:64). The Great Depression was the result. If Americans were to reconstruct society properly, wrote John Dewey in "Antitrust Legislation" at the start of the Depression, it "would signify that we had entered constructively and voluntarily upon the road which Soviet Russia is traveling with so much attendant destruction and coercion" (Dewey 1968:350).

The Founding Fathers had conceived 'rights' as entitlements to act and to keep the products of one's actions, not as claims to the actions or products of others. 'Equality' in the original American view, meant the right of everyman to independence – to make his way and sustain his life by his own effort; and 'opportunity' in the American sense of the term meant freedom. The New Dealers rejected this approach as unfeeling and cruel. While President Roosevelt believed in his "Inaugural Address"- San Francisco Speech of 1932, it was important to think less about the producer and more about the consumers, Dewey taught a generation, that "the mind was not a private possession, but a social asset" (Roosevelt 1932:64). Hence, Rand believed that America was reaching a state of bankruptcy. In her first two novels, **We the Living** (1936) and **Anthem** (1938), Rand satirizes social realism and total collectivism with all its ultimate consequences and tries to combat that absolute lack of individuality. In her major novel **The Fountainhead** (1943) Rand explores the theme of "individualism versus collectivism not in politics, but in man's soul" (**TFH** vi) and also the psychological motivations and the basic premises that produce the character of an individualist or a collectivist. In her last and most challenging best seller of the times **Atlas Shrugged** (1957) Rand pursues the theme of "the role of the mind in man's existence" (VOS 16) and as corollary the exemplification of a new moral philosophy: the morality of rational self-interest.

Rand set forth the fundamentals of her philosophy, "a philosophy for the living on earth" in her non-fiction works such as **The Virtue of Selfishness: A New Concept of Egoism** (1964), **Capitalism: The Unknown Ideal** (1967) **For the New Intellectual** (1974) **Introduction to Objectivist Epistemology** (1979) and **Philosophy**: **Who needs it?** (1984) In all these books, Rand puts forth her philosophy of Objectivism – the philosophy that holds man's life as the standard of moral values and regards Altruism as incompatible with man's nature. Rand also discusses the problems of the times namely, the validation of egoism, the evils of self-sacrifice, the nature of government, individual rights, racism, the psychology of socialism and capitalism. Rand address any man who is willing to think and challenges the philosophic doctrines of the times that creates guilt, panic, despair, nihilism and boredom for man. Rand also deals with basic issues such as love, sex, morality, values, education, money, trade, censorship, and isolation, to prove that philosophy is a fundamental force in man's life and man needs it, as Leonard Peikoff says: "to think, to act, to live" (Peikoff 1984:8) here on this earth. In writing her non-fiction Rand realizes that "non-fiction is my natural way of functioning" (**FTNI**:vii).

Rand is a polemical writer and so has roused heated reaction from various sources. Blind adoration of her precepts has even led to the formation of a 'cult' posing the question: "Is Objectivism a Religion"? This section glances at some of the important criticism available on her life, work and philosophy. It also establishes the need for the present study. **Who is Ayn Rand** (1962) by her disciples Nathaniel Branden and Barbara Branden is a close biographical study. Albert Ellis in **"Is Objectivism a Religion** (1968) & William O'Neil in **With Charity Towards None** (1971) focus their attention on objectivism as a Religion and the contradictions and ambiguities in Rand's philosophy, respectively. **Answer to Ayn Rand: A Critique of the Philosophy of Objectivism** (1974), John W. Robbins points out that Objectivity is self contraordinary and can only result in hedonism and anarchy. While in **The Philosophical Though of Ayn Rand** (1984), Douglas B. Ramussen deals with Rand as a philosopher. Barbara Branden in her The Passion of Ayn Rand (1986), gives an authentic portrait of Rand as a person and a writer.

A range of articles on Ayn Rand are also available and these can be catalogued into four major divisions.

1) Articles that study Ayn Rand as an astounding phenomenon and highlight her appeal especially among young people of the middle class, and her impact on the female psyche. For instance, Nora Ephram's article on **The Fountainhead in the New York**

Times Book Review, and an article of Barbara Grizzesti Harrison, illustrate the two views respectively. Articles of this nature view Ayn Rand as a She- Messiah, who can hypnotize an audience.

2) Articles by Ayn Rand's detractors who are concerned with the potency of Rand's effects on young people in general – Bruce Cook, a Libertine and Catholic, for example, is afraid of what Rand's damaging views on charity and contempt for religion might do to youngsters. While Jeff Riggenback in "The Disowned Children of Ayn Rand", says that Ayn Rand's novels may instigate young people to rebel against elders and also damn establishments.
3) Articles that negatively criticise the growing number of Objectivists and followers of her philosophy. This includes Nora Sayre's article "The cult of Ayn Rand", Ellis's "Is Objectivism a Religion?" and Nathaniel Branden's "Break Free". In the later, the author acknowledges his role in perpetuating the Ayn Rand mystique of intellectual repressiveness that pervades the Objectivist movement.
4) Specific and general studies on Rand's works and ideas. There are only few professional journals that treat Rand's books from a pedagogical perspective. This includes the article "**Anthem**: A Book for all Reasons" which suggests sixteen student projects for junior college readers. "Ayn Rand and Feminism - An Unlikely Alliance" recommends **Atlas Shrugged** as a book which defines feminist premises, while Philip Gorden's "The Extroflective Hero: A look at Ayn Rand" is a psychological study (which uses F.S. Perl's Ego, Hunger, Aggression as the basis for a generally negative analysis of the egoism of Rand's heroes.

Rand's anti-collectivism and defense of Capitalism have influenced politicians in & outside America. Her ideas are seen as catalysts for further innovation in Libertine thinking. While writers like Stephen E. Taylor have questioned her theories and basic tenets, a few like Kenneth J. Smith and Hazel Barnes have found similarities between Rand's ideas and the principal hypothesis of Existentialism.

Thus, from the above review of Ayn Rand's fictional, non-fictional and critical articles, it is evident that most of the existing studies on Rand have focussed mainly on her philosophy – Objectivism. Moreover, her work has so far not been compared with other writers. A rare attempt is her made to evaluate the works of Ayn Rand, the American Novelist, and a champion of 'Individualism', with Chinua Achebe, the Nigerian Novelist, and a champion of the Collective Consciousness.

The 'new voice' coming from Africa, speaking of the African in a world language was heard as far back as the eighteenth century. Literature from Africa holds great interest and fascination for people all over the globe for various reasons. Once considered an impenetrable mystery, unexplored and unrelegated as Eustace Palmer in his book, **An Introduction to the African Novel** tells us, the Continent has lately come to make significant contributions in creative writing and is no more the Conradian "Heart of darkness', or the strange abode of Cannibalic rites and jungle drums. It can rightly boast of the heritage of a rich oral tradition, extending over centuries, besides the tangible body of works published during the middle of the present century. In fact, the emergence of a very large corpus of African Novels both in English and French, has been acclaimed generally as one of the most interesting literary developments of the last thirty years (Palmer 1977:10).

There was a time when the literary image of Africa was created by non-African writers. Some of these writers were objective and sympathetic in their treatment of the African experience. Some used Africa as a kind of a backdrop, where the white man was able to work out his neuroses in stock patterns; still other non-African writers ruthlessly depicted Africa in primitive patterns which symbolically reflect the colonial rape that the Continent itself was physically undergoing. This literary distortion of Africa has also come to an end. In a period of barely twenty-five years, the situation has entirely changed. It is not so easy for the European or the American to write about Africa any more now that the African novelist has appeared on the scene. The African novel is both very young and very old; maturity was forced upon it just as African societies were going through the birth pangs of old age within a few years after they gained independence. What the Western novel became in a leisurely course of three hundred years; the African novel was forced to become, in a mere generation and a half.

The African novel was born in the 1950's which saw the flowering of African writers in English with Amos Tutuola's **Palm Wine Drunkard** (1852), which was the first to immediately gain international reputation. The second major novel, radically dissimilar in theme from Tutuola was Cyprian Ekwensi's **People of the City** (1954). The first Nigerian writer to transmute successfully the conventions of the novel as an art form into African Literature was Chinua Achebe. His **Things Fall Apart** (1958) was the first solid achievement whose explicit influence on subsequent novelists could easily be detected. The evocation of the tribal Society acquired an added dimension in the hands of this competent craftsman, with the publication of this remarkable work. Later came **No Longer at Ease** (1960) **Arrow of God** (1966) **A man of the People**

(1966) and **Anthills of the Savannahs** (1987) where he attempts to satirize the political corruptions of Post – Independent Nigeria. The variety of life in Africa is echoed in the multiplicity of approaches in the novels. A novelist usually needs a base, a point of view, an understanding, and this is not always easy to achieve in an Africa shifting from rural to urban conditions, from farming to industry, from communal values to individualism and from oral to written concepts of communication. These shifts and the tensions imposed by them are the stuff their literature is made up of.

African novelists deal with themes varying from folk culture to self-conscious literary tradition engendered in the third world. Colonialism vanishes, to be replaced by other forms of government, with corruption and turbulent armed struggle, hindering the full achievement of the Continent's immediate potential in many areas. The works of Amos Tutuola, Chinua Achebe, Wole Soyinka, James Ngugi, Camare Laye, Lenrie Peters, and Ayi Kwei Armah are amongst those well-known outside as well as inside Africa. These writings have vigour of language and that language communicates the cultural, social and racial ideas, the nuances of an expanding consciousness with all its sense of excitement and of tragedy, with all its conscious blending of the old and the new.

Much of Achebe's works are the consequences of his own personal life experience. Chinua Achebe, the son of a catechist for the Church Missionary Society, resettled at his ancestral home, Ogidi. He had his primary education at the Society School and his first lessons were in Ibo.

Achebe learnt English quite early and at fourteen, was one of the few boys selected for the Government College at the Umuafia a very considerable distinction. At eighteen, he matriculated at the New University College, Ibadan, to study Medicine, then changed his subject to Literature, and as Arthur Ravenscroft in his book **Chinua Achebe** has observed: "his formal studies in English Literature would have been very similar to those of a British undergraduate" (Ravenscroft 1969:27). British education was in a sense, sacred to the generation who sent their children to the University. The children themselves (Robert Wren, in **Achebe's World : The Historical and Cultural Context of the Novels of Chinua of Achebe** observes), may have been less reverent but they know well that the University was the sole route to senior ranks of the civil service, which was being reluctantly but assuredly nigerianised in anticipation of self-rule (Wren 1980:1).

For Achebe the British Higher Education made available not the British past but much of the Nigerian past also. At some point during his studies at Ibadan, from 1948-1953, the future novelist began to correlate his sense of literature and his sense of Nigerian history and tradition. He recalled much of his home life; and encountered in the writings of novelists, anthropologists, colonial officers and missionaries, a Nigeria at once familiar and alien – like one's own image in a distorting mirror. A profound change took place, a change that was revealed in four stories that Achebe published as a student in **The University Herald**. These were reprinted in a larger collection entitled **Girls at War and Other Stories** (1972).

Achebe had become aware that he himself being a mission school boy and University educated, had lost his ancestral knowledge and did not understand his past well enough to perceive its innate dignity. This early condition of his, Achebe describes as 'a crisis of the soul' where everything alien was considered 'good' and everything local or native, 'inferior'. This process of Europeanisation exerts a pressure on all the young intellectuals of Achebe's generation. It is true that Achebe has minimized this effect in his own upbringing. Unlike Obi Okonkwo's parents in **No longer at Ease** who reject their past, Isaac, Achebe's father, seems to have spoken freely of it and was not unduly troubled 'was' and to some extent still 'is'. Continuing festivals recur, attitudes and philosophies persist, but not everything remains. Achebe had to use whatever resources he could. What the village had lost, he had to rediscover. "I didn't do any research as such", he told Dennis Duerden in Sept. 1965:

> *This is largely picked up ... this is the life that interested me, partly the life that I lived and the life that was lived around me .... Supported by what I heard in conversation. I was keen on listening to old people and what I learned from my father (An Interview with Achebe, p.64).*

Thus, Achebe belongs to the group of African writers who began writing out of an eagerness to prove their own identity. Convinced that Africa too has her vision, Chinua Achebe says in **Morning Yet on Creation Day**, that "Americans have their vision; we have ours; we do not claim that our is superior; we only ask to keep it" (Achebe 1970:61).

Achebe's belief that the voice of Africa should be heard, is born out of his conviction, as G. D. Killiam observes in Exile and Tradition: **Studies in African and Caribbean Literature** : "Africa is not a geographical expression, it is also a metaphysical landscape; it is in fact a view of the world and of the whole cosmos" (Killiam 1976:2). Like his contemporaries Amos Tutuola and Camara Laye, Chinua Achebe began writing during the colonial encounter. Adrian Roscoe, in **Mother is Gold : A Study in West African Literature** observes that they show "an eagerness to sink a tap root into the soil of their own artistic tradition" (Roscoe 1971:11), convinced of the truth of the African proverb which Claude Wauthier quotes in **The Literature and Thought of Modern Africa** "a tree can grow by sinking its root into nourishing soil" (Wauthier 1978:66).

Chinua Achebe believes that art should always be in the service of society. So, he writes as a literary historian. The writer has to be socially relevant and be "the voice of vision in his own time" (Ibidem:69). Thus, Achebe writes "out of an African experience and a commitment to an African destiny" (Ibidem: 72). The novels therefore speak of a certain place, and "evolve out of the necessities of its history "past and current and the aspirations and destiny of its people" (Ibidem:74).

Belonging to the first generation of Nigerian novelists who are committed to the colonial struggle, its aftermath and Africa's rehabilitation, Achebe returns to the past in his novels – a past which was wiped out by two important incidents – colonialism and the slave trade. Roscoe, quoting Achebe observes that "no thinking African can escape the pain of these two important incidents as it is the wound in our soul" (Roscoe 1971:133). So Achebe recreates the simplicity, charm and significance of the traditional Ibo life, the devastating, effect of colonialism on this rich culture and the cultural neurosis that set in as a consequence. The five novels analysed in a thematic order, are a rolling survey of the history of Nigeria from 1850 to the early twentieth century. Achebe's deep and abiding interest in history is not a reverence for a lifeless subject of remote antiquity, but "an accumulation of human achievements, a testimony of the triumph of human ingenuity and will, reaching down ancestral roots" (Roscoe 1971:13). This detribalization, anxiety and the freezing of the old ceremonial order is traced out through the five novels. **Things Fall Apart** (1958) **No Longer at Ease** (1960), **Arrow of God** (1964), **A Man of the people** (1966) and **Anthills of the Savannah** (1987).

African fiction has five general subject areas, and though these areas did not appear in African fiction one after another, the basic situations within the societies did occur in this sequence, as the works of Chinua Achebe illustrate. When Achebe's own experiences and those of his society were essentially limited to traditional African life and the initial conflicts with western religion and colonialism, the novels which resulted could only be one such as **Things Fall Apart** and **Arrow of God**. After his society has undergone a more direct confrontation with western education and urbanizations, then only could Achebe write **No Longer at Ease**, illustrating, as it were, these conflicts with westernization. Then as

Achebe's society sped past independence and was confronted with the increasing problems of political and economic stability and these new problems became a part of the collective consciousness, a novel such as **A Man of the People** could appear. And about two decades later, contemplating on the solutions for the problems that affected his society, could he write his fifth novel **Anthills of the Savannah**. In this novel Achebe's increasing concern with an individual's life also appears. The theme of the subject matter of the novel becomes more inner rather than outer directed. The broadening experiences of the African writer constantly reflected the contemporary issues confronting African societies.

In the novels mentioned above, Achebe reflects upon the changes which have taken place in Ibo and by implication, Nigerian life, as a result of what he calls the 'chance encounter' (Killiam 1977:46), between Europe and Africa during the imperial colonial period. Achebe has also written a number of critical works on Africa and African writers. In his prose writings Achebe comments on the inheritance that African writers and society have received from the colonial period.

A vast ocean of criticism has been written on Achebe's fiction. Some of the most important and significant ones are mentioned below. **Chinua Achebe** (1969) by Arthur Ravenscroft is a critical comparison of Achebe's life and works with other Nigerian writers. In **Morning yet on Creation Day** (1975) Achebe illustrates the ethos of traditional Ibo society and discusses the role of the artist in his society. While David Carrol's **Chinua Achebe** (1980) gives a critical evaluation of Achebe's writings, **Achebe's World : The Historical and Cultural Context of the Novels of Chinua Achebe** (1981) by Robert Wren explores Achebe's novels in their historical context. **The Writings of Chinua Achebe** (1977) by G.D. Killiam shows the anthropological and sociological significance of Achebe's work, and Bernth Lindfor's **Critical Perspectives on Chinua Achebe** (1979) analyses how Achebe's works assist in the decolonization process of peoples who have suffered the trauma of foreign conquest. Yet another enlightening work is **African Writers on African Writing** (1978) by G.D. Killiam which also discusses the anthropological importance of writers like Amos Tutuola, Cyperian Ekwensi, James Ngugi, Wole Soyinka and Chinua Achebe. Most African writing is observed to be concerned exclusively with the reality of African life.

Achebe's prose writings reflect three essential and related concerns:

i) The legacy of Colonialism at both the individual and societal level.

ii) The fact of English as a language of national and international exchange.
iii) The obligations and responsibilities of the writer Achebe's prose, when considered with his fiction offers and assessment and an apology for his adoption of a world language, his choice of subject matter and his obligations as an African to his culture and his craft.

Glancing at his fictional and non-fictional works and the review of the criticism done so far, the researcher observes that though a variety of criticism has been done on Achebe, the proposal of comparing and contrasting the African novelist with an American novelist is an innovative adventure. For the first time in literary history, the work of Chinua Achebe is evaluated alongside the work of Ayn Rand, exploring the specific concept of "The Individual versus Society".

As a novelist, Achebe writes out of the necessity to help his society to regain its belief in itself. His word is a record of an ancient and deeply articulate culture and its gradual decay, as the materialistic outlook of an alien culture, slowly seeps into this once hallowed world of rich tradition and culture.

For the African intellectual and creative writer like Achebe the arrival of the colonizer on the continent had may repercussions. For example:

1) Disruption of the strong bonds of kinship which held the clan together.
2) Loss of identity for many elders as the traditional roles assigned to them gradually became irrelevant and this power was transferred to the Colonial administrator.
3) Economically, the land was grabbed and monopolized by the Colonizers.
4) The White missionary discussed tribal religious ideas and practises as 'heathen' 'pagan' – an attitude later condemned by leading African Nationals.
5) Socially, exchange of cultures qualified as 'civilizing process' or as Achebe statistically characterizes it, "the pacification of the primitive tribes of the lower Niger" (**TN** 46), led to sociocultural alienation and consequently a tragic protest and conflict was born.

But despite its deforming and ever stifling effects, colonialism has made for a certain dynamism in what were essentially static tribal societies. Time has come to move beyond the dualism of

1) Black versus White
2) Colonizer versus Colonised
3) Monotheism versus Polytheism

to a more carefully defined critical encounter.

In this study, the researcher attempts to show how the lives of the major characters develop from a primarily communal, tribal existence to a more western, individualistic one. The change along this dimension can best be traced through a study of the many-faceted interactions of a monotheistic, individually centred Christianity and a polytheistic socially oriented tribal religion. This process involves adjustments, denials, acceptances of each other's creeds and principles on the social as well as individual levels. Religion being a major force in the traditional communities that holds its members together, the slightest threat to its power and integrity paves the way for substantial changes in their very apprehension of life. It is this complex and subtle phenomenon symbolized by a few significant characters that one sees in Chinua Achebe's various novels.

J. Jahn Munty, in **An Outline of the New African Culture**, claims "that such as encounter is one primarily of Monotheism versus Polytheism" (Jahn 1961:58-59). It is almost incomprehensible here to have a formed distinction between the 'sacred' and the 'secular'. This lack of distinction is a key point of contrast with a more modern society. In such societies every human being belongs to the whole community. His life participates in rituals, beliefs, ceremonies, festivals of that community. Thus, deeply aware of the communal aspects of his very existence, no individual can think of detaching himself from the religion of his group:

> *For to do so is to be severed from his roots .... Therefore, to be without religion amounts to a self–excommunication from the entire life of society and African peoples do not know how to exist without religion (Mbiti 1967:1).*

Life is a profoundly religious phenomenon, with vague religious notions concretized in modes of worship: Magic, Totemism, Festishism and Ancestral worship. These symbolise the tribal power to reach out to the masses and hold them together as a solid whole. These manifestations merge into the texture of social life, assimilating every individual into its strong inescapable currents and leaves no space for individualism or aesthetic pursuits. Celebrations for a new born child, marriage and death are more social functions than a personal individual affair, because it is the interest and concern of the whole tribal community.

This socio-cultural conflict that existed and the gradual emergence of the autonomous individual, independent of the determining hold of the tribal community, gives rise to the growth of a whole new individualistically oriented structure: Socio – political as well as cultural. With the coming of Christianity, the emphasis is shifted from communal to personalized living supporting individual achievement. This symbolizes a positive dynamic future-oriented view: for example, progressive but corrupt new-found individualism and new-found humanity, sympathy for the down-trodden outcast victim, and cosmic oneness of the universe. It also symbolized a negative view: for example: selfishness, competition, materialism. Within such a world, personal realities of an individual world view are alien. It's evident that change will not be easy.

The planting of organized Christianity in Africa was a terrible exploitation politically, economically, socially, religiously. Claude Wauthier observes in **The Literature and Thought of Modern Africa:**

> *The Bible redeemed the African individual from the power of superstition, individuality, crushing tradition, witchcraft that makes not for progress. The same Bible is helping the African individual to reassert himself above colonial powers (Wauthier 1978:218).*

But three aspects resulted in the growth of individualism directly:

i) Increased formal educational facilities;
ii) Urbanisation;
iii) Independent church movements.

There was no stopping this new rhythm. Africa could not be the same anymore. Change was total and affected individuals, tribes and the whole nation. Socially, this was termed 'detribalization' at many levels:

i) Family level: Educated youth symbolized a new set of values, expectations, economic standards, cultural concerns and world view. Polygamy and female circumcision no longer existed.
ii) Urbanization: significant features of modern Africa - quest of new pastures.

Urbanization brought in new problems: e.g. economic imbalance, unemployment, broken families, social evils and desire for new ethics. The individual had to seek for a new identity in these new forms – political parties, clubs, church denominations, associations etc., There is a change from traditional 'We' to the life of the 'I' in the reality. This resulted in a painful discovery, a sense of isolation in the midst of the large masses of people. J.S. Mbiti in **African Religions and Philosophy** observes that:

> *The individual simply discovers the existence of his individualism but does not know of what it consists. He has no language to perceive its nature and its destiny (Mbiti 1967:225).*

The individual is in conflict with new forces and new values: e.g. Nwoye's and Oduche' in **Things Fall Apart** and **Arrow of God**. Their individualism is vague and blurred, they do not as Mibiti points out know of what it consists, they have no language to explain its nature and destiny. Going further from a tribal culture towards a more industrialized and urban culture, one meets characters like Obi in **No Longer at Ease**, who gropes in the dark in the same external pursuit. The forces that shape his gate are absolutely novel and different from the ones faced by his counterparts in earlier age and surroundings. The socio-economic factors that constitute the milieu of their existence and pave the way for conflicts are complex and varied. And finally, another form of 'individualism', where attempts to assert the integrity of individual as leader combating tradition and bureaucracy are portrayed in Achebe's last novel **Anthills of the Savannahs**.

The felt experience of African life has gone far beyond the pictures presented in these works to encompass entirely new perspectives in societies which in a few short years have moved from illiterate to literate, from communal to Individual from largely rural to increasingly urban, and the fiction itself has mirrored these evolutions in its own patterns. Situational plots are being replaced by works which concentrate on character and individuality. Description and the treatment of time and space are becoming more typically a western experimentation. Experimentation tends now towards Western techniques which replace the traditional conscious or sub-conscious incorporation of oral literary materials into the text. African fiction is growing out of the collective experience of the society in which the writer lives, out of the reservoir of ideas and experiences of the total consciousness of the society itself. The African writer functions as the historian of his continent's widening outlook on life, moving away from limited closed-off societal view of the village and clan to an ever-widening world view.

Rand and Achebe are significant juxtapositions, provocative as well as enlightening. In a bootstrap universe like ours, everything is related to everything else, and accordingly our search for similarities is legitimate. Again, in our world of infinite variety, multiplicity and mutability, there is never any exact mimicry or repetition. Between these extremes of total relatedness and uncompromising uniqueness, one is free to infer what parallelisms seem striking.

The chapters in this thesis offer discriminating comments on the works of Chinua Achebe, the Nigerian novelist and Ayn Rand, the American novelist. The idea is to bring the insights of these two very prominent yet totally different critics together, to compare and complement one another. Achebe has his own vantage point in viewing the cultural scene in the West, with his own optimum degree of involvement and detachment and brings to bear on it, his own sensibility, born out of his own very different cultural milieu.

There is a need to read American and African literature, to have a feel of the American and African life and understand the workings of the American and African psyche. Rand and Achebe have struggled to present various aspects of the American and African self in the context of a historical moment.

At the root of the novelist's business lies the implicit recognition that while every culture has its characteristic moral attitudes and values, no culture has an absolutely monolithic code; that alongside the voice of conformity there exists, however small and isolated, the voice of dissent. This dissenting voice provides a healthy tension between the community and the individual. Since dissension from the established code can assume various forms, a culture carries within it, a multiplicity of moral consciousness.

Both Rand and Achebe deal with self-definition as a moral and social concern in the twentieth century novel; and have expressed their moral values as part of their uncompromising dedication to truth. In contemporary American Literature, the concept of morality has been an expansive and adaptable one. The limits of morality have extended to include the idea of individualistic realization. The individual tries to extricate himself from the surrounding images, myths, stereotypes and values in order to learn to see itself. Rand and Achebe have expressed their concern for the individual by revealing the emptiness and pathos in the lives of their characters who seem to have little freedom to find the moorings in a society from which they have no escape.

Both Rand and Achebe are novelists with a purpose. Their novels attempt to prove a premise, draw conclusions from a whole category of forces, social tendencies, race impulses and their works are devoted to the study of man. While Rand attempted to restore the dignity of the individual; Achebe's objective was to restore the faith in pre-colonial humanity of African society and the dignity of the African national consciousness. Achebe found it necessary to remind the world of the pioneer role played by the African continent in providing civilization to mankind; while Rand observes in the 'Introduction' to **The Virtue of Selfishness: A New Concept of Egoism** that the goal and purpose of my writing is the projection of an ideal man and the portrayal of a moral ideal as my ultimate literary goal as end in itself" (Rand 1964:iv).

Plot, the conception of a well-made story in Rand's fiction takes on a widely different importance in Achebe's fiction. While Achebe's plots are situational, wherein not just one individual, but an entire group of people (a tribe, a clan, a village) become ultimately affected by the major event of the narration. But Rand's plots circulate around the individual character, as she believed a plot to be a purposeful progression of events. Barbara Branden in **The Passion of Ayn Rand** says that "the progression of a human life consists of a random series of disconnected, unchosen events, united by any common theme or purpose and leading in the end to the grave" (Branden 1986:155).

Unlike in Rand's fiction, characterization is almost de-emphasised in Chinua Achebe's works. There is not much of character introspection and character development in Achebe's works, because of the African concept of group solidarity; yet his characters are very emotionally gripping and fully capable of drawing in the reader, though the character is not developed in any significant relationship to events. But Rand believes character to be the novel's prime concern, as she is a champion of the individual cause. All her characters are romantic rebels pitched against restrictive and mundane societies. In all their rebellion, they act alone and on principle. They are intellectually gifted and have unusual talents. Unlike in Rand's fiction woman characters in Chinua Achebe's fiction have relatively minor and functional roles. But of Rand's five protagonists three are women; in spite of this, Rand cannot be called a Feminist writer as she believes not only in hero-worship, but the "cult of man worship" (Ibidem:361). But Rand's fiction, more especially **Atlas Shrugged** as Mimi Gladstein in her article: "Ayn Rand and Feminism " An unlikely Alliance" observes, can be prescribed for women's studies as Rand highlights a lot of feminist issues in the novel (Gladstein 1982:16).

On the contrary, Achebe does not project women characters too much because his, is a chauvinistic, male dominated society. But in **Anthills of the Savannahs**, David Maugham Brown observes "a remarkable development is seen in Achebe as a novelist, because of his attitude to women and their role in society and his concept of 'gender transfiguration' (Brown 1990:231). While Rand explores the theme of live in all her novels, Achebe tends to ignore the love theme, except for the Obi-Clara episode in **No Longer at Ease**. But Achebe's novels are quite domesticated in the sense that a lot of rituals, ceremonies, functions, marriages, births and deaths, etc., pervade his novels. With Rand, marriage, child bearing any kind of ritual or ceremony is totally missing; and the marriages that do exist like Hank Rearden's and Lillian Rearden's and Peter Keating's are scorned at, by implied contrasts to relationships like Howard Roark's and Dominique Francon's, John Galt's and Dagny Taggart's. This shows Rand to be a novelist who transcends most man-made institutions.

Hence it is not surprising that Rand is an atheist while Achebe is a theist. Rand believed in the 'cult of man-worship', Achebe believed in an 'agrarian cult' "for wherever the African went there was his religion" (Mbiti 1967:2). He deified the sky, the trees, the earth the moon and the stars, all of nature as it were. Both Rand and Achebe overflowed the petrified separative frontiers of their own times and in their attempt to describe their experiences and findings, spoke in myths and legends. Achebe is not a repetition of Rand but they are two mighty rivers that run parallel to each other and yet they meet from time to time. The proper thing then would be to see Achebe in a perspective of Rand and viceverse, and this can heighten the appeal of such a study.

Rand and Achebe lived far apart in place, time and circumstances, yet on a closer scrutiny, one lights upon much agreement in the seeming disagreement.

Both Rand and Achebe chose to write in the English language. It seemed to both of them that speaking in their native language became a conscious activity and so it had lost its premier position to another, i.e. (English language) which came more easily and naturally to them (Okara 1990:14). But unlike Rand, Achebe uses pidgin, Ibo proverbs and folk lore which enhances the lucidity of his style.

Both Rand and Achebe explore the theme of the 'Individual versus Society'. Though Rand champions the cause of the individual, she also portrays in her chapter titled 'Atlantis' her concept of an ideal society. Achebe supports the cause of the collective initially but gradually moves on to speak of a balance that is to be maintained between the individual and society.

Both writers present the ambiguities and dilemmas, the pains of involvement and the pangs of isolation within the individual's social consciousness, as it enacts its drama of self-exploration and understanding.

Both the novelists dramatize the development, the change, the adjustment and transformation of their protagonists. While Rand's protagonists exemplify Hubert Bonner's Hellenic model of excellence and a life perfected, Achebe's protagonists exemplify Bonner's Hebraic idea of responsibility and discipline in a life shared.

Both Rand and Achebe wrote against the background of myths and to explore their stand, Rand uses the myth of Atlas, the myth of Prometheus, the myth of Atlantis and the myth of Adam. Chinua Achebe explores the Cultural Hero myth.

Both Rand and Achebe can be termed epic writers attempting to write in the epic form. Achebe is a traditional epic writer celebrating the traditional cultural hero, embodying the total culture of a whole people. Rand has no native tradition, but the major theme of all epic poetry is heroism itself- heroism as the perilous mythification of man.

Both were influenced by Aristotle. While Rand follows Aristotle's principles of logic and the importance he gave to Reason and the mind, Achebe falls in with Aristotle's concept of tragedy and the tragic flaws in characters which bring about their downfall. But Rand does not fall in with the Aristotlean definition of tragedy. Tragedy must entail the threefold relationship of man, society and God. Each individual has to accommodate himself to a broader context and undermining the social system is a moral, which refers either to a specific deity or to an agreed act of guiding assumption about right or wrong. In Rand's fiction, the pendulum swings between these aspects and usually settles on the individual; Alastain Niven in "Chinua Achebe and the Possibility of Modern Tragedy", says that "the focus is more evenly distributed and the dominating faction in the relationship of Man, Society and God is the middle one- the Society" (Niven 1975:45).

Except for the above similarities, Rand and Achebe cannot apparently have much in common. On the one hand, the contrasts between Rand and Achebe are strikingly many - in temperament, attitude, style and literary tradition. And the contrast which makes a whole world of a difference is the fact that while Rand is an expatriate writer, Achebe lives in his homeland.

An expatriate writer like Rand enjoys a unique position. She is not committed, except to her private sensibility or vision. She can tell unpalatable truths, tell them slant, be a prophet, a soothsayer, a doom watcher, and her brand or apocalyptus of times can be a little too uncomfortable for the genteel taste. She looks at creeds, cultures, and countries and sees enough and tries to debunk their blue print for reconstruction. Rand is a social deconstructionist who believes in stripping the American society of its pretences and their defence mechanisms. It is obvious Rand does all this with irony, passion, and prophecy. Killiam, quoting Achebe in **African Writers on African Writing**, says that Achebe is militantly African and believes in the writers' mission "which is to teach my readers that their past was not one long night of savagery from which the first European, acting on Gods behalf, delivered them" (Killiam 1978:41). Achebe is forthright and can sound even didactic when he says that he is out to help his society regain its belief in itself and put away the complexes of the years of denigration and self-abasement (Ibidem:3).

There are enough bones of contention for the two writers to come once to a head on collision, if ever they decide to confront each other. For they assume different intellectual positions. In tone, attitude, philosophy, Achebe is aggressively confident and positive, like Rand. Unlike Rand, Achebe is a spokesman for the African way of life. Quoting Achebe, Killiam says that the African writer has a distinctive function to perform:

> *We must first of all set the scene which is authentically African; then what follows will be meaningful and deep. And setting the scene means to recreate the past, not only for enlightenment of our detractors but for our own education. Because the past with all its imperfections never lacked dignity (Ibidem:44).*

So, the African writer should learn to do without "this aura of cosmic sorrow and despair" even though it happens to be a sentiment guaranteed to win applause in the West" (**MYCD** 32:33). Quite contrary to Rand, Achebe does not totally champion individualism.

It is apparent from this, then, that the difference between Achebe and Rand is radical in attitude and perception. But this does not mean that Achebe doesn't see any cracks in his "society or ambivalences in his culture; and is out to whitewash Africa and set himself up as a conscious propagandist" (Ibidem). Though Achebe's overtly intellectual stance proclaims his African militancy, his fiction tells a different story. The novelist usually tells us the whole truth, and this qualifies in an important way his ostensible ideological stance.

Of the two writers, Rand is the more sweeping exercise. This study is no commentary on them, but just what one individual feels about probable future world order in the light of the topic : "The Individual Versus

Society" which has plagued the world ever since man evolved on this planet. But American Literature and African Literature are one, as art and humanity are one, and their literary evaluation will be strengthened because of their inter-relatedness.

Categorizing is a dangerous game. Experience themselves defy this sort of thing. Each writer is unique and so are his experiences. Where experiences are translated into fiction, there are a thousand results. The categories and the generalization in this study resulted because of necessity and practically and they admittedly have their short comings. But Rand and Achebe have been brought together for this study, as already mentioned in 'The Preface', as each author supports to a very large extent, the opposite poles of the hypothesis which, is:

> *Whether the sphere of moral and imaginative values by which an individual functions in society is at once autonomous or related to society.*

This hypothesis is analysed in three phases. Each phase demonstrates the different stages in the growth and development of individualism. This is discussed against the background of the different texts chosen for each phase. The fourth chapter is devoted exclusively to both Rand's and Achebe's philosophical views. Ayn Rand is primarily a philosopher, originating a philosophy of her own, namely 'Objectivism'. Achebe, on the other hand, is not primarily a philosopher like Rand, but has framed his stories against and already existing philosophical framework.

The next chapter titled 'The Emergence of the Autonomous Individual' attempts to portray the struggle of four protagonists, (Kira Arugounova of **We The Living**, Equality 7-2521 of **Anthem**, Okonkwo of **Things Fall Apart** and Ezeulu of **Arrow of God**) against two different kinds of claustrophobic societies: Rand's Communistic Society of Soviet Russia and Achebe's Ibo Society of Nigeria, both of which smother the life of the individual.

II

The Emergence of the Autonomous Individual

This chapter explores Phase I and proceeds with the assumption that the autonomous individual is seen emerging in Ayn Rand's **We the Living** (1936) and **Anthem** (1938) and in Chinua Achebe's **Things Fall Apart** (1958) and **Arrow of God** (1964) respectively. In the fiction of Ayn Rand, the researcher explores the nature of the individual from the socio-political context. Rand's **Anthem** follows **We the Living** chronologically and forms Phase I, as both these novels are set in Communist Russia and trigger off the rise of the individual. Though Chinua Achebe's **Arrow of God** does not follow **Things Fall Apart** chronologically, these two novels are set in the Ibo tradition and spark off the beginnings of the quest for the individual.

Both Rand's and Achebe's novels highlight the theme of "Individualism Versus Collectivism". Rand's individuals who struggle to assert their individuality in this phase are Kira Argounova, Leo Kovalensky and Comrade Andrei Taganova of **We the Living**; Equality 7-2521 and Liberty 5-3000 of **Anthem**; Okonkwo and Nwoye of **Things Fall Apart** and Ezeulu of **Arrow of God** respectively. These individuals suffer and struggle, but their cause and manner of struggle vary. While Rand's protagonists attempt to break the fetters of Communism to which they are tied and liberate themselves to individual freedom a happiness and self-fulfilment; Achebe's individuals, in this phase, struggle to maintain the dignity of their own Ibo society, which the white man ignorantly attempts to destroy.

Though both the societies represent the collective, they are totally different. In Rand's world it is the traditional communist society of Russia; in Achebe it is a well-knit meaningful communal society in this phase. But both the societies are common in their functioning in the sense, that both societies control the lives and activity of the individuals to a large extent. Kira Argounova and Leo Kovalensky of **We The Living** and Equality 7-2521 and Liberty 5-3000 of **Anthem** are portrayed struggling to combat the terrible tranny of a paralyzing, dictatorial state on the one hand; while Okonkowo of **Things Fall Apart** and Ezeulu of **Arrow of God** are trying to break away from a traditional-communal bound ethos and assert their own individuality on the other.

We the Living and **Anthem** depict the struggle of 'Man Against The

State. Both these novels depict the story of "a ruthless, blazing and courageous love, a love that flung defiance against the scavengers of human souls" (**WTL** 5). In this bitter struggle of the individual against The State, five people stand out with the mark of the unconquered in their bearing. Kira Argounova, the heroic protagonist in **We The Living** and the two men who love her, comrade Andrei Taganov, "the reddest communist" (**WTL** 9) and Leo Kovalensky, an aristocrat and Kira's" top value" ; and the heroic protagonist in **Anthem**, Equality 7-2521, "a man of intransigent mind" (**A**7) and Liberty 5-3000, "The Golden One (**A**9) "whom he chose to love". In these intensely dramatic stories, Rand portrays what the theories of Communism mean in practise. **We the Living** and **Anthem** are stories, not of politics, but of men and women who struggle for existence behind the Red Banners and slogans and hence condemn the supremacy of any State or Society over the individual consciousness. Rand, in her article "The Totalitarian Universe" observes:

> *A society that robs an individual of the product of his effort or enslaves him or attempts to limit the freedom of his mind, is not a society, but a mob, held together by institutionalized gang rule (Qtd in.* ***The Ominous Parallels****, 1982:26).*

In **We The Living**, Rand uses Kira Argounova as her mouth piece when she philosophises on the vague abstraction - society: "If you write a whole line of zeros, it's still nothing" (**WT** 633). While Rand obviously champions the cause of the 'individual will', Achebe's emphasizes the collective will when he asserts in **Things Fall Part**: "Where something stands, something else should stand beside it" (**TFA**21).

Rand's and Achebe's objectives in writing naturally evolve from their different experiences and convictions. While Rand writes with Russia in her bones, Achebe evolves as a more detached and objective artist. But unlike Achebe, Rand, born Alice Rosenbaun, a Jew, leaves behind her a blood-soaked dictatorship, the soul-shrivelling terror of a life without hope or future, and marches into the United States, boiling with energy and limitless ambition.

The rush to Collectivism had begun in America which earned the thirties, the titles of 'The Red decade'. Barbara Branden in **The passion of Ayn Rand** quotes Granville hicks, the literary terrorist of the Left who writes in the prestigious **New Masses** : "To be a good writer, a man must first become a good communist" (Branden 1986:71). Dorothy Parker announces: "There is no longer I", there is only "we". "The day of the individual is deal" (Ibidem:77). Rand now realizes the enormity of what has to be fought. And so, in 1930, Rand begins outlining her first novel. Its working title was **"Air Tight"**, later changed to **We The Living**. In **We The Living** Rand attempts to tell the world, the nature of her Russian nightmare; "that Russia was a huge cemetery and that people were slowly dying" (**WTL** 6). **We the Living** was a protest, Rand later said, and an introduction to her philosophy – "Individualism versus Collectivism". Rand shows that Collectivism destroys not only the average man but most particularly the best among men – those with the greatest gifts to offer the world. **We the Living** got Russia out of my system", Rand said. "By the time the book was finished, the issue of Russia was also finished for me" (Branden 1986:78). The Alice Rosenbaun of Soviet Russia dies and like phoenix from her own ashes is born the Ayn Rand of America. **We the Living** and **Anthem** function as a kind of catharsis for Rand. **Things Fall Apart** and **Arrow of God** demonstrate a nostalgia for Achebe. Achebe, in a 1964 lecture on "The Role of the Writer in a New Nation" speaks of "a strong temptation to idealize the African past to extol its good points and pretend the bad never existed" (Achebe 1964:67). To a certain extent, Rand and Achebe are literally reliving their Russian and Nigerian experiences. In both **We the Living** and **Anthem**, Rand explores the theme: 'The sanctity of human life'. The word 'sanctity' is used not in the mystical sense as Rand tells us in the 'Introduction' to **We the Living** (**WTL** vii), but in the essence of 'supreme value'. In the 'Foreword' to **We the Living** Rand makes explicit her theme:

> *The essence of my theme is contained in the words of Irina, a minor character of the story, a young girl who is sentenced to imprisonment in Siberia and knows that she will never return: "There's something that I would like to understand. And I don't think anyone can explain it. There's your life. You begin it feeling that it's so precious and rare, so beautiful that it's like a sacred treasure.*
> *Now it's over and it doesn't make a difference to anyone, and it isn't that they are indifferent, it's just that they don't know*
> *(**WTL** v).*

In **Atlas Shrugged**, Rand's last novel, Rand reaches the full answer to Irina's question, where she explains the philosophical, psychological and moral meaning of the men who value their own lives and of the men who do not. Rand shows in **Atlas Shrugged**, that the men who value their own lives are the prime movers of mankind and the men who do not, are the 'social suckers', 'the parasites' and the 'metaphysical killers' (VOS 19). Barbara Branden, quoting Rand in **The Passion of Ayn Rand** observes: "In **Atlas Shrugged** I show why men are motivated by a life premise or a death premise. In **We The Living**. I only show they are" (Branden 186:101).

Just as Rand has a specific aim in writing **We The Living** and **Anthem**, Achebe too in writing **Things Fall Apart** and **Arrow of God** wants, as Robert Wren tells us in **Achebe's World: The Historical and Cultural Context of the Novels of Chinua Achebe:**

> *To allow the old ways their due and to deal fairly with his ancestors, to set the scene right ....as an act of atonement with my past ... the ritual return and homage of a prodigal son (Wren 1980:3).*

In the light of this remark, Achebe's novels especially **Things Fall Apart** and **Arrow of God** becomes a record of:

> *An old and deeply articulate culture too long silenced by European cultural projection ... depicting the realities of tribal life lost behind the innumerable accounts of African primitive customs (Ibidem:15).*

Rand and Achebe explore thematically, the quest of the autonomous individual, but Achebe's concept of individuality does not permit the individual to be considered as 'supreme' or 'totally free' as Rand does. Achebe's individual is controlled by the will of the community. "No man, however, great, can win judgement against all the people" (**TFA** 16). But Rand treats man as an end in himself and the achievement of his own happiness as man's highest moral purpose (**VOS** 21). Both Rand and Achebe's protagonists in **We The Living** and **Anthem**, Kira Argounova and Equality 7-2521 are pitched against their Russian society: The State. In **We the Living**, Kira Argounova the female protagonist and Equality 7-2521 of **Anthem** are see emerging from the terrible fangs of a totalitarian system. But unlike Equality 7-2521 who successfully himself and the sacred world "I", Kira Argounova of **We The Living** is shot by Ivan Ivanov in the process of attaining freedom and self-preservation.

Achebe's protagonists Okonkwo of **Things Fall Apart** and Ezeulu **Arrow of God** are pictured struggling against a well-knit, human and meaningful Ibo society which may be stateless, but is very disciplined. Achebe's individuals are combating a communal society; Rand's individual is combating a communist society.

In the following section of this chapter, the researcher analyses the struggle of the protagonist in each author's text. Kira Argounova of **We The Living** and Equality 7-2521 of **Anthem** are set in the mould of future Ayn Rand protagonists, dedicated to two purposes: i) the work they had chosen to do ii) the men and women they had chosen to love. Rand's individuals are very assertive and confident of what they want to do; Achebe's individuals are victims of circumstances and of the colonial encounter, and hence the struggle is also totally different. Kira Argounova, "a young girl of eighteen, with a fierce independence, grey-eyed, a calm mouth, defiant, enraptured, solemn" (**WTL** 12) plans to be an engineer, but she is the daughter of a Bourgeoise, a class enemy and hence is expelled from the University in The Student Purge (**WTL** 21). The Revolution brings pestilence, disease, poverty and starvation. In the name of the people, factories and banks are nationalized. "A flight from the city stood before them as the Argounova's only course of action" (**WTL** 14). Kira's first steps on Petrograd soil makes her determined to fight the collective system. She scorns at banners that carried messages like "Proletarians of the World Unite" (**WTL** 19). "Long live the Dictatorship of the Proletariat (**WTL** 22) "Who is not with is, is against us" (**WTL** 24), "Comrades, we are the builders of a New Life" (**WTL** 26).

To Kira, the system is rotten at the root. Kira is condemned as highly anti-social', 'lacking things of the spirit', and 'most undutiful' (**WTL** 33). But Kira learns the 'Joy of being alone' (**WTL** 35). She rejects young man, treacly fairy tales and religion. Her ideas, convictions, values are very different from her sister, Lydia's. They are more like Ayn Rand's herself. While Lydia, her sister, falls in love with a grand opera tenor and admires Saint Francis of Assisi the only hero who is known to Kira is a Viking is a story, "who laughed at priests and lived but for the joy and the wonder and the glory of the God that was himself" (**WTL** 37). The end of this legend pictures the Viking on a tour over a city he had conquered, drinking a toast "to a life which is reason unto itself" (**WTL** 41). Kira Argounova is a study of the exemplification of the 'self'. Kira believes in the sanctify of life; but the leaders of the Russian Revolution defines a life as "only a brick and of no use unless cemented to other bricks" (**WTL** 44). Kira believes that she is an end in herself; the communist society believes that man is a means to a social end. On October 7, 1933, Adolf Hitler at Brickberg rendered this theory, quoted by N.H. Baynes in his book **The Speeches of Adolf Hitler:**

> *It is thus necessary that the individual should come to realise that his own ego is of no importance in comparison with the existence of his nation; that the position of the individual ego is conditioned solely by the interests of the nation's as a whole ... that above all, the unity of a nation's spirit and will are worth far more than the freedom of the individual.... (Baynes 1942:871-872).*

Kira Argounova is symbolic of the 'individual cause', and comrade Andrei Taganov symbolizes the 'collective'. Kira condemns 'The Party' because "it dares to touch things sacred in the best of us which no outsider should touch, be it any State, Collective or any number of millions" (**WTL** 80). But Comrade Taganov believes that "the millions cannot be sacrificed for the few" (Ibidem) and Kira screams:

*What 'are' your masses, but millions of dull, shrivelled, stagnant souls that have no thoughts of their own, no dreams of their own, no will of their own, who eat and sleep and, chew helplessly the words others put into their brains. And for those you would sacrifice the few who know life and are life. I loathe your ideals because I know no greater injustice than giving the underserved. Because men are not equal in ability and one can't treat them as if they were (**WTC** 8).*

'The State' Kira argues, is but a servant and a convenience for a larger number of people, just like the electric light and the plumbing system. It is absurd to claim that men exist for the plumbing and not the plumbing for the men.

*And if your plumbing pipes got badly out of order, wouldn't it be preposterous to sit still and not make an effort to mend them. I hope that when you find those pipes running with your own blood-you'll still think they were worth mending (**WTL** 82).*

In the "Ethics of Evil", quoted in **The Ominous Parallels**, Rand refers to two opposite approaches to morality: the pro-self-approach versus the anti-self-approach or the ethics of egoism versus the ethics of self-sacrifice (Teikoff 1982:81). While egoists hold that a man's primary moral obligation is to serve some entity outside himself. Morality, writes Edgar Jung, a German Rightist, consists in the self-abandonment of the Ego, for the sake of the higher values of the State. Such is the ethical base of Collectivism, which demands of each man, a life of subservience to the whole.

In **We The Living**, these two approaches of morality are well brought out through the conflict in the value-system of Rand's protagonist, Kira and those of the State. While Kira believes in the sanctity of human life, the State believes in its own sanctity. As a result of the revolution, Leo Kovalensky is about to die of Tuberculosis, but The State would not even register him, as he is not 'member of the party' (**WTL** 109), nor a State Employee (**WTL** 121). That he is going to die meant so little to the State, that he is not registered, nor a member of the Trade Union meant so little to Kira. But Leo's life has to be bought or saved any cost. Kira tries various sources. She approaches her cousin Victor, a member of "The Party" for help. But Victor's concern and loyalty to The Party membership, "is a sacred trust not to be used for purposes of personal advantage" (**WTK** 211). Kira rushes to Marisha, who laughs and says:

*With all our sanitoriums stuffed like herring –barrels, and waiting lists till the next generation, and comrade workers rotting alive waiting – and here, he's not even sick yet. You don't realize reality, citizen Argounova (**WTL** 211).*

Kira makes one last plea to the State. It takes many weeks of calls, letters, introductions, secretaries and assistants, but finally she gets an appointment with one of the most powerful officials of the Petrograd Government. Kira goes to see him in person. She looks straight at him, her eyes are not hostile, nor pleading; they are clear, trusting, serene; her voice is calm; she pleads for a life that is going to die:

*They didn't write his name on a piece of paper with many other names and call it a membership. One signature of your hand and he can go to a sanitorium and he doesn't have to die. Do you know what death is, nothing at all... never again..never..no matter what we do. Do you see why he can't die? I love him. There's something in each of us something like the very heart of life condensed and that should not be touched. Well, he is 'that' to me (**WTL** 216).*

The terror, cruelty, and inhumanity, the emptiness and hypocrisy of collectivized ethics is amply demonstrated in the response of one of the highest representative of The State: "One hundred thousand workers died in the Civil War. Why, in the face of The Union of Socialist Soviet Republic, can't one aristocrat die?" (**WTL** 216-217).

Leo Kovalensky is sentenced to die. But Kira fights one last battle. She meets Comrade Taganov, and to suit her convenience, Andrei confesses his love for her: "I'd give everything I have Kira for something you can't give me" (**WTL** 221) Kira is not thinking of Andrei nor Leo. She was thinking of Maria Petrovna and the red bubble on her dying lips and she hears the scream: "Kira I want to live. I want to live" (**WTL** 219). She is not sure now whether it is Maria Petrovna or Leo screaming, she throws the words at Andrei: "I can. I love you" (**WTL** 223). From that night, Kira Argounova becomes Comrade Taganov, the 'reddest Communist' is gradually seen alienating himself from the G.P.U. as well as the State. Andrei also realizes the double standards of his party's politics.

The State is the most senseless and useless of monsters standing in the way of human life-and that's something we call humanity's Politics. We *shoot one speculator and a hundred others hire taxis on Nevsky every evening. We raise villages to the ground, we fire machine guns into the rows of peasants crazed with misery, when they kill a communist. And ten of the avenged victim's party brother's drink champagne at the home of a man with diamond studs in his shirt. Where did he get the diamonds? Who is paying for the Champagne? We don't look into that too closely (**WTL** 319).*

The supreme value of the individual's life and the evils of a totalitarian State that claim the right to sacrifice it, is further brought out in the scene where Comrade Taganov learns the truth about Kira's relationship to both of them: Leo Kovalensky, the man she loves and fights to save his life, and Andrei Taganov whom she loves but is unfaithful to. Andrei Taganov is officially designated to arrest Leo Kovalensky, for committing the political crime of opening a private food store. At the home of Leo Kovalensky, Comrade Taganov realizes that Kira is also Leo's mistress. Andrei Taganov has Leo Kovalensky locked in a cell at the G.P.U. and returns to his house where Kira decides to lay bare the truth before him and also hurl at him, the hatred and revenge she feels for a party to which Taganov has dedicated twenty-eight years of his life. Kira tells Andrei: "For all the sorrows your comrades brought to a living world, at least one of them has been paid. I paid it. In you and to you" (**WTL** 387). Rand's satiric condemnation of the Collective is seen in her powerful description of Communism: The Party believes in the hundreds, the millions, the majority, simply because they - "stomachs, legs, hands, tongues and souls" (Ibidem) have been registered, but not Leo, since he is only an individual. "All stones are cobblestones to you. And diamonds, they're useless because they sparkle too brightly in the sun, and it's too hard under the hoofs marching to the Proletarian future, … and you smile, and you sing hymns to the toil of the Collective" (**WTL** 390). It comes as a solemn army and attempts to bring new life to men but succeeds only to tear that life knows nothing about. The party drives men into iron cellars and closes all doors, and "locks it air tight till the blood-vessels of our spirits burst. Then you stare and wonder what it is doing to us" (**WTL** 392).

The complete transformation of a collectivist to an individual is demonstrated in Andrei's conviction that the Red Party is a failure. In his speech at the Party Club, where Andrei's comrades are waiting for report on the agrarian situation, Andrei condemns his Communist party for their policy of the end justifying the means, especially when there is no end. He condemns the Red Party for its inhumanity and mass killings of peasants who refuse to surrender their leaders. He scorns The Party's 'great work' (**WTL** 390).

*You consecrated warriors of a new life: Are we sure we know what we are doing. No one can tell men what they must live for. No one can take that right – because there are things in men, in the best of us which are above all states, above all collectives: Man's mind and his values. Aren't you living for yourself and only for yourself? Call it your aim, your love, your cause – isn't it still 'your' cause? Give your life, die for your ideal – isn't it still 'your' ideal? Every honest man lives for himself. The one who doesn't, doesn't live at all. You cannot change it because that's the way man is born, alone, complete, an end in himself. No laws, no party, no G.P.U. will ever kill that thing in man which knows how to say 'I'. You cannot enslave man's mind. You can only destroy it. You have tried. Now look at what you are getting. Look at those whom you allow to triumph. Deny the best in men- and see what will survive. Do we want the crippled, creeping, crawling, broken monstrosities that we're producing? Are we not castrating life in order to perpetuate it? (**WTL** 392)*

That communist should make a speech for the cause of the individual in a dictatorial system like Soviet Russia is to record a major shift. Comrade Andrei Taganov is one of the most remarkable of characters in **We The Living**. Described as ' the reddist communist, Andrei is sincere and devoted to the cause of the collective. Through love in the person of the female protagonist, Kira Argounova and her tremendous influence on him, a rapid change and growth takes place in Comrade Taganov's life. He displays great virtue and humanism and begins to realise and discover the importance of personal values. When after 'The Purge', both Kira and Leo are expelled from the Institute and the University respectively, it is this member of the G.P.U., Comrade Taganov, who functions as a life-saviour. Andrei's great love for Kira Argounova makes him give her his whole salary, leaving him "only what she could spare" (**WTL** 264). It is Andrei's money that sent Leo Kovalensky to a tubercular sanitorium in the Crimea. It pays for the life of a man she loves long before she meets Comrade Taganov. Joseph Sobran, in his article: "Mussolini Shrugged; Ayn Rand Revived", published in the **National Review**, portrays Andrei as the nobler of the two men. Unlike Leo, he prefers death to dishonour. He serves Communism only as long as he can believe in it. Except in his love for Kira, he serves it incorruptibly. Leo on the other hand is willing to compromise himself. When Andrei sees the truth, he sacrifices himself for Kira as she sacrifices herself for Leo. But Leo is incapable of such love being what he is Kira never tries to explain her actions to him, rather mysteriously, she simply allows him to think the worst about her and to sink further into cynicism (Sobran 1989:53). One wonders whether she is sparing him the torment of full knowledge or whether she feels it futile to try to keep his love, and pointless to justify herself.

Be that as it may, Kira loves Leo, and not the more deserving Andrei. When it comes to winning maiden's affections, the smart money still on reckless virility rather than moral rectitude, and reckless virility happens to be Leo's long suit. He tells off Soviet officials (including Andrei) with a courage that frightens Kira for him, even as makes her admire him all the more. "Andrei has his own courage, as his final Sydney Carton gesture shows, but as a G.P.U. officer, he is hardly in a position to display it: in executing his duties he simply appears ruthless" (Sobran 1989:52). Andrei Taganov is seen as an individual, who, in the beginning turns away from himself and seeks to be one with the social substance, thus alienating himself from his essence or particular self. After his encounter with Kira, Andrei seems to concentrate on developing his inner self and turns his back on the social substance. Andrei's life, before he meets Kira can be described in the Hegelian sense as 'a negation of personality' (Hegel 1967:114). Personality development, Hegel contends, is characterized by one's freedom to express himself freely, which Andrei initially lacks but later acquires, as portrayed in his speech on the agrarian situation.

Pavel Syerov and Victor Dunaev are also part of the collective, but unlike Andrei Taganov, they function as the most detrimental characters to human happiness. Both are not only opportunists but parasites who use people to further their own ends. Victor marries Marisha because he thinks his proletariat background will help him in the Party; when that is not, he turns in his own sister and her fiancé Irina and Sasha, for counter revolutionary activities to prove his loyalty to the Party; when he has neither loyalty nor honour in his demeanour. Pavel Syerov, a ladies' man, uses Comrade Sonia to further his Party's aim as a revolutionary. While spouting the party line, Syerov secretly backs the black-market speculations of Karp Morozov and Leo Kovalensky. His party saves him when his black-market dealings are uncovered; his hypocrisy continues when he uses Andrei's funeral as an opportunity for self-aggrandizement.

Andrei Taganov was not a famous man, but he bore proudly and gallantly one title; that of Communist. He and I grew up together and together we shared the long years of toil; side by side we fought in the ranks of the Red Army. He is dead but his work, our work, goes on. The individual may fall, but the collective lives forever... Thousands of us are gathered here to honour one man-But one man means nothing in the face of the mighty proletarian Collective, no matter how worthy his achievements. We would not be here, if that man were not more than a *single individual, if he were not to honour-the birth of a new humanity, with a new race of men, with new standards. The first and basic one is the loss of a most dangerous, the most insidious, the evilest of human words- The word 'I'. We have outgrown it. 'WE' is the slogan of the future: The 'Collective' stands in our hearts where the old monster 'Self' has stood. Our only badge of honour is the consecrated unselfish service of the collective (**WTL** 419).*

While the protagonist Kira Argounova and the sub-protagonists Andrei Taganov and Leo Kovalensky are Rand's prime movers of mankind, Pavel Syerov and Victor Dunaev are the 'metaphysical killers' and the 'social suckers' and the 'parasites', symbolizing 'Good' and 'Evil' in life (**VOS** 19).

In Anthem (1936) Rand's next novelette, Rand projects this society of the future, which has accepted total collectivism with all its ultimate consequences. Men have relapsed into primitive savagery and stagnation; The Word 'I' has vanished from the human language; there are no singular pronouns; a man refers to himself as 'we' and to another as 'they'. They are conceived in 'Controlled Palaces of Mating" (**WTL** 15). They die in "The Home of the Useless" (**WTL** 17). From the womb to the tomb, the crowd is one: 'A Great we', They exist only to serve The State. In all that is left of humanity, there is only one man "who dared to think, to seek and to love" (**A** 9). He is Equality 7-2521, "a man of intransigent mind" (**A** 11), who lives in the dark ages of the future. In, a loveless world he dares to love the woman of his choice, Liberty 5-3000. In an age that has lost all trace of science and civilization, he has the courage to seek after knowledge, a treacherous blasphemy. But these are not the crimes for which he would be killed. He is marked for death because he has committed and unpardonable sin; he stands out from the mindless human herd. He is a man alone and rediscovers the lost and holy word 'I'.

In this novelette, Rand portrays the horrors of dictatorship where none among men may be alone. Over the portals of the Palace of the World Council, these words of Truth are cut in marble:

*We are one in all and all in one. There are no men but only the great We-One, indivisible and forever' (**A** 14).*

Each night, raising their right arms, they proclaim the pledge, along with their Teachers:

We are nothing. Mankind is all. By the grace of our brothers we are al-

*lowed our lives. We exist through, by and for our brothers, who are The State, Amen (**A** 28).*

Rand's protagonist, Equality 7-2521 is condemned by the State as evil, and lashed because "his body had grown beyond the bodies of his brother's (**A** 13); he "found learning too easy, when it was considered a sin to be born with a head that was too quick" (**A** 15). "He sang aloud without reason and was guilty of the great 'Transgression of Preference' in choosing the work he liked to do" (**A** 17); and "in noticing Liberty 5-3000 at a time when men and women were forbidden notice each other (**A** 19). Equality 7-2521 is a thing set apart from his brothers: The Collective. With bowed heads, eyes dull, never looking at one another in the eyes, "their muscles drawn, shoulders hunched, their bodies shrinking with fear, without name, without shape they walked through the city" (**A** 47). Fraternity 2-5503, "a quiet boy with wise kind eyes", cries, "their bodies shaking with sobs, they cannot explain". Solidarity 9-6347, "a bright youth, fearless at day, screams in their sleep... "Help us!... Help us", and the doctors cannot cure solidarity 9-6347. union 5-3992, "a sickly lad with convulsions was always frothing at the mouth" (**A** 49).

The Society here is a disease-stricken, pestilence-polluted society. The political system of such a society created psychological freaks. In contrast to this sick society, Equality 7-2521 "wished to know and loved the great science of things an asked many questions and wished to be sent to the House of Scholars (**A** 23) but The State condemns him to be "a street sweeper", along with International 4-8818. Together they discover a dark tunnel where they secretly learn much more in those two years than all the ten years in the home of the student. They realise:

*We are false in the face of our brothers we are defying the will of the councils. We alone of the thousands are doing a work which has no purpose save that we wish to do it... And yet we feel no shame, no regret, no burden in our spirit, no fear in our heart. Strange is the heart of evil. In our heart there is the first peace we have known in 20 years" (**A** 36).*

"If this be vice, then we wish no virtue" (**A** 40). In their enthusiasm for work, knowledge and quest for the unknown, they discovered electricity.

A discovery of such a nature by 'street sweepers' was a concept the world council of scholars could not digest. They considered the candle a great boon to mankind approved by all men, therefore it cannot be destroyed by the whim of one.

How dared you think that your mind had greater wisdom than the minds of your brothers? How dared you gutter cleaner to hold yourself as one alone and with the thoughts of one and not of the many... What is not done collectively cannot be good (A 82).

The State council considers it a sin to give names which distinguish them from other men. But Equality 7-2521 names Liberty 5-3000, 'The Golden One", and takes no heed of the law which says that men may not think of other men, save at the time of mating, when the council of Eugenics assigns (each Spring) one woman of over eighteen to a man of over twenty. Children are permitted to be born each Winter, when parents never see their children and children never know their parents. "Equality 7-2521 went twice to The Palace of Mating, but found it is an ugly and shameful matter" (A 42), when Equality 7-2521, disgusted with this social system, flees into the Unchartered Forest, The Golden One follows him. The Golden one looks upon Equality 7-2521 as a God

*Your eyes are a flame, but our brothers have neither hope nor fire. Your mouth is cut of granite, but our brothers are soft and humble. Your head is high, but our brothers cringe. You walk, but our brothers crawl. We wish to be damned with you than blessed with all our brothers (**A** 94).*

Many words are lost in the unmentionable times, especially one word which is not in the language of men, but which has been. And this is the unspeakable word which no man can speak nor bear. There is no crime punished by death In this world save this one crime of speaking the unspeakable word. And slowly, haltingly, like the words of a child the 'we' becomes the 'I' (**A** 113). Rand champions the cause of the 'I" here. "I am. I think. I will" (A 108). Of all the words granted to man, false and wise, only three words are considered holy: "I will It".

*My happiness is not the means to any end, Neither am I the means to any end others may wish to accomplish. I am not a tool for their use. I am not a bandage for their wounds. I am a man. The miracle of me is mine to own kneel before. And we shall join hands when we wish and walk alone when we so desire. For in the temple of his spirit each man is alone. Let each man keep his temple untouched and undefiled. Then let him join hands with others if he wishes, but beyond his holy threshold (**A** 115).*

Rand believes that the word 'We' must never be spoken save by one's choice, nor should it be placed first within man's soul else, it becomes a monster, the root of all the evils on earth, the root of man's torture by men, and unspeakable lie. Rand condemns the word 'We' because it crushes all beneath it, "and that which is 'white' and that which is 'black' is lost in the 'grey' of it" (**A** 125), it is the word by which the depraved steal the virtue of the good, by which the weak, steal the might of the strong, by which the fools steal the wisdom of the sages (Ibidem). This creed of corruption, this monster 'We', the word of serfdom, of plunder, of misery, falsehood and shame is over and the face of this God- this one word: 'I' by this word, man is taught the reverence of his own spirit-the spirit of Freedom.

In both **We the living** and **Anthem**, Rand condemns the State's right interfere with individual rights. Hand portrays in this first phase how the individual's right is evaded, distorted, perverted, and seldom discussed. Rand believes 'right' to be 'a moral precept' as she observes in her article "Man's Rights" (Rand **VOS** 1964:96). Hegel in his book **Phenomenology of the Mind** argues that:

> *Rights provide a logical transition from the principle guiding an individual's action to the principles guiding his relationship with others. Individual right are the means of subordinating society to moral law (Hegel 1967:121).*

Rand attempts to restore the dignity of the individual through both her protagonists, Kira Argounova and Equality 7-2521 in **We The Living** and Anthem. In **We The Living** even though the protagonist is shot while crossing the Latvian border to freedom and to Leo, the overall emotional tone of the book is not tragic, but life – affirming. The State has the power to end Kira's life, it does not have the power to destroy her spiritually: she remains as he had begun, loyal to her knowledge of what life could be and should be. In **Anthem**, the protagonist Equality 7-2521 escapes with Liberty 5-3000, to rediscover themselves and their identity. Joseph Sobran, in his article; "Mussolini Shrugged: Ayn Rand Revived", says that "Rand's characters (in this phase) seem to speak on Rand's behalf and not for themselves" (Sobran 1989:53). In writing **We the Living** Rand knew that the major protagonist is not yet Rand's 'ideal man', rather Rand is concerned to demonstrate (here) a woman's feelings for her ideal man. The ideal man is born only in the world of **The Fountainhead** which will be dealt with in the next phase.

Through these novels, **We The Living** and **Anthem** Rand introduces the main concept of her Objectivist philosophy; Individualism versus collectivism. Rand observes in **The Virtue of Selfishness** that her aim is to condemn the altruist-collectivist premises "that the misfortune of some is a mortgage on others" (**VOS** 81). Rand offers her philosophy in its foetus form in this phase. It is a challenge to the modern conscience and is Rand's clarion call to all those who are concerned about preserving one's right to individual freedom. Rand shows in "The Objectivist Ethics" that:

*It is only to the frozen unreality inside a collectivized brain that human lives are interchangeable, and only such a brain can contemplate as "moral" or "desirable", the sacrifice of generations of living men, public benefits will bring to the unborn (**VOS** 27).*

Soviet Russia is the nearest, but not only illustration of the achievement of collectivized mentalities. Two generations of Russians have lived and toiled and died In misery waiting for the abundance promised by their rulers, who pleaded for patience while building public hope in five-year instalments. The waiting has no end. The unborn profiteers of that wholesale sacrificial slaughter will merely breed new hordes of sacrificial animals, as the history of all tyrannies has demonstrated while the unfocussed eyes of a collectivized brain will stare on, undeterred and speak of a vision of great service to mankind, mixing interchangeably the corpses of the present with the ghosts of the future, but seeing no men. Progress can come only out of men's surplus, that is, from the work of those men whose ability produces more than their personal consumption requires, those who are intellectually and financially able to venture out in pursuit of the new. Rand conceives of the present age a rapid epistemological degeneration, when men are being brought down to the level of concrete bound animals who are incapable of perceiving abstractions and this "makes it necessary for me to give the following warning to my readers: "Do not be misled by those who tell you that **We The Living** is outdated or no longer relevant to the present, since it deals with Soviet Russia in the 1920's".

*We The Living is not a story about Soviet Russia in 1925. It is a story about dictatorship, any dictatorship, anywhere, at any time, whether it be soviet Russia, Nazi Germany, or (which this novel might do its share in helping to prevent a Socialist America. What the rule of brute force does to men and how it destroys the best will be the same in 1925, in 1955- whether the secret police are called G.P.U or N.K.V.D., whether men eat millet or bread, whether they live in novels or in housing projects, whether the rulers were red shirts or brown ones (**WTL** 9).*

We The Living and Anthem does not satisfy Rand stylistically. Certain aspects of it are a deep and lasting pride to her. Mimi Gladstein in The Ayn Rand Companion : An Analysis of her Fiction observes: "What Rand liked most was the plot structure; it was a single-tracked series of events leading to a dramatic climax, a highly personal novel set against a social background (Gladstein 1982:57).

But there are other issues that presented the greatest difficulties. Rand is writing a new language. Sometimes she thinks in English, sometimes in Russian, at times even in French. American idioms come to her automatically, but Rand says, she is not fully satisfied with her way of saying things, with her narrative linguistic aspects. For example, many of the early passages pertaining to Kira's reactions to Leo are not quite right, they are too brief, too understated, particularly in emotional scenes, she feels that there is so much she wants to project, that she does not know how to capture it all, she is not yet at home in writing in essentials about emotions and moods, one has to do that by practice, one can't do it theoretically (Ibidem:61).

In We The Living the influence of Victor Hugo is seen on Rand. Quoting Rand, Gladstein observes that his influence shows itself in a certain kind of over assertive, an slightly over dramatic turn of sentences:

> *My mind worked in those forms. I could not have any of my own yet, not on a first novel. The events leading to Andrei's suicide and the suicide itself were among the very few places where I was able to achieve deliberate under statement and indirection and implication (Ibidem).*

It is only in **The Fountainhead** that Rand starts writing in her own style, and fully succeeds in the art of implication that is, building a strong emotional situation, then not naming it for the reader but writing around it. That makes the emotional impact stronger, according to Rand.

The section that follows analyses the rise of individualism in Chinua Achebe's **Things Fall Apart** and **Arrow of God** respectively.

The world of **Things Fall Apart** and **Arrow of God** is a composite and compact world where characteristic Ibo rituals and practices are interspersed with the structural requisites of the major themes explored in them. Though these two novels do not follow each other, both deal with the pre-colonial, and early colonial days in the eastern part of Nigeria, occupied by Ibos. Historically **Things Fall Apart** and **Arrow of God** portray a phase of transition. The Nigerian people are faced with aliens in their midst. Christian missionaries establish themselves in this region by the nineteenth century only. So, religion precedes politics in this particular entry into the 'exotic existence of Ibos. But the entry is extended beyond politics into all aspects of socio-cultural life.

Things Fall Apart portrays a vivid picture of Ibo society. It is remarkable for the recapturing of the buoyancy and vigour of traditional life. Order and significance exist. The plot revolves around the protagonist Okonkwo. It is as much the story of the whole clan as a single individual. The voice of Achebe, a wise sympathetic one is very much part of the tribe, his Ibo society, unlike Rand. But even in Achebe's novels, a transition from the 'communal' to the 'individual' is seen and implies a tension, but Achebe's achievement is not just the balancing of the two, more important is that the presentation of the social glide is from a narrative point of view, that is firmly from 'within' the tribe. There is no distinction between the sacred and the secular. Okonkwo symbolizes the values of pride and glory of his tribe. The divine directives are manifested in three powerful forces: The Oracle of the Hills and Caves, the Chi and Mother Earth, the Goddess. The protagonists in each of the books come into direct contact with the supernatural powers dwelling in their midst and feel what is means to submit to them. For instance, the Oracle of the Hills and Caves is deeply involved in the tragic fate of Ikemefuna: "Yes, Umuofia has decided to kill him. The Oracle has pronounced it" (**TFA** 5). The death of Ikemefuna could be viewed as calculated murder especially a son by a father, because there is a shift in values in the whole community. The involvement and relieves it of the guilt associated with bloodshed and wins the approbation of "communal consciousness' (**TFA** 9). But Achebe places the event in an individual perspective too, raising the incident to the fore and suggesting a very subtle alternative. It echoes the beginnings of a new individualistic humanism. The response of the individual consciousness is seen through Obierika and Nwoye. Max Weber says in **Sociology of Religion** that the 'savagery' associated with primitivism' (Weber 1971:45) makes itself manifest in the most ruthless manner in the case of Ikemefuna. Ezendu informs Okonkwo that Umuofia has decided to kill the boy calls you his father. Here Ezendu proposes human predicament neither to defy the gods by resisting, nor offend one's conscience by assisting in the death. Okonkwo's vision is blinded because of his fear to be thought weak to fulfil his desire to the Oracle and his idea of masculinity. Wisdom and maturity seem to be the touchstone of the tribe. Okonkwo tries to win the tribe's praise but ironically loses it and that is Okonkwo's personal tragedy too. Okonkwo is likened to one who dares to wrestle with his spirit, for even as a man of eighteen, he had earned popularity by throwing, an unbeaten wrestler "in a fight which the old men agreed was one of the fiercest since the founder of their own town engaged a spirit of the wild for seven days and seven nights" (**TFA** 1). Later, in the sacred Week of Peace, he beats one of his wives thus showing that he had no respects for the gods of his clan. His enemies said that his good fortune had made him proud and likened him to the little bird Aza who so forgot himself after a heavy meal that he challenged his chi" (**TFA** 26).

Using proverbs Achebe reinforces the image of Okonkwo as a man who struggles with his Chi, when everyone at the kindred meeting took sides with Osazo. When Okonkwo called him a woman, the oldest man present tells Okonkwo "that those whose palm-kernels were cracked for them by benevolent spirit should not forget to be humble" (**TFA** 39). Okonkwo apologises.

> *But it was really not true that Okonkwo's palm-kernels had been cracked for him by a benevolent spirit. He had cracked them himself... At an early age he had achieved fame as the greatest wrestler in all the land. That was not luck. At the most one could say that his Chi or personal god was good. But the Ibo people have a proverb that when a man says "yes", his Chi agreed. And not only his Chi but his clan too, because it judged a man by the work of his hand (**TFA** 22-23).*

In his exile he had come close to understanding that his personal god or Chi was not made for great things. A mind could not rise beyond the destiny of his Chi. The saying of the elders was not true-that if a man said 'yes' his Chi also affirmed. He was a man whose Chi said 'no' despite his own affirmation (**TFA** 117).

However, he returns with the false hope that his Chi and his clan would now be making amends for the past disaster. He is unable to resume his former position of leadership for the village has changed. So, even though he says "yes" very strongly, his chi and his clan say "no". Okonkwo's tragedy is that he is unwilling to adapt himself to the changing times. He tries to recreate the old way of life which is gradually disappearing. He makes rash steps to resist the forces of colonial change, stumbles and falls. Okonkwo's fall is symbolically the fall of the traditional Ibo society. For his hero, Achebe

> *...wanted a character who could be called representative of this particular group of people... who may admire a man of strength ... The weakness of this particular society is a lack of adaption, but being able to sense... I think in (Okonkwo) time, the strong men were those who did not fend, and I think this was a fault in the culture itself (**TFA** 120).*

Achebe's sympathies are not entirely with Okonkwo for he believes as he observes in "Cultural Events in Africa", that "Life has to go on and if you refuse to accept changes, then tragic though it may be, you are swept aside" (Achebe 1967:11). Achebe's portrayal of Ibo society is compassionate. He shows how this noble, simple, poetic way of life gets frozen. Yet he does not hide its occasional inhuman practices like ritual murder, killing of twins and its emphasis in manliness which brings down both the hero and the society.

Obierika admits that tribal ethics, for all its flexibility does not provide an easy answer when it comes to choosing between personal claims and social commitments. The Ikemefuna incident highlights both the overpowering 'traditionalism' and the streaks of 'individualism' that would seem to be on the rise, and results in the unique form of individualism pioneered and championed by Nwoye.

> *As soon as his father walked in that night, Nwoye knew that Ikemefuna had been killed, and something seemed to give way inside him, like the snapping of a tightened bow. He did not cry. He just hung limp (**TFA** 59-60).*

The concept of individualism and its relations to the coming of Christianity brought about subsequent changes in Ibo life. The individual is invariably in conflict with the force that is society or tradition preserved with religious sentiments. Emmanuel Obiechina, in his scholarly enquiry into the **Culture, Tradition and Society in the West African Novel** maintains that : "The identification of the individual with the group of which he forms a part, and its social and cultural outlook, is the very essence of traditionalism" (Obiechina 1975:202). Besides Acquiescing the beliefs and customs of the group (Ibidem:18). This is the value often emphasized by most novelists, who contrast it with the opposite value based in self-interest that marks a more "developed" situation. But along with social conformity and the discouragement of deviation from the common norms, traditionalism involved a certain amount of the repressive curbing of individual freedom. Erich From in **The Sane Society** uses the word 'submission' to denote the various ways in which an individual relates himself to the rest of the society (Fromm 1956:30).

He maintains that the individual in this way "transcends the separateness of his individual existence by becoming part of somebody or something, bigger than himself and experiences his identity in connection with the power to which he has submitted" (Ibidem:38). It leads us to assume that any movement contrary to this coordinating gesture any attempt at the severance of the total integrity of the can is taboo and anathema to a tribal society. Irrespective of the means employed, the individual is bound to the milieu inseparably. He can achieve this coordination by integrating himself wilfully and consciously to its entire body, by transcending the individualistic traits in him, or by mens of pure 'submission'.

Things Fall Apart is a record of a steady transformation of the individual from his integrated existence to independent existence. It is a long process. The contradictions, tribal commands and its values, lead to its own downfall in Umuofia. The inscrutability, and arbitrariness of the religious dictates puzzle Obierika and Nwoye equally. The technique Achebe employs is juxtaposing the tribal and the personal very effectively, bringing out the paradoxes that sustain a social superstructure. Obierika thinks for us when he asks, "why should a man suffer grievously for an offence he had committed inadvertently?' (**TFA** 113). The anguish is terrible for the new individual thinking. Achebe does not probe deeper into the nature of the inner adjustment of the individual being torn between loyalties from within the structure of the tribal society itself. Focussed from that point of view, the incompatibility of human and divine values, and their paradoxical and inextricable involvement creates a stasis, a stagnant equilibrium, which admits of no synthesis and suggests no possible dialectic.

Achebe's treatment of Christianity is so detached that it has not been possible to decipher his attitude towards Christianity. There is no sudden conversion or dramatic confrontations. This new religion enters quietly and touches vulnerable points of their culture. There is no urgency and no fear of the tribal. The early converts were "excrement of the clan, the new faith a mad dog that had come to eat it up" (TFA 13). Okonkwo's son, Nwoye is converted much to Okonkwo's displeasure.

For Nwoye, a new "frame of orientation" (Obiechina 1975:222), much more flexible and appealing to the human emotion is tangible in Christianity. Obiechina observes that in the new religion the whole tribe mattered, not individuals:

> *It is not the mad logic of the trinity that had captivated Nwoye. He did not understand it. It was the poetry of the new religion, something felt in the marrow. The hymn about brothers who sat in darkness and in fear seemed to answer a vague and persistent question that haunted his young soul – the question of the twins crying in the bush and the question of Ikemefuna who was killed. He felt a relief within as the hymn poured into his parched soul. The words of the hymn were like the drops of frozen rain melting on the dry palate of the panting earth (**TFA** 137).*

Nwoye's instantaneous response is not expected but very consistent with the logic of his consciousness. It appeals to a deed neatly and deeply felt, but not neatly formulated. The point is not whether the Christian

God equals in power to the great Chukwu but the loving personal care appeals to the whole unresolved fear-syndrome, so rampant in Umuofia.

The progress of Christianity meant the re-assimilation of all that was considered undesirable by the tribe-the Osu, the slave, the twins the effeminate, into a confraternity of love: For them: "The new religious profession of basic human quality, the universal fatherhood of God and the universal brotherhood of man constitutes an awakening of submerged hopes, a resurrection of a sense of human worth, long buried under the grave mound of custom" (Obiechina 1975:224). The appeal is largely on the emotional and psychological level. Nwoye sees it as a liberating force. David Carrol says in **Chinua Acebe** that for Obi, this new religious awareness implies acceptance for the outcasts of the tribe (Carrol 1980:56). Critics view the alien religion as disrupting Africa's culture. The novel features it that way, but the Christian religion does have its contributions to African culture. Economically education widens the outlook of life. But it also has undermined the solidarity of the tribe. With Mr. Smith on the scene, there was no negotiated attempts between rival myths and the slaying of the Gods of Baal. Sacred practices of the tribe like the unmasking in public 'an egwugwu' was defied (Ibidem).

The tribal narrative voice, so far authoritative seems to be less confident and shakier (**TFA** 168-169).

*That night the mother of the spirits walked. ...weeping for her murdered son. It has a terrible night. Not even the oldest man in Umuofia had ever heard such a strange and fearful sound, and it was never to be heard again. It seemed as if the very soul of the tribe wept for a great evil that was coming – its own death (**TFA** 171-172).*

The tribe here mourns its own demise, a unique act of rebellion, an expiration of a crime, where even the narrative voice falters, never to be heard again. Umuofia yields & disintegrates. Along with the tribe sinks its own value system, religious as well as socio-economic. A new administrative setup and a fresh economic growth give rise to individualism. Assessment of wealth has its dual aspects – the extinction of a compact system that believes its corporal ownership and the development of individual ownership. It means advanced thinking on the economic lines:

"Mr Brown triggered off a new trend in the thinking patterns in schools and managed to win the affection of the clan" (**TFA** 160), because he treads softly on its faith. He realizes a frontal attack will not succeed.

Even the narrative voice seems to appreciate the manner in which Mr. Brown approaches the tribe, its religion and leaders, though it is in his interest. Schools, and religion go hand in hand from the beginning (**TFA** 164). Young Nwoye, now called Isaac, undergoes training as a teacher.

The change that Umuofia visualizes, the growth of formal educational facilities, personal approach to religion and a new economic thinking is so instantaneous and effective, that Okonkwo, on his return from exile, finds himself amidst a different social order, "one based on individual contractual relationship as opposed to the traditional and collective kinships hitherto existed" (Weber 1930:59-76).

The white men have taken over the administration of the tribe. Obeirka says that his own men are against the tribe. "He has put a knife on the things that held us together and we have fallen apart" (**TFA** 158).

Thus, an eventual release from conventional social ties gives the individual an impetus and motivation to reshape his whole pattern of life rather than maintain the status quo. Nwoye severed from his family, but accepted and established in the new dispensation, holds forth the image of this new individual. There is a change from the 'communal', to the 'individual'. This brings about a conflict, but Achebe manages to balance the two. There is also a social glide from the point of view of the narrator from within the tribe. Neil McEwan in **Africa and The Novel** observes two distinct narratives voices: 'traditional-communal', and the modern individual (McEwan 1983:22-25). In the first two thirds of the novel, the 'communal' voice is heard through a mixture of anecdotes and gossip, folk-tales and proverbs, in which the emphasis is on experience that is shared rather than as it appears to any individual consciousness. In the last part of the novel is heard the voice of the 'modern individual' – the urban editorial voice, who sees beyond the view point of the villagers, who are now 'they' rather than 'we' and who presents the decay of traditionalism. The colonial mentality and the coming of Christianity form a large, more balanced and detached perspective, in a more distanced and elaborate style:

> *They were many men and women in Umuofia who did not feel as strongly as Okonkwo about the new dispensation. The white men had indeed brought a lunatic religion, but he had also built a trading store and for the first-time palm-oil and kernel became things of great price and much money flowed into Umuofia (**TFA** 126).*

The narrative of **Things Fall Apart** modulates, through this interchange of narrative voices, from the communal voice of the village to the voice of the individual consciousness and back again, so that the two interpenetrate.

Arrow of God, a fitting sequel to **Things Fall Apart** takes us one step further away from the socio-political situation portrayed in the latter, where the narrative ends as the tribe realizes that it comes to terms with the alien force which is powerful and irreversible. **Arrow of God** is a richer, more dynamic and complex world with an elegance that comes of its multi-dimensional capturing of the Ibo society in 1921. It explores simultaneously the depth of three elements evolved in the artistic apprehension of a particular historical movement. The tribal world of Umuaro created around its chief Priest Ezeulu, the colonial administrator's world and its political concerns, symbolized by Colonial Winterbottom, the Missionary world represented by Catechists John good country and Moses Unachuku. These three have independent existence put together they form a totality, vast and mature, with revealing portraits of personal and social modes. Achebe is at his best in **Arrow of God,** which is a rich and renewed representation of traditional Ibo ethos within which Ezeulu tries to assert his individuality. The role of the white men here as agents of change is different from **Things Fall Apart.** In an article title, "The Human Dimension of History in **Arrow of God**", Obiechina writes:

> *The local school and mission station, irreverent strangers like the catechist Goodcountry and the inarticulate though palpable reality of the white man's administrative presence, all these have undermined traditional confidence and shakes the sense of common purpose and solidarity which in the past constitutes the spirit of traditionalism (Obiechina 1979:170).*

The people of Umuaro have come to view these changes without bitterness. Ezeulu contains the contradictions relating to the privileged role he plays, when the priest as Max Weber terms 'specially called' or 'set apart' from the category called 'most men' has been perceived as somehow more in touch with the transcendental realities than other men, as a spiritual leader, a divine sportsman, an intermediary between men and deity, and even the bearer of the people's spiritual burdens, he ministers at all stages of man's rites of passage and his personality may at times be defined in terms of the attributes of the God whom he serves (Weber 1930:20-31). But he is only the servant of God. It is not his individual will, but the will of the deity that guides him along. The tragedy of Ezeulu is that he tries to be 'himself', 'individualistic', identifying himself with the God whom he is expected to serve; defying the precept that

"... no matter how strong or great a man he was he should never challenge his chi" (**AOG** 27).

It is within this broad framework that Achebe establishes once again that and individual, priest or no priest, has real valid existence only in terms of the community. The norms of the society exact conformity from the individual, discouraging deviations and subversions of the common will and emphasize the primacy of the group over the individuals who compose it. This is reinforced in the fate of characters like Okonkwo and Ezeulu who are important and powerful in their own rights, yet as one sees, in their conflicts with their communities, the supremacy of the latter is soon established.

The Feast of the Pumpkin Leaves (**AOG** 66-73) is a dramatic realization of the major priestly function of Ezeulu. David Carrol says it is private as well as public drama: "The power of the scene comes from the effortless interaction of the individual & community, which at the climax, merge in the ritual gesture" (Carroll 1980:90). On the one hand Achebe seeks to give unity and authentically to the festival through the drums, the dancing in union, the cloud of dust and the imagery. The llo sounds like a vast swarm of giant flying insects. But this unified reality is repeatedly intruded upon and fragmented by the intervention of individual perspective artistically blended into it, like the fears and rivalries of Ezeulu's wives, the meeting of friends which are then gathered up into the totality of the larger ritual. This part is the most representative gesture of the fundamental vital rhythm of Ibo life (**AOG** 60).

The whole novel can be read as a search for individuality in the context of strong tribal affirmations, a quest for identity, characterized by personal idiosyncrasies. Ezeulu's misgiving as he tries to assess his powers, takes one right into the heart of the problem:

> *No. the chief priest of Ulu was more than that, must be more than that. If he should refuse to name the day there would be no festival-no planting and no reaping (**AOG** 3).*

Achebe goes on to follow Ezeulu's consciousness in argument with itself: "what kind of power was it if it would never be used?" (**AOG** 4) Ezeulu the man cannot be separated from Ezeulu the Chief Priest. Because of this, some critics regard the novel as depicting the desperate attempts of an individualistic high priest to redefine his relation to the society. The paradox of his office is indicated in his ceremonial appearance. He is half man and half spirit. In the world of man, he is very powerful, in the world of spirits he is a servant. The duality of his person and position is almost incomprehensible to the 'man' Ezeulu, which leads his to shifting loyalties from the 'Divine' to the 'Human'.

This discrepancy between 'Divine' and 'Human' becomes more acute and apparent in **Arrow of God** than in **Things Fall Apart**. Every minor event in the novel testifies to the theme that is explored and one's attention is immediately focussed on Ezeulu whose character embodies this dilemma in its most acute form. In complexity too, Ezeulu, far outdoes the hero of **Things Fall Apart**. Okonkwo's pride and assertiveness springs from his literal loyalty to the tribe and values upheld by it. That Ezeulu is proud and arrogant in his own right, and his personal drives and ambition in constant conflict with the expectations of the tribe, is highlighted throughout. But as Okonkwo discovers:

*A society based on a flexible balancing of competing claims is not the most comfortable place for a domineering personality. No one, not even a God is safe from criticism; there are always other people, other Gods, ready to supplant their predecessors in these shiftings, of sceptic Ibo communities (**TFA**: 92).*

The main threat is that Ezeulu attempts to identify himself with Ulu and imposes his will as the gods come from Nwake, the most titled man in the whole of the six villages. Nwaka's insight into the personality of Ezeulu maintains that "He is a man of ambition: he wants to be king, priest, divine, all. His father they said was like that. But the Umuaro people showed him that Ibo people knew no kings" (**AOG** 27-28). But as Ezeulu sees it, since the highest spiritual values are attached to his priestly tasks, any autonomous individual would tend to regard his achievements as a quasi-divine mastering of the whole situation and environments. Obvious that Ezeulu is quite conscious of his vulnerable position and this explains his closely scrutinizing the nature of his power in the beginning of the novel. He recalls how his authority was challenged five years ago over the war with Okperi. He advised Umuaro not to fight for a piece of land which was not theirs and warned them that Ulu would not support an unjust claim. But "Umuaro is today challenging its Chi … some people are still talking of carrying war to Okperi. Do they think that Ulu will fight in blame?" (**AOG** 27). Nwaka, however, refuses to accept the priest's authority and exclaims that his powers should be exclusively limited to the rituals as "the man who carries a deity is not a king. He is there to perform his God's ritual and carry sacrifices to him" (**AOG** 27). The significance of 'Chi' is once again brought to the limelight, whereas Ezeulu thinks that it is an offence to challenge one's 'Chi'. Nwaka asserts that "if a man says, 'yes', his 'Chi' also says 'yes' (**AOG** 28). Though Nwaka won the argument,

Umuaro lost the battle, the disputed and being given to Okperi by the white men. But the question of Ezeulu's identity in terms of his deity is still in a crisis and shrouded in mystery. Now his position as the unifying symbol of the tribe appears shaky.

In a sense, the inadequacy in the tribal set up, the fact that it has no room at all for individuality, in some ways parallels the problems of Ikemefuna and the twins in **Things Fall Apart**. What it points to is the limits of an old humanism prevalent in the tribe and how a socio-political order uses it. In the long run it leads to strangers making steady inroads into the traditional communities and creating wide chasms out of mild cracks. What interests us is the thought process of certain individuals in such a transitional phase, revealing the conflicts involved in the mental adjustments demanded of them. It is indeed fascinating in West African fictional locus, that against the innumerable literary creations celebrating the purely communal ethics in **Arrow of God**, Achebe has upheld the validity of an individualist mode of thinking. Hence there is no lamenting over things falling apart, but a very objective, realistic picture of Ibos at a phase where the encounter with the European values meant accommodation and assimilation rather than protest and conflict. Ezeulu is far more aware of the changing responds to it in an exceptionally more mature manner than the rest of his clansman. "The world is changing", he had told him (oduche). "I do not like it. But I am like him". When he was asked why he was always on the wing he replied, "men of today have learnt to shoot without missing and so I have learnt to fly without perching" (**AOG** 45). This renders him capable of deeper perception into the nature of things and a greater adaptability to changing conditions: Ezeulu's experience is treated by Achebe as something that is of little validity to the tribal world, that of the inward moral being of the individual. Thus, though Achebe does not release his hero from the determining ties of his society, the delineation of Ezeulu's character is marked by a radically individualistic approach. And in **Arrow of God**, self-examination, introspection and personal reflection lie interspersed with social documentation. The hero's consciousness is the Joycean Stream of Consciousness. His reflection over his image as the priest of Ulu, his decision to send Uduche to the white man's school, his leading role in the colourful celebration of the Feast of the Pumpkin Leaves, his witnessing against Umuaro in the land dispute with Okperi, his rejection of the 'warrant chieftaincy' and finally his refusal to proclaim the day for the New Yam Festival-everything is elaborated and gathered into a crescendo of controlling perfection from which Ezeulu has no escape. What happens in the course is a steady progressive alienation from his surroundings, a denial of normal human relations. By the end of the novel, the alienation is complete and turns out to be fatal, and his friend

Akuebue tells him, "no man however great can win judgement against a clan" (**AOG** 131).

The consciousness of the hero provides us with a glimpse into its depths will all its subtlety and complexity. He is not merely an appendage of the clan, but a world by himself, confined as it is, and conceived in 'Superhuman' proportions. The reader shares doubts and fears and ambitions of the High Priest wholly partaking of their eventual development into an obsession, until they reach a natural climax. Thus, the thematic progression is made logical and lucid rather than super-imposed. However, an element of Ezeulu pervades Ezeulu, befitting a Priest who dwells in a sanctorum, the sublimity that is part of the transcendental scheme of things. As Ezeulu himself says:

*I have my own way and I shall follow it. I can see things where other men are blind. That is why, I am thrown and at the same time I am throwable, ... you cannot know the things which beats the drum which Ezeulu dances (**AOG** 132).*

But this new internalized democratic, individualistic ethos evolves out of Ezeulu's own theistic apprehensions, and does not add to his priestly stature in the existing milieu. His final confrontation with the demand of the collective body of the tribe, is prior to the New Yam Festival which he manipulates to assert his own rights. Ezeulu refuses to accept warrant chieftaincy, infuriates Winterbottom the District commissioner and this results in his imprisonment for thirty-two days. This unexpected event adds a new dimension to the jealousy among the tribes of Umuaro. In his return from prison, Ezeulu recounts and broods over hid grievances against Umaro. The fights between Ezeulu and Ezidemili, mainly represented by Nwaka, is always seen as a threat to the power and authority of the chief priests of Ulu. Vengeance fumes in his mind, yet he is overwhelmed by the warmth of the welcome he receives from the whole of Umuaro on his return from captivity. Oscillating between the two options of revenge and reconciliation with his community, he begins "to probe with the sensitiveness of a snail's horn, the possibilities of reconciliation, or if that was too much, then narrowing down the area of conflict" (**AOG** 191). His imaginative recreation of tribal harmony attempts a striking balance between his human and divine roles, Ezeulu in fact does not feel any more the need to affirm that his power over the tribe is absolute.

This new-found sense of the community is described by the one direct intervention of Ulu in the novel, where his voice falls on Ezeulu like a thunderbolt:

Ta: Nwanu: barked Ulu in his ear, as a spirit would in the ear of an impertinent human child. "Who told you that this was your own fight?" Ezeulu trembled and said nothing, his gaze lowered to the floor. "You want to save your friends who bought you palm wine: Beware you do not come between me and my victim or you may receive blows not meant for you : Do you not know what happens when elephants fight? Go home and sleep and leave me settle my quarrel with Idemili whose envy seeks to destroy me, that his python may again come to power. As for me and Idemili, we shall fight to the finish; and whoever throws the other down will strip him off his anklet (AOG 191-192).

Ulu reasserts his control over the divine-half of Ezeulu's ambiguous nature in an unmistakable way, and all doubts and perplexities are resolved. The assertive priest's ambition and eagerness to identify with his God, and act on his behalf only provokes his wrath. The priest is nothing more than the remote agent of Ulu:

*After that there was no more to be said. Who was Ezeulu to tell his deity how to fight the jealous cult of the sacred python. It was a fight of the Gods. He was no more than an arrow in the bow of his gods. This thought intoxicated Ezeulu like palm-wine. New thoughts tumbled over themselves and past events took on new exciting significance. Why had Oduche imprisoned a python in his box? It had been blamed on the white man's religion; but was that the true cause? What if the boy was also an arrow in the hand of Ulu? (**AOG** 192).*

Ezeulu's madness takes the form of an extreme individualism, which means an assertion of complete independence from the reality of his existence.

The next part of the novel, till the end, depicts the struggle embodied in the person of Ezeulu. Presumptuous as he might be called, he lets himself to be ruled by the 'Secular' half in him rather than the 'sacred' and decides to hit Umuaro at its most vulnerable point-the Feast of the New Yam. He is a conformist with a vengeance; and considers himself 'sinned against rather than sinning'. The Feast takes on a new significance. Everything is made subordinate to the conflict with the rival God. Ezeulu should exact punishment from Umuaro for dividing its loyalty to him with the sacred python of Idemili. Achebe follows at length the 'subjective' in Ezeulu where he tries to rationalize his 'ungodly' approach and seeks peace with himself. Thus, he keeps up the enduring image of Ezeulu in his single-minded pursuit of a solid individuality.

The image of the unplacable Ezeulu has been highlighted. He refuses to proclaim the Feast of the New Yam. He is determined to manifest that he is not just an 'Arrow of God', rather, some body more potent and powerful. "I only call a new festival when there is one Yam left from the last. Today I have three yams and so I know that the time has not come (**AOG** 27). He means to make them wait the next two moons to eat the remaining sacred yams. "Ulu did say that two new moons came and went there was no one to break kola nut to him and Umuaro kept silent" (**AOG** 208). The yam harvests rot in the field and Ezeulu remains unappeased, the question of his power over the clan occupies our concern once again. Is it absolute or confidential? The question on the opening pages of the novel takes on a new relevance and depth here: "If he should refuse to name the day... But could he refuse? No Chief Priest could ever refuse. So, it could not be done" (**AOG** 3). He has refused and now tries to establish that it was done on the authority conferred on him by his God, extending a purely human act of personal revenge to a transcendental dimension.

With the same skill seen in **Things Fall Apart**, Achebe insinuates the growing challenge faced by Umuaro by the growth of Christianity, which seizes this moment of discord very effectively. One begins to hear the sound of the mission by the very heart of Umuaro; near the sacred shrine of Ulu. The narratives gain a powerful effect by the juxtaposition of two polarities embodied in two different religions:

> *As Ezeulu cast his string of cowries, the bell of Oduche's people began to ring. For one brief moment he was distracted by its sad, measured monotone and he thought how strange it was that it should sound so near – much nearer than it did in his compound (**AOG** 210).*

In a point of deadlock and despair the missionaries intervene and announce their own harvest festival, "whoever made his thanks offering to God, they could harvest their crops without fear of Ulu" (**AOG** 215). Desperate and confused the people turn to the Christian religion for help. They send their sons with yam offerings to the Church and harvest their crops in the name of new God. The sudden death Obika, Ezeulu's famous son serves as the end of the human drama. It disturbs Ezeulu's mind and sparks off the madness in Ezeulu's family and finally resolves the tension built up between Ulu, his priest, and clan. Ezeulu, broken, does not understand Ulu's desire to strike him down and cover him with mud. It shook Umuaro to the roots; they felt that "a man like him, did not come into the world too often" (**AOG** 229). The final act of the insane proves to be a blessing in disguise. "It allowed Ezeulu, in his last days to live in the haughty splendour of a demented high priest and spared him knowledge of the final outcome" (**AOG** 229).

A scrutiny of the text reveals a certain strain placed on the plot in the novelist's attempt to interrelate the three worlds into a coherent whole and almost all the characters are conspicuous for their inability to handle their situations and an immature grasp of events. The author is unwilling to commit himself with any precision as to the nature of the interior and exterior realities of the tribal religious world. One accepts the element of the inexplicable and the mysterious, as part of the world. Achebe tries to convince us that the ways of Ulu are untraceable and beyond the reach of man. However, for Umuaro it is simple.

> *Their Gods had taken sides with them against his headstrong and ambitious priest and thus upheld the wisdom of their ancestors – that no man however great was greater than his people; that no one ever won judgement against his clan (AOG 230).*

The last word belongs to the novelist who sees the whole narrative in its total historical context. He argues that of Ulu had meant to teach his priest loyalty and tribal wisdom, he had chosen a dangerous time for this, for "a deity who chose a time such as this to destroy a priest or abandon him to his enemies was inciting people to take liberties, and Umuaro was just ripe to do so" (**AOG** 230).

The mass defection of the tribe to Christianity must be seen as the result of the failure of the old dispensation to provide security to the people. As in **Things Fall Apart** the inadequacies of a disintegrating system provides space and accommodation for more flexibility of values, which acquires a stronger foothold in a time of crises.

With this historical dilemma, Achebe exposes the human realities faced by men and women who are caught up in it. The human dimension of it is concentrated on the high priest, the most fully individual character in the novel, who at the end of the novel stands free of all rituals and abstractions. He is defeated because his grasp of the situation is inadequate. Yet the changed valued and attitudes reflected in **Arrow of God** prepares us for a more radical departure from the tribal modes in thinking as well as in lived realities.

Thus, both Ayn Rand and Chinua Acebe can be considered as social realists in this phase, as both the authors highlight realistically the different situations in their respective societies. While Rand portrays the realism as existed in the Communist Russian Society and shows the individual's struggle to emerge from such a claustrophobic system in her fiction **We the Living** and **Anthem**, Chinua Acebe portrays the realism that existed in the traditional Ibo Society and depicts the transition from a communal to an independent, individual existence, in his fiction, **Things**

Fall Apart and **Arrow of God.**

Rand's power lies in her depiction of the grim terror, that prevailed even in the supposed golden age of Lenin. Everyone is reduced to a debasing dependence on The state, not because of the fear of arbitrary arrest but because of the total absence of property rights and economic freedom. One can be suddenly deprived of anything, job, possessions, living quarter, that is coveted by some Party hack. The characters are driven to corruption, prostitution, and treachery by the system that promised them 'liberation'. **We The Living** and **Anthem,** make the issue of property rights vivid and vital. It also shows the formation of a malign status system in a society where connections are everything and talent is next to nothing.

Achebe, in **Things Fall Apart** and **Arrow of God**, reveal the depth and inclusiveness of the pre-colonial Ibo society, and shows a clan of people who live a rich and rhythmic way of life that gradually becomes frozen. Through the stories of Okonkwo and Ezeulu, Achebe pays a tribute to the dignity of the Ibo tribe and their ancestors. But while Achebe recaptures the vigour of traditional life, where the life of individual, the beliefs, rituals and ceremonies of the community are merged into an order and significance, presenting a centre that will hold, Rand shows how her individuals are unable to cope with the Communist system. Even at the cost of their lives, they preserve their own 'sense of life' till the end. Though Kira is killed, Andrei shoots himself, and Leo chooses to live as a prosperous gigolo, the protagonists could be considered successful, unlike Achebe's protagonists who meet with defeat. Okonkwo, is like Kira in one sense, they never change. They are in the end as they were in the beginning. They never give up their 'sense of life' though life and society deal hardly with them.

Both societies throw light on a different kind of a collective system. Rand depicts an opportunistic, parasitical communist society, Achebe depicts a peaceful, well-knit communal Ibo society. Rand and Achebe's objectives in writing the fiction belonging to Phase I evolve from their different convictions. While Rand wrote **We The Living** and **Anthem** to warn America of her Russian nightmare, Achebe in **Things Fall Apart** and **Arrow of God** laments the loss of a rich and glorious past.

Thematically, Rand explores the sanctity of individual human life in this phase while Achebe depicts the crisis of the Collective Soul. Both Rand and Achebe hold up a gripping plot and a property almost unique, which portrays the individual's struggle against a society which attempts to overpower them. Here in this first phase, Rand's protagonists' lives end drastically. This is because Rand's protagonists live up to their own 'sense of life' and do not give up their struggle to maintain their own individual status quo, unlike Achebe's protagonists, who succumb to the social norms of their society and are unable to flout completely the restraint of the Ibo society on them. So, while Kira of **We the Living** succeeds to reach the Latvian border, beyond which her 'top value' Leo Kovalensky has escaped, she is shot in the process of the struggle. The individual is destroyed physically but not mentally or spiritually proving that "life undefeated existed and could exist" (**WTL** 446). Okonkwo of **Things Fall Apart** is unable to accept the flexibility of his society and commits suicide. There is a conversion that takes place in the heart of Ayn Rand's most remarkable character Andrei Taganov, 'the reddest communist ever' (**WTL** 24) and in Chinua Achebe's Character, Nwoye. Both Andrei and Nwoye are gradually convinced of the absurdity and the inhumanity of the Communist party and the tribal ethos respectively. While Andrei loses all faith and hope in his G.P.U. becoming almost an individual in the end, Nwoye loses all faith and hope in his tribal society; and finding the logic and humanity of the Christian religion more meaningful, joins the Christian Church as Isaac. Ezeulu of **Arrow of God** is also unable to relate his own selfish desires with those of his society's demands and becomes mad in the end.

In this first phase, the individuals hold out little hope, except in Anthem where the worthwhile protagonists exhibit abilities that are 'society shaking' (A 6). Equality 7-2521 is a creator and inventor in the tradition of Galileo, Edison and Einstein. In a world where all technological advancement has been lost, he discovers electricity and is able to move beyond the shackles of his limited education. He not only invents but defies. When his society is unable to accept what he offers, he escapes through uncharted forests to form a new colony of his own, where he and the others who wish to throw off the chains of collectivism can develop individually.

What is highly remarkable in this first phase is that the seeds of 'individualism' in the fiction of both Rand and Achebe are deeply planted. All the protagonists in the four books chosen to represent this early phase, are seen striving to assert their own individuality. In the overall perspective of Rand's philosophy. The State evolves a loser and the individuals are the winners. The individuals begin their evolution and is seen growing in the next phase into the 'man-child' of The Fountainhead; believing that the Ego is the fountainhead of all human progress and society is nothing but an empty shell. In the next phase, the Randian concept of society further deteriorates, when society is no more "The State" or any dictatorial system as in Phase I, but the evil men-'second handers', 'social suckers' or 'parasites.

With Achebe, the individuals are seen emerging from a well-knit, harmonious, ordered and disciplined society, unlike the corrupt and inhuman society of Rand. In this phase, Ibo society is at its best, but with the intervention of the white man, things fall apart, and the centre can no more hold them together. Gradually as the seeds of individualism sprout here, the clan no longer can think or feel as one, and succumbs to the influences of an alien force. The socio-cultural richness of the Ibo society if seen deteriorating gradually in the next two phases and the Ibo's are no longer at ease as they were. The individuals are portrayed as heroic, chivalrous and courageous men of dep thought and action, but as they emerge as individuals, they grow more corrupt and cowardly and also deteriorate. Okonkwo is cast in a better mould than Ezeulu; and Obi Okonkwo and Odili Samulu are still lesser men than Okonkwo and Ezeulu. In Rand's fiction, society deteriorates but the individual changes and develops in a linear progression. In Achebe's society the individuals change for the worse, though Achebe believes that change is a must.

Ayn Rand, being an emancipated woman writer, casts three of her, five protagonists as women; but Achebe, hailing from a chauvinistic, male-dominated society casts all his protagonists as men, except for Beatrice in **Anthills of the Savannah.** In this early phase, Rand introduces her first woman protagonist. Kira Argounova, and Liberty 5-3000 in **Anthem,** who follows the male protagonist, Equality 7-2521 to the Uncharted Forest. In phase I, Achebe depicts only male protagonists, namely Okonkwo and Ezeulu. Women characters have no significant part to play except for Ezinma in **Things Fall Apart and** are merely objects performing a junction.

In **We The Living** and Anthem Rand has not yet fully developed her concept of the ideal man, nor her concept of the parasitical society. The protagonists here, as the protagonists of Achebe are not portrayed as productive, since they do not contribute materially, as they do in the next phase. Kira Argounova, Leo Kovalensky, Andrei Taganov of **We The Living**, Equality 7-2521 and liberty 5-3000 of **Anthem,** and Okonkwo and Ezeulu of Things Fall Apart and Arrow of God respectively, are all 'chief strivers' and heroic individuals. But the two characters of actual achievement are Andrei Taganov of **We The Living** and Okonkwo of **Things Fall Apart**. Andrei is a hero whose bravery has been demonstrated in the battle of Melitopol. He risks his life to convince the White Army soldiers in the trenches that the red flag should be their flag. Okonkwo can also be called a man of great ability as he was:

> *Cut out for great things. He had won fame while still young as the greatest wrestler in the nine villages. He was a wealthy farmer, had two barns full of yams and had just married his third wife. He had taken two titles and had shown incredible prowess in two inter-tribal wars (TFA 5-6).*

Though Kira Argounova and Leo Kovalensky of We The Living and Ezeulu of Arrow of God have the raw materials for later achievement, none of them in this phase, are allowed to develop those natural resources. Kira has grand aspirations; she wants to be a builder and build bridges and buildings. To that end, she is a good student at the Technological Institute. The readers are convinced that she could be an able engineer, but she is prevented from becoming one. She is expelled from the Institute because she is the daughter of a former factory owner. Her talents are buried in a deadening job as an excursion guide. Leo Kovalensky's only demonstrated talents are in the attraction of women. Though Kira believes in him and though he does begin his studies in the University, his promise is also stultified by the reverse discrimination practised against children of those who were once in power. Leo's only accomplishments are a bitter bravado and black marketing.

Ezeulu, the Chief Priest of Ulu, tries to regain his power which he feels has been slowly slipping away from his position. Owing to a misunderstanding with Captain Winterbottom, Ezeulu is exiled and jailed for more than a month. By the time he returns, it is time for the New Yam Festival, and only Ezeulu can announce the yearly cycle. But Ezeulu refuses to announce the New Yam Festival and the yams begins to rot in the land, the village enmasse make their sacrifice to the Christian God instead, and the old traditional religion loses its vestiges of power almost overnight.

There is a noticeable development seen in the growth of the protagonists in the second books of the very same phase. Ezeulu of **Arrow of God** is a much more significant than Okonkwo of **Things Fall Apart**, just as Equality 7-2521 and Liberty 5-3000 of **Anthem** are much more significant than Kira and Leo of **We The Living**. The protagonists in **Anthem** and **Arrow of God** are characterized by what they do rather than by the lengthy authorial commentaries or description. There is a lot more introspection both in the form of dreams and in conversation that these protagonists indulge in. Ezeulu is as much an enigma as Kira. It is difficult to understand their attitude and actions. Kira Argounova, Leo Kovalensky, Equality 7-2521, Liberty 5-3000 and Ezeulu are much less gregarious individuals than Okonkwo.

In this phase, Rand also sows the seeds of her concept of a parasitical society. Rand calls her society 'parasitical', as the Communist system does not permit productivity. But Achebe's society is depicted as a 'productive' society, not parasitical nor opportunistic like Rand's. Achebe's society on the contrary promotes ability and appreciations men of courage and achievement.

The 'negative characters' like Pavel Syerov and Victor Dunaev are more specifically opportunistic than parasitical. Pavel Syerov and Victor Dunaev in a real sense are feeding off the productivity of others. Pavels Syerov trades upon his supposed friendship with Andrei Taganov, who is a real hero. He also benefits from the dangerous activities of speculators. Victor Dunaev has some real abilities, but he uses them to further his political aims, not to accomplish anything concrete. But there are not many negative or opportunistic characters in this phase of Achebe's world, unless the white man can be considered so; however, Achebe himself declares that the white man's invasion brought its own advantages and disadvantages.

Rand places great importance even in this early phase on the love theme, as an instantaneous recognition of a breed apart and sows the seeds of one of her major philosophic premises that 'Love is a response to values' (**AS** 987). In Achebe's fiction, in phase I, the love theme is totally missing. This is because the emphasis in Achebe's world, unlike in Rand's is more on communal life rather than on the individual's aspiration. Moreover, **Things Fall Apart** and **Arrow of God** are situational novels, not novels of character like Rand's **We The Living** and **Anthem.** The prime concern of Achebe here is recording the destruction of a traditional culture, and not depicting character, like Rand.

There is a difference in the way Rand and Achebe treat their individuals and their societies. In Rand, the triumph of individuals like Kira Argiunova, Andrei Taganov of **We The Living**; Equality 7-2521 and Liberty 5-3000 of **Anthem** symbolise the triumph of the individual and the death of the Communist society. But Achebe's handling of the tragedy of individuals namely Okonkwo of **Things Fall Apart** and Ezeulu of **Arrow of God** Symbolises the death and decay of a rich, traditional society, because in this society, and so their fall is also the beginning of things falling apart in the Ibo Society. But in another sense, the emergence of these individuals as independent beings, standing apart from the rest of society, speaks much for them as individuals who did stand alone with nothing and no one else beside them.

While Rand depicts her ruthless society as one where no alien force is responsible for freezing the life of the individual Achebe depicts his society on a very compassionate basis and shows how alien forces froze a noble, simple, yet rich poetic way of life.

Unlike in Rand's fiction, Achebe's novels show how Christian missionaries and The British intervene by the end of the nineteenth century and the Ibo society experiences a transitional phase at the socio-cultural, religious and economic levels. Rand's fiction does not depict such a transition, she condemns the political dictatorship that wrenches at the hearts and lives of men and women in a blood-thirsty society.

Even in this first phase, Rand and Achebe's attitude to God and religion stands out in sharp contrast. Joseph Sobran in his article, "Mussolini Shrugged : Ayn Rand Revived", tells us that just as some Christian could only see Communism as Jewish Bolshevism, Rand seems to have thought of Communism as the logical extension of Christianity, for which her euphemises were 'mysticism' and 'altruism' (Sobran 1989:53). An atheist herself, she makes no connection between Communism and atheism and never expresses sympathy for Communism Christian victims. "Religion", she writes in her private notebook in 1934, "is the first enemy of the ability to think… Faith is the worst curse of mankind". Championing the cause of reason, she believes that 'Man as he ought to be' is worthy of worship and hence all her major protagonists are depicted as men who ultimately evolve into 'demi-Gods'. Thus, evolves her cult of 'Man-Worship'. Kira Argounova of **We The Living** and Liberty 5-3000 of **Anthem** love and worship Leo Kovalensky and Equality 7-2521 to such an extent that they are willing to follow them blindly to the end of the world.

But in Achebe's world, the Ibo society is in direct contact with the supernatural through their various rituals, ceremonies, beliefs, myths and legends, all which one finds missing in Rand's world. Though the type of religion practised in the Ibo world is primitive, yet it is sincere and honest. There is hardly any life activity from birth to death that is not intimately punctuated by a religious exercise. This traditional Ibo religion is based on the forces and elements of nature, as Dalafosse in his book The Negroes of Africa: History and Culture observes that this type of religion an "agrarian cult" (Dalafosse 1981:219).

Phase I depicts Rand's doctrine of Objectivism in its embryonic stage. The villains of **We The Living** The and **Anthem** are depicted as 'selfish' people; whereas Kira Argounova engages one's sympathy because she loves another so much that she commits a monstrously 'unselfish' act. Kira becomes the mistress of Andrei in order to send her lover Leo to a Tuberculosis sanitorium. True, the concept of selfishness underwent a drastic high redefinition in Rand's hands as Sobran in his article "Mussolini Shrugged" tells us," but it is still stretching a point too far to call Kira 'more' selfish, in any sense, than the grubby little Party worms she has to contend with. She no doubt had more self-respect, but we didn't need Ayn Rand to point this out to us" (Sobran 1989:53).

Achebe's philosophic concern in these two novels is not very different from those he wrote later. He respects communal living, Brotherhood of man and individual men of courage and achievement. But in Phase I Achebe shows through the tragedies of Okonkwo and Ezeulu, that no man can exist outside his society, and if they do, they pay a high price.

Both Rand and Achebe wrote in the English Language out of choice, as they felt they could express themselves better in English rather than in their own native tongue. But Rand admits, unlike Achebe, she was not fully satisfied with the way she said things in this phase. For example, Rand felt that Kira's reactions to Leo were not quite right, they were too brief and understated. Rand's characters in this phase seem to speak for themselves and not for Rand. Again, unlike Achebe, the authorial commentary in this phase is not fully heard; there are numerous examples of authorial commentary heard through oral illustrations and proverbs in Achebe's fiction. The most revealing of these comments is often presented through a second character, reflecting upon another. In such a manner Ezeulu's son, Edogo thinks about his father. The trouble with Ezeulu was that he could never see something and take his eyes away from it. That was what their father could never learn. He must go on treating his grown children like little boys, and if they ever said 'no' there was a big quarrel. This was why the older his children grew the more he seemed to dislike them (Achebe 1960:103-104).

Sometimes the oral illustration is related to a more personal desire or need. When released from jail, Ezeulu says:

I cannot stay another day ... I am the tortoise who was trapped in a pit of excrement for two whole markets, but when helpers came to haul him out on the eight day he cried; "QUICK, QUICK: I cannot stand the stench" (AOG 204).

The use of these oral examples is a primary means of characterization, and it is the adults in Achebe's novel who make the greatest use of these materials, giving the impression of great wisdom. The majority of the proverbs in Arrow of God are spoken as dialogue rather than as a part of authorial commentary. The unique aspect of Achebes characterization, then, is the use of oral literary materials. He uses it far more frequently than other African writers.

In the next chapter the researcher traces the growth of individualism in the second phase of the fiction of Ayn Rand and Chinua Achebe. In Rand, the individual is seen evolving from the 'foetus' to the ideal 'man-child' of **The Fountainhead**; and Achebe's individuals in **No Longer at Ease** and **A Man of the People** are seen emerging from a secure solidarity to a new form of 'identity crisis' resulting from their assimilation of the Western culture and their inability to accommodate the two.

III

The Producer and the Parasite

Phase II comprises Rand's **The Fountainhead** and Chinua Achebe's **No Longer at Ease** and **A Man of the People**. With Rand's first novel **We the Living,** which Rand herself dismisses as "only an exercise, it was not my full novel yet" (B. Branden 1986:212), Rand is not ready to bring forth into her fictional universe either literary or philosophically, this concept of the ideal man. In **We the Living**, the foetus of the ideal man is only suggested in her feminine protagonist, Kira Argounova and in hero Leo Kovalensky; and the potential they might have realized, had they been born into a free country. This foetus grows into the 'man-child' of **The Fountainhead**. Rand identifies the theme of this novel as Individualism Versus Collectivism not in Politics but in Man's Soul". Rand THF 1943:11 In **The Fountainhead**, Rand attempts to contrast 'the Soul of an Individualist' with the 'Soul of a Collectivist'. Rand states the goal of her writing:

The motive and purpose of my writing is the projection of an ideal man, the portrayal of a moral ideal as my ultimate literary goal, as an end in itself (Rand 1971:16).

It is this aspiration of the ideal man that becomes the fundamental theme of Rand's fictional world and gives birth to the concept, the primacy of the individual, which consequently results in an estrangement from the collective mass, moulding her protagonists in this phase, as outsiders. The birth of the ideal man becomes the core of both her literary and philosophical interests; it is the very radiance of her soul.

The fiction of Rand radiates superlative values that are unique in this age. **The Fountainhead** offers profound and original philosophical themes expressed in logical and dramatic plot structures. They illustrate an uplifted and dignified vision of man, in the persons of her protagonists. Like Kira, the protagonist in **We the Living**, Howard Roark the Protagonist of **The Fountainhead** is characterized by strength, purposefulness, integrity and creativity. He is a happy idealist, self-confident, serene and very much at home on this earth.

The plot portrays a gifted young architect who believes that the ego is the fountainhead of all human progress. Roark has an explosive love affair with a beautiful woman, Dominique Francon, who claims to love him excruciatingly but struggles to destroy him and his career. But Roark, the protagonist, conquers all the obstacles in his path, overcomes all struggles and difficulties and for the first time in Rand's fiction, the individual evolves triumphant, steadfast in his goal and the pursuit of his own happiness.

The concept of the individual versus society in this phase arises from the conflict and tension that exist between the producer and the 'second-handers' or 'social-suckers'. The experience that helps Rand grasp this distinction between the two basic types of human motivation, is her meeting with a young woman whose goal is to possess what no one else has in life, and if someone has an automobile, she desires two. This young woman, it appears, is seeking to make an impression on society. She wants to feel superior as a social climber (B. Branden 1986:357). This realization fills Rand with a contempt that she never forgets. It dawns on her that she now has the key to the questions that she has pondered over for years- the question about people whose values and actions seem incomprehensively and unintelligible irrational (Pruette 1943:31). From her experience with this young woman, Rand creates her Peter Keatings, Ellsworth Tooheys, James Taggarts, who are all to be formed in the mould of this young woman. This concept that names the essence of the difference between the young woman and Rand, leads Rand to define two different ways of facing life, two antagonists, two types of men: the creator and the 'social-sucker'; the individualist and the collectivists; the 'first-hander' and the 'second-hander'; a Howard Roark and a Peter Keating, modelled after Rand and the young woman, respectively.

The producer, creator or the 'first-hander' is described in all the works of Rand as the man of self-sufficient ego, of independent judgement, who lives for his own sake and whose convictions, values and purposes are the product of his own mind. He is the prime mover whose source of movement is within his own spirit.

Rand, advocating the creator concept, attempts to state her objective in writing **The Fountainhead,** which is quoted by Peikoff in his book **The Early Ayn Rand: A Section from her Unpublished Fiction:**

... a defence of egoism in its real meaning. The question of what makes a person an individual or a collectivist ... what is the principle had interested me. The conversation with the girl, gave me not just the key to personal motivation, but to political motivation as well (Peikoff 1984:136).

In an article entitled "The only Path to Tomorrow", quoted in William

O'Neil's **With Charity Towards None**, Rand states her definition of Individualism and Collectivism:

> *Man is an independent entity with an inalienable right to the pursuit of his own happiness, in a society where man regards each other as equals; and Collectivism is the subjugation of an individual to a group, be it a race, a class or a state (O'Neil 1971:43).*

In **The Virtue of Selfishness**, Rand observes that life is a process of self-sustaining and self-generated action which leads to happiness" (Rand 1964:19). But when an individual is condemned by society for that 'self-generated action and happiness', and is subordinated to a group or state, he becomes estranged from the collective group. There exists a dichotomy between the individual's quest for happiness and the society's standard of happiness. The spontaneous assertion of the individual's initiative, feelings, wishes and opinions are stifled. In some extreme cases, such an alienation may throw an individual off his or her psychological balance.

Howard Roark, the protagonist in Rand's **The Fountainhead**, is the victim of such an estrangement from society. The whole focus of Roark's life is to promote life and action: that is the creative and the innovative. Rand tells us in **The Virtue of Selfishness**, that which sustains life and enriches it is termed 'the good' and that which negates and impoverishes it is termed 'the evil' (Rand **VOS** 1964:10).

The most significant element in the fiction of Rand is her characters. Part of her credo of Literature is that the writer should populate his or her stories with individuals who inspire the reader, ideal characters or, 'people we would want to meet rather than the characters like the people who live next door (Rand **TFH** 1943:39). The Protagonist, Howard Roark is projected as the 'Ideal man' in a corrupt society. From Kira Argounova in **We the Living**, there is a linear progression to the development of the individual as the "Ideal Man" in **The Fountainhead**, to the Man-God of **Atlas Shrugged**. The society here is not 'The State', but the social unit of man with the parasites and social suckers who stand in direct contrast to the protagonist. One of the purposes of this chapter is to analyse the character of the producer, Howard Roark and contrast him with the 'social-suckers' of **The Fountainhead**:

Howard Roark, is a young architect, who fights a violent battle against conventional standards in architecture. A man of exceptional calibre, he sets his own standards. His genius and integrity are as unyielding as granite. **The Fountainhead** throws light on Roark's explosive love affair with a beautiful woman who loves Roark passionately but struggles to defeat him by marrying his worst enemy, Peter Keating.

Juxtaposed against Roark are three other men: Peter Keating, Ellsworth Toohey and Gall Wynand. Wynand is a cynic who has qualities of greatness; but disillusionment with his fellowmen causes him to seek control over others. He becomes a political outsider functioning as a dictator. Ellsworth Toohey undermines ability by extolling ineptness and mediocrity. Toohey suffers from self-alienation along with Peter Keating, who rises to the top of his career by being a 'parasite' and a 'social-sucker'. He luxuriates in manipulating people, rather than creating sound architectural designs. Dominque Francon, Rand's heroine, is convinced of the triumph of evil over good, that she submits herself to every possible degradation.

Each of these characters represent a variation on the theme of good and evil. Roark, the protagonist in **The Fountainhead**, and a brilliant architect, is based on the model of the then leading architectural genius of the times, Frank Lloyd Wright. However, Rand contends that this is not true, as the only similarity is that both Roark and Wright were innovators fighting for modernism, as opposed to traditionalism in architecture. At the beginning of the novel, Roark is encountered naked and laughing, an innocent Adam, poised on the edge of a cliff. An uncompromising man of unswerving integrity and exceptional ability, he is guided by no values but his own. The plot follows his career from the day of his expulsion through his difficulties in establishing himself as a working architect, to his professional and personal vindication. He diverges from his code on rare occasions but even then, only in full awareness of what he is doing. Sometimes Roark compromises for the sake of Dominique Francon, the woman he loves or Gail Wynand, his friend.

In these cases, he is still true to himself for they are his 'top value'. The quality he demands from his friends is a 'self-sufficient ego'. He does not see a love-relationship as an amalgam of beings.

Roark lives up to his own definition of the creator as an individual who not only looks Nature in the face but also conquers it. He looks at the world around him and transforms Nature as it were.

He looked at the granite. To be cut, he thought and made into walls. He looked at a tree. To be split and made into rafters. He looked at a streak of rust on the stone and thought of iron ore under the ground. To be melted and to emerge as girders against the sky. These rocks, he thought, are here waiting for me, waiting for the drill, waiting to be split, ripped, pounded, reborn, waiting for the shape my hands will give them (TFH 31).

Roark has just been expelled from the Architectural School, for refusing to design buildings in the tradition of the past, and for designing instead buildings such as had never existed before. Roark is dismissed because he wants to express his own ideas and set his own goals. The Dean of the Institute wants to subordinate him to a group, a class. "Everything beautiful in architecture has been done already ... We can only choose from the great masters. Who are we to improve upon them?" (**TFH** 23). Roark tells the Dean that he does not care what anyone thinks about architecture. He decides he has only sixty years to live and he has chosen the work he wants to do in joy and happiness, not the condemnation of sixty years of torture in the Institute. Roark can find fulfilment only if he does his work in the best way possible to him. "The best is a matter of standards. And I set my own standards. I inherit nothing. I stand at the end of no tradition. I may, perhaps, stand at the beginning of one" (**TFH** 25). Roark wonders about the principle represented by men like the Dean, that alienates him from them. Years later, he identifies it as the phenomena of the 'second-hander', the 'social sucker' or the 'parasite'-"the man who lives off the productivity of others and contributes nothing to production itself" (**TFH** 31).

It is interesting to have an insight into Rand's speculations. What Roark feels and thinks is entirely a matter of his own; it cannot be influenced by anything or anyone on the outside. His feelings are, in the words of Leonard Peikoff in **The Early Ayn Rand**, "a steady unruffled flame, a profound joy of living and of knowing his power, a joy that is not even conscious of being joy because it is so steady, natural and unchangeable" (Peikoff 1984:140). Rand intends her ideal man to represent the creative principle of man and so she chooses architecture as Roark's profession. Architecture assists Rand to glorify the skyscraper as a symbol of achievement and of life on earth. Since architecture involves art, science and business all in one, she can with ease and grandeur illustrate the creative principles in man's three major types of productive career (B. Branden 1986:211).

Roark in Rand's early notes as Leonard Peikoff observes has been described as "a man who was in conflict with the world in every possible way, but at complete peace with himself" (Peikoff 1984:142). The life he lives in **The Fountainhead** confirms Hegel's second concept of alienation from the self that man is essentially spirit and the social substance is one form of the spirit, a form that has objectified itself. Roark, though in Randian terminology, is at peace with himself; in Hegelian ideology, Roark is alienated from the society which is his objectified spirit.

There are two instances in **The Fountainhead** which illustrate Roark's alienation from society: The Hopton Stoddard Temple case and the Cortlandt Homes Trial. Roark designs a temple for Mr. Hopton Stoddard on the premise that a temple should symbolise man's experience of exaltation. So, Howard Roark builds a temple to the Human Spirit. He sees man "as strong, proud, clean, wise and fearless. He sees man as a heroic being" (**TFH** 355). And he builds a temple to that spirit. But society, in the person of Ellsworth Toohey and Hopton Stoddard sees it as "a monument of profound hatred to humanity …as depraved" (**TFH** 355). They reject Roark's temple because society's standard of value s does not harmonise with Roark's sense of value and hence they flout it. The second instance of the Cortlandt Homes trial reveals the society's attempt to force its value, hollow as it is, on the individual creation. There exists an estrangement from society with the individual flouting the values of society.

Hegel contends that personality development is characterized by one's freedom to express oneself freely. By creating an object, one makes the object an extension of one's personality, reflecting the will of the individual and thereby objectifying it. In both the instances of the Stoddard Temple case and the Cortlandt Homes Trial, Roark's spirit and will is objectified, but in the language of Dominique, it is like:

> *Casting pearls without getting even a pork chop in return, and when a man casts pearls before swine, it is not against the swine that you feel indignation, but against the man who valued his pearls so little that he was willing to fling them into the muck (TFH 356).*

The Cortlandt Homes incident is the climax of **The Fountainhead**. Peter Keating grabs the designing of the Cortlandt Homes, a gigantic, government housing project to be built on the shore of the East River, a model for the whole world, as his only opportunity to rise from the debris of his failing career. He realizes he cannot design it. He asks Roark to do it for him and to allow him to present it as his own work. Roark agrees. He has spent years working on this problem of low-cost housing and he knows he will never be hired by any group, board, council or committee – public or private. Roark attaches only one condition to his agreement. Cortlandt Homes is to be built exactly as Roark designs it; that is his purpose, his goal and his reward, his own work, done his own way. Keating agrees. Roark designs Cortlandt Homes. The building commences and Keating fights the first fight of his life to save it from so many people Involved, each with authority, each wanting to exercise it in some way or another. He fails to save it, Roark's structural and engineering plans without which the project would not have been possible, are retained. But the finished building has only "the skeleton of what Roark had designed, with the remnants of ten different breeds piled on the lovely symmetry of the bones" (**TFH** 610) with a charge of dynamite, Roark destroys the butchered body of his creation.

A malevolent world in the form of these collectivists of the spirit tries to destroy and humiliate the spirit of Roark, which is objectified in the Cortlandt Homes. Roark is condemned to court trial. At the trial, Roark summarises the philosophy which the events of the novel and of Roark's life illustrate and this is also the philosophy of all Pand's protagonists. Her ideal men are victims of society and socially-alienated outsiders, because they uphold the dictum that progress and achievement come only from an independent mind; that altruism is the second-hander's weapon for enslaving the creator; that man is not a sacrificial animal but has the right to exist for his own sake.

Social reviewers renounce **The Fountainhead** and Roark's action, as a selfish betrayal – the assumption being that Roark dynamites Cortlandt Homes "because someone changed the look of his building and he didn't like it – so he blew up the home of the poor" (**TFH** 84). The issue involved is a breach of contract. The contract of the building guarantees that it would be erected as it is designed. It was not. The building was a government project and the government could not be used or forced to honour its contract without its consent. Roark has no legal recourse to undo the butchering of his work. Rather than have his "objectified spirit" mangled in Cortlandt Homes, he chooses to devastate it totally. "I agreed to design Cortlandt Homes, "Roark told the jury at the trial,

> *For the purpose of seeing it erected as I designed it. That was the price I set for my work. I was not paid. The owners of Cortlandt got what they wanted from we – a scheme to devise a structure as cheaply as possible, they took the benefit of my work and made me contribute it is a gift. But I am not an altruist. I do not contribute gifts of this nature (**TFH** 686).*

Roark argues that but for him, the destitute would not have had this particular home. Those who are concerned with the poor. They imagine they have a right to his own work and a claim to his life. He is not willing to let them have either, because he does not recognize anyone's right, to a single minute of his life nor any part of his energy, not any achievement of his; no matter who makes the claim, how huge the number nor how great their need. Roark testifies that 'I wish to come here and state that I am a man who does not exist for others. It has to be said. The world is perishing from an orgy of self-sacrifice" (**TFH** 687). The Cortlandt Homes is destroyed because it is a "double monster, in form and in implication" (**TFH** 684). Both have to be blasted because its form is mutilated by second-handers who assume the right to improve upon that which they have not made and cannot equal.

Rand, like the psychologist Erich Fromm, disapproves of this social contract theory advocated by Hobbes, Locke and Rousseau who state that man must lay down his property rights and resign it to the hands of the community. Rand, through her protagonists like Roark, Dagny Taggart, John Galt, Rearden and others, lashes out violently against such a theory. Rand believes in the doctrine of rational selfishness which she expresses in her article entitled "What is Capitalism?" in **Capitalism : The Unknown Ideal** "Every man is a sovereign individual who owns his person and no man is a 'natural resource' at the (rightful) disposable of others" (Rand 1967:54).

Howard Roark and all Rand's heroes and heroines are romantic realists and rebel against restrictive and mundane societies. In their rebellion, they act alone and on principle; they are all gifted and have unusual talents. Roark's triumph is given great emphasis by contrasting his success with the hardships and obstacles he goes through. These obstacles evolve only from one source: other men or society with all its chaos of selfishness and compromise; servility and lies that stand in the path of Roark. As he moves on, it is every second-hand living that combats him and tries to crush him in every possible manner but fails in the attempt. To every second-hander, Roark stands as a contrast, a reproach, a lesson a successful outsider. These second-handers are represented in the person of Peter Keating, Ellsworth Toohey and to a certain extent, Gail Wynand. They represent four distinct psychologies and ways of dealing with good and evil. But they may also be taken as realistically possible individuals, engaged in realistically possible courses of action. Only Dominique Francon stands solely as a symbol-a symbol of idealism frozen by contempt (B. Branden 1986:21).

It is interesting and important to observe the manner in which Rand arrives at the creation of her outsiders. Quoting Rand, Barbara Branden observes in The Passion of Ayn Rand:

> *If I took the ideal man as the creator, in relationship to him I would show three other types. Every character was devised in relation to the main theme. Roark is the man who could be the ideal man –and was;*

> *Wynand is the man who could have been –but wasn't; Keating who wasn't-and didn't know it; Toohey who wasn't-and knew it (Ibid:197).*

These are not fundamental definitions but helpful analysis of why she chose these as her key figures. Rand wonders what would happen to Roark if he surrenders to society and concludes that he would be the man of good premises who has given in, and thus is born Wynand. Rand contemplates on the arch villains and the enemies of Roark and Wynand and arrive at Ellsworth Toohey and Peter Keating. While Roark is shown as the individual who does not subordinate himself to the whim of the society and the looters, Gail Wynand, is a brilliant newspaper publisher whatever his readers want to read. He is the man who could have been the ideal man but was not; rather a man who gives in to the looters and becomes a political, dictatorial outsider. Gail Wynand becomes the victim of two types of alienation: Karl Marx in his **Early Writings** discusses his theory of alienation where 'the product does not reflect the individual's personality' (Marx 1975:26). The individual is forced to produce an object in accordance with another's desire. Man's creative instincts, because it is governed by the laws of the markets, are destroyed and man is dehumanized. The second concept of alienation that Wynand suffers from is described in the language of the psychoanalyst, Erich Fromm in **The Sane Society** as "the negation of personality". This is a situation where "one adopts the kind of personality offered to one by cultural patterns and hence ceases to be one's own self" (Fromm 1956:24).

Rand explains that she does not consider individuals, who are generally regarded as ambitions, 'truly selfish'. The problem, as she sees it is, that most ambitious men of the times achieve success by 'pandering to the masses' and in doing so negates the 'self', thus becoming in her view, 'selfless' (B. Branden 1986:214). The character of Gail Wynand is the personification of the man who becomes a slave to those he thinks he controls but who control him instead. In **The Ayn Rand Comparison**, Gladstein tells us that Rand believes "If a man goes after power by appealing to mob taste, he has the least power over anyone" (Gladstein 1982:18). Wynand is one of Rand's most tragic characters. At the green age of twelve he pulls himself out of his miserable environment, "Hell's Kitchen", in search of beauty and integrity. This quest brings him disillusionment. Two instances in his early life educate him. Wynand recognizes nothing but the accuracy of his own judgement and had always been the leader of his gang. When he is fifteen, he is beaten up into a bleeding pulp by a longshoreman; both his legs are broken and he is thrown into a gutter. Conscious of his inability for action and needing help for the first time in him life, he knocks on the door of a near-by saloon. The saloon keeper opens the door, looks at Wynand, conscious of the injustice of the act, but shuts the door in Wynand's face, as the saloonkeeper does not want to get mixed up with gang fights. This saps Wynand's concept of mercy and humanity dry. The second instance in when Wynand, reading an article in the newspaper on 'Integrity' rushes to the editor of the newspaper and pleads with him to defend only honest man he has ever met in his life, Pat Mulligan, a police officer who is framed. The editor yells at Wynand: "Do you expect me to remember all the swill I write?" (**TFH 408**). Wynand's education of life is complete. He realizes that love, humanity, mercy, integrity etc. are floating abstractions never to be realized in this world and this makes Wynand a cynic. Nothing a young writer of profound calibre, Wynand tries to buy him over to his newspaper, **The Banner**. But the youngster refuses to work for Wynand stating, "You have no ideals" (**TFH** 410). Wynand's cynicism reveals itself in his spontaneous reply:

> *You can't escape human depravity kid. The boss you work for may have ideals but he was to take orders and beg money from many contemptible people. I have no ideals... but I don't beg. That's your choice ....there is no other (TFH 412).*

Wynand, another variation of spiritual collectivism, has all the qualities of greatness like Roark, with visions of the clean, the good, the beautiful and the perfect; but his disillusionment with his fellowmen causes him to become a power-seeker, seeking control over others, buying man's spirit, not to make them but to mar them. He does not believe, like Roark, that it is important to one's integrity, to project the best that is within the individual. For Wynand, there are no bests. He decides to give the masses what they want and thirst for. Wynand himself asserts that **The Banner**, his newspaper, was the voice of the collective: "I am representing the majority" (**TFH** 409). He was a power-seeker as he observes to Dominique: "Power, Dominique, power... the only thing I ever wanted. To know there's not a man whom I can't force to do anything ... anything I choose. The man I cannot break would destroy me (**TFH** 498). This power he achieves through 'The Banner'. He surrenders himself to the vulgar and the mediocre, turning the newspaper into a cheap scandal sheet full of crime and punishment. Paying with his honour for unlimited power leaves him with nothing more to conquer. Bored and in a state of misanthropy, he is ready to play Russian Roullette with the lives and the spirit of man. Wynand delights in breaking the spirit of industrialists and financiers. Once he loses interest in such men, he finds a new kind of sport, a new kind of victim. He begins breaking honest men, men of integrity who are passionately devoted to their convictions. The first victim is Dwight Carson who champions the cause of the individual over the collective. Wynand brings Carson out and forces him to write an article for **The Banner** where he preaches the superiority of the masses over the individual man of genius. Wynand then forces an atheist to write on the glories of religion. He makes a disciplined scientific method. Wynand has no mercy for his prey nor does he show any interest in men of glittering success. His victims have a single attribute in common: their immaculate integrity. Once they are all broken, he continues to pay them scrupulously but he feels no concern for them and no desire to see them again. Dwight Carson becomes a dipsomaniac, two men become drug addicts one commits suicide. Alvah Scarret tries to stop Wynand's sadistic pleasures and destructive forces. But Wynand's only defence is:

> *"If lightning strikes a rotten tree, it's not the fault of the lightning".*
> *"But what do you call a healthy tree?" ask Alvah Scarret.*
> *"They don't exist, Alvah", said Wynand cheerfully, "they don't exist" (**TFH** 416).*

Toohey, knowing Wynand's fascination for things exquisite and beautiful, sends Wynand the statue of Domique which renews Wynand's interest in life. But unfortunately, Wynand meets Dominique and Roark too late. Having given himself to the parasites and the second-handers, Wynand cannot use his newspaper effectively when he decides to battle for positive values. Wynand attempts to fight for the first time for the cause in which he believes. He then sees the public rising against him and realization dawns on him that it was not he who had directed public opinion, but public opinion that had controlled and directed him. He capitulates and cannot forgive himself. He divorces Dominique, closes down **"The Banner"** but gives Roark the building commission which includes a proviso that he and Roark are never to meet again. Commenting on Wynand's alienation as he thirsts for power, Rand asks:

> *What is accomplished if the man attains power and prominence at the cost of playing to the masses? It is not he that triumphs; it is not his ideas and standards (Rand 1943:376).*

Wynand, though a power seeker, can be analysed as a virtuous character of equal stature with Roark. Like Dominique Francon, he is the embodiment of similar values and both of them serve as adjuncts in the quest to discover and maintain the good.

Dominique Francon, Rand's heroine is an outsider and like all Rand's protagonists and sub-heroic protagonists, she is also alienated from society and the world. Dominique's premise is a withdrawal from the world, not out of bad motives or cowardice, but out of an unbearable idealism. She does not know how to function in reality as it is. She becomes an interesting case study in perverseness. She is so convinced of the triumph of evil over good that she submits herself to every possible degradation. Dominique Francon has twin sources regarding her characterization: one is Rand "in a bad mood" and the other is Frank O'Connor " had he been a woman" (Branden 1986:261). These twin sources may be the reason why Dominique Francon is a beautiful woman with a body so exquisite that she models for a statue of tribute to the indomitable human spirit which the Hopton Stoddard Temple, designed by Roark, exemplifies. Proceeding from the conviction that good has no chance in this world, a premise, the opposite of Rand's belief, she chooses to be careless in order not to let anything or anyone have power over her. Masochistic in the extreme, she marries men she despises, in order to prove her careless spirit that she is too worthy of this world. The perversity does not stop there. She loves Roark but spends years attempting to destroy his career. It could have been more intense and carefully structured a vendetta, had she hated him. Whenever she does something particularly hurtful to him, she would go to him that night, to draw strength from him for her future battle. She spent years trying to destroy, herself and her own vision of life, which is, what the world ought to be. This is the cause of her torture-the state of the world as it is. She is to do it by leaving Roark, the man she loves and by marrying two men she despises, first Peter Keating and then Gail Wynand. She marries Peter Keating because he is the representation of the lowest breed of men and in her opinion herself degradation would be perfect if she married him. Gail Wynand buys her from Peter Keating for 250,000 dollars, and the Stoneridge commission. Dominique marries Wynand as an expression of a similar self-contempt but grows to care for him in the end. When Gail Wynand gives up his battle in order to save Roark, it is them that Dominique openly, and in a scandalous manner, gives Wynand reason to divorce her. But, by the end of the novel, after the Cordlandt Homes trial, Dominique is trained to harmonize her conflict with the world and accept happiness to live openly and unafraid as 'Mrs. Howard Roark' (**TFH** 341). Dominique Francon, condemns the Stoddard Temple because it is not part of its site; and Roark builds his temple for a world which is not worthy of it. Against this site, the Stoddard Temple that glorifies man's spirit is an 'unspeakable indignity'. The Stoddard Temple is a threat to many things-man's wealth, fame, love, brutality, murder and self-sacrifice and it symbolizes man's self-respect. Dominique's criteria are:

What is the use of being a martyr to the impossible? What is the use of building for a world that does not exist... The Stoddard Temple should *be devastated not to save men from it but to save it from men, because mankind has been reduced to moles and object to mountain peaks (**TFH** 360).*

Dominique feels like Raork, helpless in such a depraved world. The one and only time that she battles openly uphold the cause she believes in, is when she asserts: "This is my Stoddard Temple… my first and last" (**TFH** 357).

Rand's protagonists, be it a Roark or her sub-protagonists, be it Wynand or Dominique, are cast with over whelming and persuasive reality and are characters who are genuinely heroic and able. This is one of the chief reasons for the enormous popularity of Rand's fiction. Her characters, especially her heroic ones, have served as a source of moral and psychological inspiration for thousands of readers, especially the young. That she has been able to project convincingly such heroes and heroines is made possible not only by her literary spirit but by the nature of her philosophy, by virtue of the fact that hers is a philosophy for 'living on earth'.

Having dealt with the protagonist who forms the world of the creators and the producers symbolizing 'The Good' in **The Fountainhead,** the researcher, in this section of the chapter, proposes to analyse the arch villains and sub-villains who live as 'spiritual parasites', 'social-suckers' and second-handers', symbolizing 'The Evil' force in **The Fountainhead**. In this phase, Rand has juxtaposed the creator against the parasite. Rand is convinced that man as he exists, not what he is ordained to be.

'The parasite', the Social-Sucker', or the 'second-hander' has been defined by Rand as the man who rejects the responsibility of judging; who is moulded and shaped by other men who set his goals and standards for him. The parasite is the man who is the collectivist of the spirit, the man who places others over self. He is the soulless being who is motion without an internal motor. Ellsworth Toohey, Peter Keating and Gail Wynand are the parasites in this phase and symbolize a sick society. Roark, the protagonist, in his trial speech very aptly distinguishes these two concepts of the creator and the parasites:

The creator originates. The parasite borrows. The creator faces Nature alone, the parasite faces nature through an intermediary. The creator's concern is the conquest of nature, the parasite's concern is the conquest of men (TFH 681).

From the beginning of time, the two antagonists have stood face to face;

the first-hander and the second-hander. When the first creator invents, the second-hander responds, and invents altruism – the doctrine that preaches that man should live for others. Using this ideology as a weapon of exploitation, the altruist or the second-hander teaches man the concept of dependence as a virtue.

While the virtuous characters aid in the morality of the novel, the arch-villains and the sub-villains in the persons of Peter Keating, Ellsworth Toohey support the immoral in the novel. These serve to counteract the good. They embody and perpetuate the evils of Collectivism, Altruism and Mysticism. Rand's secondary villains swarm over her literary canvas. Rand's satire of, and inventive against a large part of society, are often capsulized in her portraits of the villains. How these archvillains use and exploit the sub-villains to reach their goal of destroying man and his spirit and thereby achieving power over them, will be briefly dealt with in this section of the chapter.

The major arch-villains who stand for the sick parasitical society are Peter Keating and Ellsworth Toohey, against whom the major protagonists combat to retain their individuality. Mr. & Mrs. Dale Ainsworth, Atherton Beasley, Sally Brent, Dwight Carson, Lancelot Cloakey, Jim Davis, Neil Demont, Jules Fougles form the sub-villains, who assist the arch-villains in their pursuit of the immoral and the evil. But the focus of analysis here, as in the previous chapter, is limited to the major protagonists and archvillains.

Ellsworth Monkton Toohey, like Gail Wynand, is a power seeker, who knows the concept of the ideal man and realizes that he is not one. He is cast as an archvillain, alongside Peter Keating, who knows the path of good but deliberately indulges in evil. Toohey symbolizes a kind of Hitler and Stalin presence in his quest for power. They serve as obstacles to prevent Roark from attaining his goal. In the process they also attempt to destroy Roark. Rand creates two types of negative characters:

1) those who are weak and ignorant. And
2) those who actively choose to do evil.

Keating belongs to the first category and Toohey to the second. Both of them are archvillains, perverse by nature, whose behaviour and attitude are repulsive and detrimental to human happiness.

Ellsworth Toohey is as vicious a villain as contemporary literature presents. His goal is power. His aim is to rule. He is cognizant of the effects of the destructive means he employs towards his end. By extolling ineptness and mediocrity, Toohey undermines ability and quality. The talentless thereby remain under his influence and the forces that would oppose him are reduced. Toohey wants Roark imprisoned, not to kill him, as he tells Keating but to subordinate the spirit of Roark. Toohey desires to get an intense gratification from seeing Roark locked up behind bars, strapped, but alive. He gloatingly tells Keating:

*He'll get up when they tell him to. He'll eat what they give him. He'll move when he's told to move and sleep when he's told. They will push him if he doesn't move fast enough and slap his face when they will feel like it. And he will obey. He will take orders. He will take orders (**TFH** 634).*

Toohey believes that man's soul must be ruled. If one man's soul is ruled, the rest of mankind could be easily conquered. It is the soul that is the hardest to break and the most difficult to vanquish. An aunt who sees through Toohey's treachery, tells him "you are a maggot, Elsie ... you feed on sores". To which Toohey replies: "Then I'll never starve" (**TFH** 298). Toohey thinks man is depraved and low and hence must be made to feel 'small' and 'guilty'. His aspiration and integrity should be destroyed and he should be taught 'selflessness' because he should live for others and not for himself. Altruism is the ideal. Altruism teaches man to become aware of his own worthlessness. Since the supreme ideal is beyond man's grasp, he will ultimately give up his ideals and his sense of personal values. Man will learn to distrust himself and to consider himself unclean. Such is the philosophy Toohey lived by. He uses this philosophy as a means to his end; the destruction of the human spirit! He laughs at a Roark and praises a Peter Keating. Toohey's desire is to be the great leveller, to extinguish all desire to excel.

Toohey preaches sacrifice and collectivism because he is convinced that every system of ethics that advocates sacrifice grows into a world power and rules millions of men. As he says one has to camouflage it and 'dress it up differently, sugar it over and promise people that they would achieve a 'superior kind of happiness' by giving up everything that makes them happy. "Use vague words like: 'Universal harmony, eternal spirit, divine purpose, nirvana, paradise, racial supremacy, the dictatorship of the proletariat ..." (**TFH** 635). Toohey is the kind of villain who has the most self-awareness. Thoroughly conscious of his actions, he continues to mutilate and hack the spirit of his fellowmen mercilessly. His self-awareness is revealed in his dynamic dialogue with Keating where he reveals his deviousness, his cunning mind, his perverse nature, his knowledge of the truth that an Individualist is the man who leaves another with enough space to breathe, while an Altruist is the man who thirsts for another's soul.

*The man who speaks to you of sacrifice speaks to you of slaves and masters. But if ever you hear a man telling you that you must be happy, that it's your natural right, that your first duty is to yourself, that will be the man who is not after your soul (**TFH** 639).*

Everything that Toohey advocates could be contained in one word- 'Collectivism'. A spiritual collectivist, Toohey is aware of the glorification of the individual man of genius, the co-creator or the god. That is why Toohey's betrayal to himself and consequently to the world at large, is more tragic. He is like the Roman Emperor who wishes that the whole of Humanity had just one neck, so that he could hack if off at one stroke. Toohey follows only one technique in the drama of his life. He offers "poison as food and poison as the antidote" (**TFH** 640). His only purpose and motivation of life is to "kill man's soul … Kill the individual" (**TFH** 641). Ellsworth Toohey is not just the figment of Rand's imaginative powers. He is modelled after a British socialist Harold Laski; Lewis Mumford, the writer on architecture who wrote in **The New Republic**, and Clifton Fadiman the editor of the **New Yorker,** and Heywood Brown, the columnist of "It Seems to Me" (**TFH** 656). The men who seek power make real their profound inferiority, intellectual self-doubt, furtive lust to deceive and manipulate the consciousness of others, resentment towards anything confident, able, benevolent, self-assertive, and above all their virulent rebellion against reason. And so, it is with Toohey.

Peter Keating is classified under Karen Horney's concept of psychological alienation analysed in the book **Neurosis and Human Growth**, where the individual is alienated from two dimensions of the self; the actual' and 'real' self. The actual self consists of negating all that a person actually is and the individual silences 'his genuine feelings, thoughts and emotions. Horney characterizes the 'the real self' as the most alive centre of one's self and to be cut off, as Peter Keating is, from his 'real self is to be hacked off from the "spring of emotional forces of constructive energies, of directive and judiciary power" (Horney 1951:47).

Keating belongs to the group of the parasites. "I am a parasite", Keating tells Roark, and in that statement of self-recognition, he aptly characteristics his villainy and his weakness. Because he wants to feel superior, Keating blackmails, plagiarizes and beguiles his way to the top of his field. His dark, good looks and easy popularity are used to ingratiate himself with his superiors. He moves easily from the star at the Stanton Institute of Technology, to the rising young architect in the firm of Francon and Heyer, by becoming whatever people want him to be. He marries Dominique whom he does not love. Keating's last meeting with

Catherine Halsey throws light on the abject selflessness of his entire life and the futility of his quest to survive by means of adjusting blindly to the values of others:

*Katie, I wanted to marry you. It was the only thing I ever really wanted. And that's the sin that can't be forgiven that I hadn't done what I wanted ... Katie, why do they always teach us that it's easy and evil to do what we want. And it takes the greatest kind of courage. I mean what we really want. As I wanted to marry you. Not as I wanted to sleep with some woman or get drunk or get my name in the papers. Those things-they are not even desires-they're things people do to escape from desires-because it is such a big responsibility really to want something (**TFH** 599-600).*

Keating sells Dominique for the Stoddard Commission. By the age of thirty-nine, he is a miserable 'has-been', and though he understands the nature of his betrayal of self, he is too weak and dependent to change. His presence at Roark's trail has little impact because there is on being left in the shell of his body. Peter Keating possess a modicum of talent, but rather than develop his gift, he guides his life by pursuing what other people think is important. He never learns his craft and when important commissions are called for, he must put his name on other people's work, as in the Cosmo-Slotnick Building and the Cortlandt Homes Housing Project. When he achieves everything he should want, he does not understand the hollowness of it. He is never satisfied because he has never gone after what he wants. While Roark does not need any one's approval for his work. Since he knows his worth, Peter Keating needs Committees, Unions, Groups to reinforce themselves. Peter Keating, like Ellsworth Toohey also represents a variation of spiritual collectivism. Rand's concept of the 'second hander', is a landmark of psychological analysis. The character of Peter Keating is the psychological analysis of the spiritually dependent; the man who rejects the responsibility of living by the judgment of his mind. **The Fountainhead** can be read as a modern version of a Medieval Morality play. Each of its characters represent a variation of the continuum between good and evil.

An individual's human life should be the standard by which his religious, moral, ethical life is judged, according to Rand. Rand further develops her concept of 'man-worship' in this phase. Mr Stoddaed tells Howaed Roark, "You are a profoundly religious man, Mr Roark" (**TFH** 320). Roark acknowledges his religiosity in a whisper after a long contemplation; "that is true" (**TFH** 320). Roark's spirit within, harmonizes with what he projects on the without. Stoddard wants Roark to build a temple to his spirit: "I wish to call it God. You may choose any other name, but what I want in that building is your spirit. Your spirit Mr. Roark" (**TFH**-320), thus, the Stoddard Temple to the Human spirit is built. Its symbol is man-worship. It is glorification of that which is intelligible, probable, grasp able and the definable, which is the exact opposite of institutionalized religious worship, not to the Divine Creator, but to a heroic vision of man.

This concept of Man-worship, Branden observes in the **Passion of Ayn Rand**, evoked a storm of reactions to **The Fountainhead**, condemning the book as 'too intellectual', 'too controversial', that it goes 'against the prevailing climate of opinion'- collectivism, that the story is 'improbable', the hero 'unsympathetic', and no one can identify himself with Roark and that 'no audience existed for it and hence it will not 'sell'. Thus, **The Fountainhead**, like Rand's protagonists, is condemned for being too good, too idealistic. But today, Barbara Branden observes, the book that was too controversial is studied in university classrooms and has achieved the status of a modern classic. Letters poured in from all areas of life, saying that they find in Roark:

*a moral intransigence, a personal ideal that the image of Roark had given them a greater courage to stand by their own convictions, that **The Fountainhead** had liberated them from any guilt they had experienced for their failure to live by the ethics of Altruism-that it had given them a sense of what is possible in life, what is possible in Man what is possible to them (Ibid., **TFH** 415).*

This leads Ayn Rand to believe that there is hope for humanity because the sales of The Fountainhead confirm that man ultimately responds to values, which is the reason why she chooses Frank O'Connor's painting for its cover, titled: 'Man Also Rises' (**TFH** 417).

When one moves on to the second phase in Achebe's fiction, one sees how Achebe's concept of the emerging individual in **No Longer at Ease** and **A Man of the People** is very difficult from that of Ayn Rand's, and portrays a new concept.

Individualism seems to be acquiring a new meaning and dimension as one examines it in relations to the multiple reality of the urban ethos. The factors weaving up to this particular fictional milieu are numerous, and essentially different from and more complex than those of the tribal world in **Things Fall Apart** and **Arrow of God**. Two major factors mentioned in the previous chapter i.e., educational factors and economic advancement have come to exercise a wider and more potent force on the characters of **No Longer at Ease**, and **A Man of the People**, reshaping their total thought pattern. In **No Longer at Ease**, the quest for knowledge and power becomes a pronounced motif. The emerging individuals here are inextricably related to the socio-economic climate dealt with in the narrative, simultaneously effecting a further severance of the individual from his tribal affiliation. **No Longer at Ease** could be described as marking the initial stages of individualism, where it involves an enormous amount of conflict and tension, as Obi is still very much part of the corporate existence of the traditional type. It is his wide exposure to Western values that creates a new awareness in him and his rights as an individual is divorced from any collective responsibility. Individualism is thus upheld as an ideal and fought for by Obi. Thus, in **No Longer at Ease** and **A Man of the People** we move on to the second stage of the steady phase of the progression of individualism in the context if Achebe's world. The encounter with European values and Christianity is no more a conflicting issue; rather it has become an accepted thesis and effectively constitute the social framework of the novel. The focus is on Obi, son of Nwoye, and grandson of Okonkwo of **Things Fall Apart**.

Aboile Irele, in his article "The Tragic Conflict in the Novels of Chinua Achebe" says that **'No Longer at Ease** is a sequel to **Things Fall Apart**, not only in the fact that a lost generation of Okonkwo's family is involved, but also in the theme. It treats of the dislocation in the African psyche that followed the disintegration of a situation in which a meaningful social and moral orientation is made difficult (Irele 1967:12). It is also the story of an individual, Obi Okonkwo who is caught up in this situation, which demands the individual to create a firm moral order out of the flux of values in the world in which he lives – a situation that demands an exceptional moral and intellectual initiative. Obi's dilemma is contained in the conflict between his developed intellectual insight and his lack of moral strength to sustain it .Irele argues that the whole novel is built out of the profound gulf that exists between Obi's western education and its practical relevance to his individual place in the world. "Obi is something of an aesthete, but his culture is manifest in an attachment to things that are of no real consequence" (Ibidem:16).

The various forces at work are made comprehensible only with an accurate understanding of the political situation, social stratification and the economic problems of a definite historical context of the Nigeria of 1950, a composite product of the intermingling of Europe and Africa. The theme of **No Longer at Ease** is, in one sense, as G.D. Killiam says, in **The Novels of Chinua Achebe**, the price of modernity for an African society: it is Nigerian society itself which is "no longer at ease" and not merely Obi himself, though of course the social unease centres in Obi, the "only palm-fruit" (Killiam 1969:64). There is a conflict between

Obi's at-times wayward individually and the expectations of the group which has been responsible for subscribing to the loan which has enabled Obi to go to England for a university education that is intended to benefit society first and foremost. The Umuofia Progressive Union expects Obi to pay back the money loaned to him, and to maintain a European standard of living, and at the same time to fulfil his financial obligations according to the requirements of the 'extended family system' (**NLAE** 47). Although Obi is made to appear exceedingly, if not incredibly careless about money, and the financial demands to which he is to be subject (Killiam 1969:66), there is nevertheless a real sense of irrevocable beliefs and Christianity, and between both these, a non-religious superficial rationalism.

Adrain Hastings, in his book **African Christianity** discusses the traditional belief most crucial in Obi's fate, which is the opposition of his parents to his relationship with the 'Osu' (Hastings 1976:17) girl Clara; for it is at this point that he gives way under pressure, and Obi realizes partially and too late his own hollowness, that in the face of his father's objection "there was nothing in him, with which to challenge it honestly" (Ibidem:18). Obi tries the argument of Christian compassion as a means of persuasion, but there is in Obi no real commitment to Christian belief. Yet, Isaac's own Christian belief is real. He has been through a fire that Obi does not even know exists, and Isaac's retention of the prohibition against the "Osu", is a sign that he, like so many others, is a divided man in a divided society.

Obi therefore returning to transform society, or at least to make it more honest, or to resist corruption himself, finds a society full of conflicting demands. All those around him are divided as fragmentary beings in one way or another: his friend, Christopher, an economist, has his religion of sex (Christopher's bed is flippantly called the 'Holy of Holies') and a specious line of reasoning about corruption; Joseph, Obi's countryman, is both urbanized in his employment and sufficiently traditional to warn both Obi's parents and the Umuofia Progressive Union about Obi's involvement with Clara; Mr. Green, Obi's boss is a man born out of his time, in power yet powerless, totally unable to see that it is the civilization of which he is a member, that has been responsible in large part for the historical element in Obi's fate; finally, Clara too is divided, an 'Osu' and a modern nurse, a 'been-to' who is yet unable to escape from her traditional role and divided, in another way, between a real relationship and cinema fantasies.

Achebe is therefore dealing with a many-sided fragmentation but is doing so in a highly structured formal discipline.

The novel is more than a refutation. It shows a society radically changed from that in Things Fall Apart; it shows a city Lagos, not to be imagined in the context of the earlier novel, it shows a phenomenon, 'corruption' in the city, Lagos, and most of the changes that are manifest. The city, in its complexity, is symbolic of the aspiration and corruption of the new society.

At the risk of being simplistic, **No Longer at Ease** can be said to be depicting a decisively transitional phase in the history of West Africa and the social milieu is an amalgam of values carried over from Umuofia and borrowed from England, represented in the urban reality of Lagos. The values upheld in **Things Fall Apart** and Arrow of God have lost much of its validity yet is not totally irrelevant and continues to be a binding force through the powerful Umuofia Progressive Union, which is symbolic of the eventual transference of tribal values to the urban milieu. The religious atmosphere that pervades the two novels in the last phase has been lost considerably. Instead there is an atmosphere of 'peaceful coexistence' (**NLAE** 45) where religion as understood and practised by the earlier generations, has ceased to be a decisive force and has come to signify a solemn, social celebration, as in the reception given to Obi on his return from England.

An effortless blending of two religions and the ease of its employment, symbolizes the leap made from the earlier novels in their social vision. Despite its initial conflicts, Christianity has made a palpable impact on the tribal people within a time span of two generations. A new dilemma is enacted further on with the inevitable breakdown of the religiously orientated world view in the emerging urbanized ethos. There is a marked absence of any new creed with which it is to be substituted and has an equal grip on events and individuals. Society here is caught in the process of a fast change. Values are vague and in a flux; objectives are confused; allegiances are not clearly defined. J. V. Taylor in **The Primary Vision** says that the economic motif logically entailing a devaluation of their modes of thought, is on its way to replacing all other considerations (Taylor 1963:72). Thus, what happened in West Europe applies to West Africa as far as it led to a reorientation of their values.

In Chapter II of **No Longer at Ease**, Obi gives us a comprehension of the city of Lagos as it would mould his career and reshape his destiny. Obi, while in England for four years, realizes that Nigeria is more than a name to him. His predicament is ironic, because he is unable to come to terms with the Nigeria he discovers after his studies.

It also exposes the irony of the situation, because the people have shifted their attention from the 'great light' (**NLAE** 8) that was Religion in **Things Fall Apart**, to the 'great light' (Ibidem) that is Education in **No Longer at Ease**. This shift from the 'sacred' to the 'secular', results in respective sequential reorientation embracing their total apprehension of reality.

The tribe still asserts its hold on the individual, Obi. The most interesting feature of Achebe's fictional world is, as C.R. Larson points out in **The Search for the Past, East and Central African Writing** that in the present context, Obi is expected not only to defend the status quo; the establishment of which his grandfather died trying to prevent, but also to transform it as well, as he leaves his country in quest of more knowledge which ultimately aims at the economic emancipation of his tribesmen. In the next stage of this dialectical process, "the old synthesis has without their knowledge become the new thesis which will in turn be questioned by the new values Obi brings back from abroad (Larson, 1978:12-15). The Umuofians (or even the people of Lagos for that matter) do not anticipate that the knowledge which brings power will bring detachment and alienation too in its train. And hence one witnesses this inevitable process of the growing pains of a new mode of all the decisive stages of the unfolding of the 'Ibo Saga'-an outlook which needs with hostility at every stage and emerges, triumphant. Obi's fate is no different.

Obi's alienation becomes apparent to the Umuofia Progressive Union at the reception it holds in Lagos in his honour. Four years of study in London, invests Obi with a new vision, a radical awareness, that in unconventional to the core. For him, education means initiation into a highly personalized grasp of reality which makes him utter confidently to Joseph: "I'm going to marry the girl. I wasn't actually seeking your approval" (**NLAE** 72). He has moved away from ideologies still valid to the tribe's men, and the numerous clashes are a result of mutual inapprehension of Obi's deliberate assertion of his individual rights. Obi's moving away from the collective to a potentially subjective level of existence implies two basic attitudes:

i) The individual is fully responsible for his actions.
ii) An increased and intense consciousness of the self as an ultimate entity.

This presupposition gives one a deeper penetration into the thematic development of the novel beyond its formal realism. It is worked out through social relationship where Obi struggles for freedom of thought and action, inconceivable to the tribal mind. Pressure forces him to give up his idealism. He retraces his steps and attempts to recede into introspection, verging on egocentricity, yet strangely lacking in perception, as a character.

Obi's idealistic individualism makes him fall short of the great expectations of the Umuofia Progressive Union. The Union's major interest is in tribal solidarity and self-interest and the meeting ends with a discussion of bribery and influence. The 'Cultural Conflict' (Ibidem:18) of Obi, manifested in his first encounter with his tribesmen is explored. Numerous conflicting issues orbit him;

i. His estranged relationship with his tribe.
ii. Obligations towards the family.
iii. Relationship with Clara.
iv. Mounting financial pressures.
v. The allurements of city life and his professional idealism.

The whole series of events are almost spatialized, constituting a highly suggestive spectrum of the prevailing social morale. Disillusioned with the system and alienated from his own society, Obi himself sounds like a colonial describing the natives.

*What an Augean Stable! he muttered to himself. Where does one begin? With the masses? Educate the masses? He shook his head. "Not a chance there". It would take centuries, handful of men at the top. Or even one man with vision, an enlightened dictator. People are scared of the word nowadays. But what kind of democracy can exist side by side with so much corruption and ignorance? Perhaps a halfway house -a sort of compromise (**NLAE** 40).*

H. Barba observes in "Image of the African in Transition": the novelist, with a sustained irony repeatedly unravels the "cultural dislocation of his hero" (Barba 1963:251-21). The roots of this unique 'schizophrenia' could be traced back to his early childhood in a very logical manner. Obi's lack of grip on any single life principle and his "mission house upbringing and European education had made him a stranger in his country" (**NLAE** 71-72). Fed on diverse religion-cultural elements, the seeds of an unresolved conflict and unsteady affirmations were absorbed into his mental make-up as a child. The Nigeria of the first half of the century possessed a hybrid culture, which accommodated elements of tribal religious values and Christianity. His father, as village catechist, insisted dogmatically upon Christian upbringing, whereas the mother tried to modify this quietly but insistently with her native fork lore (**NLAE** 57-58). This double heritage frustrates him and leaves him in a spiritual void without anything substantial to hold on to.

The cultural conflict is made manifest through two main issues: duty and marriage. There is a discrepancy between Mr Green's concept of ideal duty and the view of duty and loyalty envisaged by the Umuofia Progressive Union. Mr Green's diligence and rectitude makes him almost an abstraction. Obi is forced to step too low, to the level of being demoralized. Obi perceives the full implication that has followed him into Lagos. From one point of view, it is an impressive continuation of the communal solidarity into the modern city and the tribal ethnic one witnesses in the previous chapter. Obi is expected to help fellow Umuofians, using his position to pay back his debt to his tribe. The tribe fails to see that commendable ideal of tribal fellow feeling, when transferred to the town becomes nepotism and self-interest. It is also a question of viewing the whole situation from a totally different individualised framework. The task performed by individuals are mostly roles ascribed to them by the society. They expect whatever they come to inherit. This inevitably results in conformity to the prevailing modes and prevents any form of unconventionality. Having been exposed to a different pattern of thinking, and being strongly influenced by it, Obi's norms are now personally validated ones, which naturally turn out to be inacceptable to the tribe. Within the new bourgeois scale of values, one's personally achieved status is what matters and that points to the inviolable rights of the individual as against those of the tribe upheld in the earlier circumstances. Obi is in debt to the community, yet his concept of duty demands he act as an independent agent. The ambiguity of relationship, a stifling phenomenon curbs the growth of Obi as a person and nullifies his individualism.

The two versions of 'duty' represented by Greene, and Obi reinforce the contradictory views of the individual in the society. David Carroll in his book **Chinua Achebe,** uses two potential terms in this connection; the 'atomistic view', which holds the individual solitary and self-sufficient, where "duty is a means of exercising his will and testing, his integrity", and the second is the 'Organic View' which incessantly affirms that "the individual is a member of a community", a fact which guides and controls his action. Here, "duty is the constant awareness of the self as an integral part of the organic whole of the village or "tribe through which one acts and achieves identity". It provides one with a concrete example of the meeting of European individualism and African tribalism, "in the confused no-man's land of the city which represents-both" (Carroll 1980:49); and one is compelled to restate the earlier assumption that within the context of tribal values, one's individuality is realized only in terms of the corporate body. The tragic inevitability of the situation is fully captured in the fact that he has been educated at great cost by his clan, but the lesson he has learnt is inviolability of the freedom of the individuals. Obi's sense of individualism is treated rather ironically by Achebe, because the increased awareness of his potentials, somehow transforms him into a misfit, incapable of responding effectively to the demands of the situation.

Another facet of Obi's identity crisis is eventually brought to light in spite of his consistent attempt to reconcile conflicting claims. Here again Obi is trapped between two different value systems in the choice of a life partner. He wants to marry Clara, but the tribes set up arms against him because Clara is an 'Osu'. Obi refuses to be controlled by outdated practises:

> *It was scandalous that in the middle of the twentieth century a man could be barred from marrying a girl simply because her great-great-great-great-grandfather had been dedicated to serve a god, thereby setting himself apart and turning his descendants into a forbidden caste to the end of Time (**NLAE** 65).*

He insists they get engaged, confident he can master his own life. But he is summoned home by his father, to meet the fiercest opposition of all and when he tells his father, whom he wants to marry, "His father laughed. It was the kind of laughter one sometimes heard from a masked ancestral Spirit" (**NLAE** 120).

Disconcertingly, one is back in the world of Things Fall Apart and Arrow of God, where Obi is told that if he marries an Osu,

> *....your children and your children's children ... (until the third and fourth generation) will curse your memory. It is not for myself I speak; my days are few. You will bring sorrow on your head and on the heads of your children. Who will marry your daughters? Whose daughters will your sons marry? Think of that my son.*
> *We are Christians, but we cannot marry our own daughters (**NLAE** 12).*

Obi argues that being Christians, they cannot accept Osu prohibition, and professes to meet the challenge … but his father rejects Christianity and reverts to tribal law. This regression to earlier beliefs, states that apparent assimilation of cultures and faiths are built on shaky foundation, in the case of both father and son. This implies that society is still in the process of change and no new values have taken deep root. Beneath all innovation and change, lies the solidarity of the tribe.

Obi's professional ethics is challenged. Obi lives now in the cult of despair and experiences almost a dismembering of the self.

> *His mind was troubled not only by what had happened but also by the discovery that there was nothing in him with which to challenge it honestly. All day he had striven to rouse his anger and his conviction, but he was honest enough with him, to realise that the response he got, no matter how violent it sometimes appeared, was not genuine (**NLAE** 124).*

He finds it hard to accept his parents' values, and also to reject it. The hybrid nature of his individuality is neatly drawn, as he is a product of Umuofia, Lagos and Europe. His manner in relation to people, display deep rooted inner conflict and lack of grip. He is no longer at ease with Clara. When he returns to Lagos he wants to break off his engagement. This is financially a breakdown too. With his mother's death, all ties with the past are dissipated. Engulfed in social impasse, he attempts a series of rationalizations aimed at self-justifications, in the repudiation of Clara and in the acceptance of bribes. His attempts to preserve his 'old self' is seen in his efforts to draw distinctions between accepting bribes from those candidates who are likely to win and those who cannot.

With a feeling of guilt, he senses extreme loss at his mother's death. He tries to redefine his relationship with her and finds solace in "the memory of his mother (which) seemed to release this kind of peace... the peace that passed all understanding" (nlae 149). He attributes his despair and guilt to a new philosophy, a new vision of reality. This is suggestive of a more objective vision, yet it speaks of a passive acceptance of life as it is. His thought process reflects unresolvable conflicts in the present, aggravated by his almost mechanical surrender to it. Yet his attitude is nebulous, which puts it outside the confines of neat formulations and renders it rather abstract. His 'idealism' is unable to struggle for survival and dies a natural death. The novelist has not been very eager to unravel the psychic mysteries of his hero. No pattern of consistent thinking can be formed from the narrative. This inherent ambiguity contributes to the tragedy in a very unique and modernistic sense of the term.

Obi's 'identity crisis' is due. He is lost in a world of contradictions and oppressive forces. He feels victimised by his own people. The final paragraph flashes back to the first chapter and reminds the reader of the inexplicability of the whole dilemma, and suggests what a vicious circle it has been:

*Everybody wondered why. The learned judge, as we have seen, could not comprehend how an educated young man and so on and so forth. The British Council man, even the men of Umuofia, did not know. And we must presume that, in spite of his certitude, Mr. Green did not know either (**NLAE** 154).*

Emmanuel Ngara in Art and Ideology in The African Novel, says that Obi, a hybrid product in search of a stable point of view, faces the dilemma of idealism, and "the effects of the flashback is to concentrate attentions on the causes for Obi's conviction and the complexity of events, actions and decision which lead up to it" (Ngara 1985:22).

The understanding of 'individualism' which Achebe portrays in the character of Obi, is one which leaves no doubt as to the impossibility of synthesising two opposite values-those of Umuofia and Europe. It is vital to see beyond the surface conflicts of social moves and view it as a predicament of the individual who contains diverse conflict within his own self and those of religion and its values. This inherent dualism forces on him irreconcilable demands. The 'divided' commitment (Ibidem) is further deepened as the narrative proceeds and leaves Obi with a sense of the lack of a unified view of life and a specifically relevant awareness.

This could be viewed as his inability to assert himself in the face of pressures, because this premature death of an idealist takes us to Colin Wilson's analysis of the outsider in his book, The Outsider. In his eagerness to repudiate the falsity around him, and possessed by a desire for action, the outsider tries to find an act, "a definite act that will give him power over his doubts and self-questioning" (Wilson 1970:163). He looks for an effective way of establishing contact with the power within him. Obi returns from England positive about his goals to build a New Nigeria, free from corruption and constraining outlooks. In a society where 'duty' and 'individuality' involves contradictions, the chances of relating effectively, is gauged. For Obi, it leads to estrangement from society and strained personal relationship, where once cherished values cease to hold any possibilities any more. Like the magi in T.S. Eliot's epigraph, he can only say in despair:

We returned to our places, these kingdoms. But no longer at ease here, in the old dispensation, with an alien people clutching their gods I should be glad of another death (The Journey of the Magi).

Achebe concludes his tetralogy with **A Man of the People**, a book which brings the historical record right down to contemporary times and deals with a single theme: the moral relations of the individual with his society. Indeed, this novel, published on January 24th, 1966, only nine days after the first military coup in Nigeria, also ends with a military coup. This extraordinary coincidence has led many reviewers and critics, like D.A.N. Jones to hail the novel as 'prophetic work' (New statesmen 1966:132-133); one in which Achebe predicts with uncanny accuracy, the end of his country's First Republic. But Bernth Lindfors observes that Achebe intended "the coup as a parable, not a prophecy" (Linfors 1979:130-136).

Nevertheless, this completely fortuitous correspondence between fiction and reality should not blind the reader to the fact that Achebe has not changed his underlying theme; he is once again dramatizing against the background of a particular era in Nigeria's history, the consequences of a collison of cultures. The only major difference between this novel and the earlier ones is that, the entire narrative bristles with sharp satire which at times explodes into hilarious burlesque. In an uncommonly happy ending, the villain is brought low, the hero gets the right girl, and the country is purged of politicians.

There is no doubt that Achebe presents the ideals of Okonkwo's society as admirable, when they are properly balanced and Okonkwo's opposition to them as unusual and misguided, though noble; or that he sees Odili as right, in opposing his apathetic, immoral society. In Achebe's two historical novels, the society chooses to reject grand dreams propounded by ambitions individuals, and opts instead for survival, but the way to survival lies through fragmentation of the community and confusion of moral values. In **A Man of the People**, the instinct to survive, which leads Umuaro to choose life and Christ over starvation and Ulu, produces the self-seeking spirit of Anala and Urua. Things have indeed fallen apart, and the community which was once the source of wisdom and law now apathetically endorses any corruption which will bring it food.

Achebe may on the surface seem to have turned to a new kind of social commitment in **A Man of the People**, but the novel is closely linked in its essential argument with the earlier ones. As Rosemary Colmer observes in "The Development of moral Values in **A Man of the People**: "There was the place where the rain began to beat the people; here, now, is where they must begin to dry themselves" (Colmer 1990:89). **Anthills of the Savannah** continues the argument, two decades later, in a world where the necessity to identify the right moral behaviour, and to find the courage to see it through, still confronts the central characters. **A Man of The People** looks at the possibilities of a right government and finds a dearth of right-minded men to make up such a government.

As in the earlier novels, Achebe is dealing with a central character who is regarded by most of his society as a misfit. **Things Fall Apart** examines the traditional Ibo ideal by showing how Okonkwo, who aims to embody it, in fact fails to realise it. **Arrow of God** shows a man exalted by his community who abrogates to himself the power which is in the gift of the community. **No Longer at Ease** investigates the modern ideal by comparing the practical expectations of the Umuofians with the abstract moral principles of Obi, and by showing through Obi's failure, (both in relation to the bribery charge and in his behaviour towards Clara) the sort of social pressures which have produced the Umuofian way, and against which Obi's idealism must be strong enough to stand, if it is to justify itself.

In **A Man of the People**, one sees a protagonist who sets himself against the tide of public judgement, but because he capitulates on some of the material issues, he survives. For the same reason, he is a less sympathetic character than Obi, whose swiftly narrated lapse of principle is not allowed to detract from the effect established by his idealistic stand on corruption in the rest of the novel, and whose treatment of Clara is shown to be, to some extent, forced on him by his concern for his mother. Okonkwo and Ezeulu are nobles in their stand for a principle, even if it brings them into conflict with the valid (and pragmatic) terms of reference of their community. Obi's principles are equally admirable, but he fails them.

Odili Samalu, the protagonist in **A Man of The People**, comes across as an honest, intelligent, somewhat naïve but engaging, idealist-an individual who attempts to swim against the tide of materialism, corruption and immorality that is engulfing his society. He is both sensitive enough to understand the currents that swirls about him and sensible enough to comprehend the motives of those who drift with the tide, while he struggles against it. However, one wonders if a man possessed of such good sense, moral courage and unyielding integrity would behave as Odili does on occasions, For example, it is hard to believe that a man, too timid to check an assault on his mistress, would have the bravado necessary to carry out dangerous political campaigns of his own. Also, Odili's readiness to exploit sexually any compliant female, who crosses his path makes it difficult to believe in the sincerity of his sudden love for Edna, the girl he wins away from Nanga and plans to marry. These inconsistencies in Odili's conduct diminish his stature as a hero, for they prevent us from viewing him as a stable moral being in an unstable, immoral world. The issues however are not directly political, but moral.

Achebe focuses on the moral dilemma of the protagonist, the way in which his ideals clash with the community ethic, and the extent to which he is true to his own beliefs. From the first scene in the novel, Odili is faced with the question of what are the proper standards to apply: "I knew I ought to be angry with myself but I wasn't. I found myself wondering whether perhaps I had been applying to politics stringent standards that didn't belong to it" (**AMOP** 9).

The society depicted in this phase is an immoral one. Almost any crime is tolerated, and the criminal admired for his success. Town and clan loyalties are carried into the political arena as well as into personal life. Odili is critical of his friend Andrew Kadibe, who feels he cannot oppose Chief Nanga's visit to the school because they come from the same town; but once this behaviour is translated into political terms, it becomes more sinister. Odili's candidature is welcomed in his home town, Urua, when Max makes the point which Odili finds unworthy of him or of C.P.C., namely that the town will share in the good fortune of its elected son, and that it is time for:

*Our own son to go and bring our share ... that word entered my ear. The village of Anata has already eaten, now they must make way for us to reach the plate. No man in Urua will give his paper to a stranger when his own son needs it (**AMOP** 141).*

Achebe's indictment of this new spirit in society which measures good only by the immediate benefits in cash or kind, is nevertheless tempered with an understanding of its causes. The expansion from village to nation has made it impossible for the enlarged community to control the behaviour of its member.

Odili suggests at the end of the novel that only the individual can act against those who are beyond the control of the community. Eunice can avenge the death of Max Kulamo, when the society would not. Odili's own stand against "P.O.P. and P.A.P., and the way he conceives the role of the C.P.C., suggest again the importance of the stand of an individual for an ideal, in the face of public apathy" (**AMOP** 140). Odili's most sympathetic feature is his belief in the effectiveness of honesty as a weapon against cheating and corruption. He is deeply disturbed by Max's venture into a further realm of dishonesty than even Nanga has tried: accepting a bribe and then refusing to honour the agreement. Odili insists that while the agreement may not have been legal, it had moral force (**AMOP** 142) and he fears that "Max's action had jeopardised our moral position, our ability to inspire that kind of terror which I had seen so clearly in Nanga's eyes despite all his grandiloquent bluff, and which in the end was our society's only hope of salvation" (**AMOP** 144).

Odili's refusal to accept Nanga's bribe has impressed Nanga in a way which Max's duplicity has negated.

One significant stand by an individual is Odili's father's refusal to dissociate himself from his own actions by signing Nanga's document. He attributes his action to a respect for traditional behaviour: 'Our people have said that a man of worth never gets up to unsay to what he said yesterday. I received your friends in my house and I am not going to deny it" (**AMOP** 152), but the parallel with Odili's refusal to sign a similar document (**AMOP** 132-133) is too close to be ignored. Traditional morality and individual idealism are united in this action.

In the first half of the novel Odili makes his loudest claims to idealism but succumbs to the temptation of Nanga's patronage. The period under Nanga's influence is a valuable experience which gives him some real knowledge and understanding of the world. In the second half of the novel, Odili brags less about his ideas (recognising instead that his motives may be ignoble or personal), but some of the moral choices and cash bribe (**AMOP** 118-119). His earlier experience has enabled him to withstand this temptation, but he has not yet acquired the experience or the self-knowledge to resist temptations which may come in other forms. "He that knows not and knows not that he knows not is a fool" (**AMOP** 117) is a warning Odili should heed. He is blindly, wilfully ignorant of many things he should make it his business to know, from the source of his party's funds, to his own father's character:

> *I thought to myself: You do not belong in this age, old man. Men of worth nowadays simply forget what they said yesterday. Then I realized that I had never really been close enough to my father to understand him. I had built up a private picture of him from unconnected scraps of evidence. Was this the same D.O.'s Interpreter who made a fortune out of the ignorance of poor, illiterate villagers and squandered it on drink and wives or had I got everything terribly, lopsidedly wrong? Anyway, this was no time to begin a new assessment; it was better left to the tax people (**AMOP** 135).*

With such flippancies, Odili dismisses the need to know. And yet the whole novel affirms the importance of knowledge as the basis of right moral judgement.

One reason why Achebe's criticism of Nigerian society is sharper in this novel than in any of the others, is that he allows his hero to tell the story in retrospect. As narrator, Odili not only reports events but criticizes, corrects judgements and editorializes on them, voicing strong protest against what is evil in his world. His observations are shrewd, penetrating and just. At times he is devastatingly honest about past mistakes:

> *Sitting at Chief Nanga's feet I received enlightenment; many things began to crystallize out of the mist-some of the emergent forms were not nearly as ugly as I had suspected but many seemed much worse. However, I was not making these judgements at the time, or not strongly anyhow. I was simply too fascinated (**AMOP** 45).*

Most importantly, Odili knows little about practical politics and nothing at all about people, individually or collectively. Worse, he is not aware that his knowledge is dangerously limited, and he passes up many chances to improve his understanding. David Carroll in his book **Chinua Achebe** points out that because of his family background Odili has grown up lonely, alienated and selfish (Carroll 1980:124). He has learned a few lessons about people, and this has made him both genuinely more idealistic and more cynical. He is still demonstrably selfish, still alienated from the people, but he has learnt to recognize his past actions and attitudes as ridiculous.

Odili faces his first moral trial when Nanga's arrives at the Anata school. This is the beginning of Odili's real education in life. In a delightful comic reversal, one-minute Odili is scowling icily at the display of enthusiasm by Nanga's constituents, and the next he melts in the sunny rays of Nanga's recognition, as Nanga greets him as a former pupil revives an old nickname, 'Odili the great'. In that moment he learns what it is to be singled out by a man of the people for praise and attention.

> *I became a hero in the eyes of the crowd. I was dazed. Everything around me became suddenly unreal, the voices receded to a vague border zone. I knew I ought to be angry with myself but I wasn't. I found myself wondering whether-perhaps I had been applying to politics stringent standards that didn't belong to it (**AMOP** 10).*

Odili has faced his first trial and had failed it. He is ashamed of a great deal of his past behaviour, not always from the best of motives. Odili's defensiveness echoes throughout the first part of the novel. Once he ceases to defend his own actions and begins to criticize those of other people, like Max's speech for the C.P.C., one is dealing with an Odili whose values have matured to the level of the narrator's.

On his visit to the capital Bori, Odili's moral equivocations cannot conceal the fact that he willingly lays himself open to temptation. Yet while he is dazzled by Nanga's life, he is not completely blind to the moral contradictions he sees. Even at the time he is aware of the irony in Chief Koko's belief that he has been poisoned when he tastes the home-grown product his government promotes, and he greets Nanga's fear at the suspected poisoning with an appropriate proverb: "When one slave sees another cast into a shallow grave he should know that when the time comes he will go the same way (**AMOP** 40). Yet Odili's revolt against Nanga does not spring from political motives. He is inclined to enjoy the luxury of being a minister. He confesses "if I were at that moment made a minister I would be most anxious to remain one for ever" (**AMOP** 41).

Odili's split with Chief Nanga has nothing to do with politics or corruption; it is Nanga's appropriation of Odili's girlfriend, Elsie. Odili is horrified when Elsie deserts him and detests Nanga for invading into his territory. Odili ignores the fact that he himself referred to Elsie as 'just-a-good-time-girl' and forgetting his own annexation of Jean Odili determines on a much more serious incursion into Nanga's bride-to-be, Edna.

As he walks the street in a fury of resentment, Odili sees the slums and the night-soil men emptying the bucket latrines he has despised, but the sight means nothing to him. Achebe is emphasising Odili's blindness, at this stage in the novel, to the social issues which ought to concern an idealistic young politician. Uppermost in his mind is his sexual humiliation. Elsie has changed in his mind from the friendly, generous girl he goes to see at the hospital (**AMOP** 63-66), and to whom he laughingly suggests that Nanga might want to swap girls, into "a common harlot" (**AMOP** 80), and then, when his image in the eyes of others is concerned, she is "a casual acquaintance whom both Chief Nanga and I knew" (**AMOP** 87). Odili's judgement is formed according to the enthusiasm others show for him. His remark that the talk at Jean's party was very good is immediately followed by the reason for this judgement: 'My closeness to the Minister gave everything I said, heightened significance. And-I don't know whether this happens to other people, but the knowledge that I am listened to attentively, works in a sort of virtuous circle to improve the quality of what I say (**AMOP** 55). Nanga's appropriation of Elsie is taken as a personal insult, and Odili's overreaction is proportionate to his former enjoyment of Nanga's regard for him. Odili realizes that he has become not the Minister's pal, but the Minister's pimp, and it is the attitude to himself which he bitterly resents.

In his political activities, Odili begins to show signs of a new maturity. He still enjoys recognition and watches the placards of the opposition for his name, but he also shows that he understands the nature of his own rather limited power. His only hope is in his honesty. Max's attempt to appeal to the greed of Odili's electorate is recognized as a betrayal of the ideals which Odili wants to uphold, while his father's refusal to deny his past actions is seen as morally correct behaviour. Odili is learning to understand the people's cynicism, but he is learning also the value of his own idealism. The Odili of the present sees his past actions of this period as naïve but right. He still runs from Nanga (**AMOP** 133), but he knows that Nanga is more afraid of his honesty than of Max's political opposition. He is able to dismiss his chagrin at the fact that Max's bribe is four times the size of the one he is offered, and to see that the real issue is one of honesty. By refusing two hundred and fifty pounds he has made himself greater than Max, who accepted a thousand.

In a novel which is deeply concerned with the question of who the guardian of the public conscience shall be, Odili's refusal to accept the bribe shines out as the one gesture which raises him above the others in the novel, and it is this moral stance which Nanga fears. Odili's incorruptibility makes him a potential watcher set upon the watchman. Honesty in the electorate may keep the elected politicians honest.

Odili's stand against Edna's father has marked a new kind of maturity in his approach to Edna. His final confrontation with Nanga is distinguished by a similar access of courage. Publicly accused by Nanga of dishonesty, Odili confronts Nanga and calls him a liar. In a practical sense, the incident saves Odili by putting him out of action until after the election, when it is again safe to be the man who opposed Chief Nanga. Morally, it puts him in open opposition to the values Nanga represents.

Yet so great is Odili's ignorance and moral blindness that he cannot see the extent to which his own behaviour has come to resemble Nanga's. Odili's moral laxity, his unwillingness to apply stringent standards to his own behaviour which he still applies elsewhere, leads to his own implication in a world of violence. Odili's standards are certainly less than stringent when it comes to enquiring about the source of his own campaigning funds. Those same funds from dubious sources have an even more damning end. Odili has learned how to survive from the cynicism of the people, and quietly helps himself from the party funds entrusted to him.

The main evidence on the moral state of Odili at the end of the novel must come from the voice of the narrator throughout the novel. He approves of his past idealism but laughs at his own naivety. He invites us to admire his prowess, both as speaker and as lover, and his recognition of his own craving for admiration does not lead him to any radical reappraisal of his own self-concept. He is honest enough to let the truth appear to the reader, but not honest enough with himself to change his concept of himself. The most important change in him is his recognition of the importance of honesty and integrity in the individual, coupled with his new understanding of what it means to be 'a man of the people'; but these are not enough to prevent him, by the end of the novel, applauding murder as an unselfish act and embezzling party funds. Odili's trials and his many errors have not brought him to any firm moral ground. He has acquired a vast cynicism, a limited experience, and very little appreciation of the extent of his own ignorance. One may well say, in Odili's own words, that "a man who avoids danger for years and then gets killed in the end has wasted his care" (**AMOP** 109).

Odili begins the novel idealistically opposed to Nanga, and contemptuous of the villagers; "they were not only ignorant but cynical" (AMOP 2). He ends the novel guilty of most of the same moral errors and even the same crimes as Nanga; he is guilty too of the same moral errors as he villager's ignorance and cynicism.

The message Achebe wants to get across is that there are new injustices in Africa which Africans cannot blame wholly on Europe. In an essay "The Black Writer's Burden" published in the same year as the novel, Achebe states that:

One of the writer's main function has always been to expose and attack injustice. Should we keep at the old theme of racial injustice (sore as it still is) when new injustices have sprouted all around us? I think not (Achebe 1956:138).

In style as well as theme, Achebe introduces several new innovations in **A Man of the People,** e.g., first person narration and an extensive use of pidgin in dialogue, but he does most of his work with tools he has used effectively before. His opening paragraphs not only establishes an appropriate mood and setting but penetrates to the very heart of the subject he is to explore. By fastening on the significant and avoiding the trivial and irrelevant, he builds a tight, cohesive structure which never lacks point or direction. And in the last page he rounds off his story with a wry ironic twist, his characteristic signature. These feats are quite impressive, but more impressive still is Achebe's sheer eloquence. Take, for example, the last sentence in the novel:

*I say, you died a good death if your life had inspired someone to come forward and shoot your murderer in the chest without asking to be paid (**AMOP** 167).*

Here, in a fine rhetorical flourish, Odili sums up his experience and utters a fitting epitaph to an ugly era in his nation's history. Achebe engineers this pejoration with characteristic grace, simplicity, urbanity and syntactical sophistication.
But in spite of these impressive achievements, **A Man of the People** cannot be considered Achebe's strongest novel. Indeed, it may well be his weakest. What mars it most is not Odili's instability of character, but his involvement in a rather torrid succession of sensational events. One is willing to concede that politics is a very dirty business and that politicians in newly, independent, African nations, seldom lead serene lives. It is difficult to accept the hasty pace at which Odili and Nanga confront their numerous crises and catastrophes. Characters caught in such a whirlwind of events are inevitably twisted into melodramatic poses.

Although **A Man of the People** is a comedy and ends happily, it remains like Achebe's other novels, a disturbingly pessimistic work. While censuring Africa for allowing itself to be corrupted by forces from within and without, Achebe indicts Europe for contributing to the moral confusion and political chaos that beset independent Africans states. His characters are representative men and women of their time, yet emblematic of the ills and insanities that afflict modern African society. Odili himself is not without his 'civilized' affections. Nothing seems completely right in so debauched a world.

Thus, in phase II the progression of the concept of the individual versus society moves on to the next stage of individualism, as depicted in **The Fountainhead** and Achebe's **No Longer at Ease** and **A Man of the People**, the three novels chosen for analysis in this chapter. Here both Rand and Achebe examine the concept of individualism against totally different backgrounds. Unlike in Phase I, where Rand argues the cause of the individual against the State, here in phase II, Rand argues the cause of the individual as producer against a parasitical society. Individualism in this case is more at the psychological and philosophical level as Rand discusses two types of men, symbolizing 'The Good' and 'The Evil' in Society. Here the herd not only lives on the production of the individual creators, but also attempts to swallow up the individual. Achebe's individuals, on the contrary, struggle against a chaotic, corrupt and complex, urban society quite different from the disciplined collected and peace-loving Ibo society of Phase I. The encounter with European values and Christianity are no longer a conflicting issue, as in Phase I, rather it has become an accepted part of the social framework of these novels.

This phase is a sequel to the first phase for both Rand and Achebe. The

Rand's study of individualism moves on from the Political (Man against The State) level to the spiritual level, as Rand herself states in the "Introduction" to **The Fountainhead** ("Individualism versus Collectivism not In Politics but in man's soul" vii). It is a sequel in Achebe's case as this phase also develops the theme of the dislocation of the African psyche. It is also the story of the growth and development of individual protagonists. In phase I, Kira-Argounova is just the foetus of an individual which grows into the ideal 'man-child' in the person of Howard Roark of **The Fountainhead**; Achebe's Obi of **No Longer at Ease** and Odili of **A Man of The People** are caught in the shackles of a very corrupt society, not to be imagined in Phase I, and which demands from them a firm moral order out of the world in which they live. In phase I, Okonkwo and Ezeulu are cast as courageous and heroic men of integrity, but Obi Okonkwo and Odili are seen as fewer heroic individuals swallowed in by the corrupt society. Consequently, a quest for creative knowledge and power is seen as potential forces that operate on the protagonists.

The theme of the individual versus the society is more fully developed in this Phase, but while the linear progression of the individual is seen in Rand's fiction; in Achebe's world, there is a gradual liquidation in strength and character as seen in the protagonists of Achebe. The individuals in Phase I, to a certain extent, are failures in the sense that they do not evolve triumphant. For example, Kira Argounova of **We the living** is shot while crossing the Latvian border, Leo Kovalensky chooses the life of a Gigolo and Andrei Taganov, the most remarkable character of **We the Living** commits suicide. In Achebe's **Things Fall Apart**, Okonkwo hangs himself, Nwoye dissatisfied with the rituals and customs of the Ibo society, converts to Christianity and Ezeulu turns mad. Though the individuals struggle in this phase, they do not evolve triumphant; society to a large extent becomes the winner. But in this phase, Howard Roark, the protagonist of **The Fountainhead** triumphs for the first time Rand's fiction. Though in **Anthem,** the beginnings of a triumph are seen in the protagonists Equality 7-2521 and Liberty 5-3000, who escape from the State into the Unchartered Forests to discover and invent, it's only Howard Roark, the architect who actually bears the badge of triumph. Expelled from the Architectural Institute, he sets his own standard and never comply with the Institution's traditional norms. He is considered an innovator because his buildings are of a nature and quality that has never existed before. Achebe's Obi and Odili of **No Longer at Ease** and **A Man of the people** respectively are not creators and innovators like Howard Roark, but they attempt to uphold a cause and live by it. Obi and Odili are influenced by educational factors and economic prosperity which gives them, not the creative power and energy of Roark, but a knowledge and strength to relate their knowledge to the socio-economic climate dealt with in **No Longer at Ease** and **A Man of the People** respectively. In this manner, Roark is covered from the other traditional architects of his time and Obi and Odili from their primitive tribal affiliations. Roark, Obi and Odili mark this initial stage of individualism. Conflict and tension become very much part of Obi and Odili, but never Roark. While Roark is depicted as one who always believes in his rights as an individual creator, Obi and Odili experience a new awareness because of their sudden exposure to Western education and values. Gradually their rights as individuals are divorced from any collective responsibility. In this phase the quest for creative knowledge and power becomes a pronounced motif.

These protagonists, are in direct contrast with the archvillains Rand's Howard Roark (The Good) is cast opposite Ellsworth Toohey and Peter Keating (The Evil). While Roark knows exactly what he wants and is not the least bit interested in what other people think of him, Keating not only acknowledge to Roark that he is a parasite but guides his life by what other people think is important. In architectural terms while Roark's work is original, Keating plagiarises and needs Toohey to tell him that he is a great architect. Toohey is a maggot who feeds on sores. A spiritual collectivist, his only mission in life to kill the individual.

The protagonist Obi Okonkwo of **No Longer at Ease** is estranged from his tribal ethos and is torn between two worlds, Africa and Europe. Never did he realise that with Western Education comes power and with power corruption, which results in gradual detachment and emancipation from his tribe. Odili, the protagonist of **A Man of the People** is cast opposite the corrupt politician Nanga. He stands as the symbol of political chaos, confusion and culture-conflict in Nigeria. He believes that just, because he led the political struggle for independence, he uses people for his own purposes, and buys off the opposition. His death symbolizes that there is still hope for Nigeria and the possibility of purgation. Ellsworth Toohey, Peter Keating and Chief Nanga are bloated parasites who draw their strength from the weaknesses of their society and thrives on chaos, confusion, disorder and instability. All of these arch-villains in this phase symbolise a parasitical society.

David Carroll in his book Chinua Achebe refers to the following two versions of duty:

i) Atomistic View which includes protagonists who live solitary lives but who are self-sufficient and fulfilled like the protagonists of Ayn Rand.

ii) The Organic view refers to those individuals who function as members of a community like the protagonists in Achebe's fiction.

The concept of the love theme is also further developed here in this phase. In Rand's fiction love plays a dominant role and finds a place in all her fictional works, but in Achebe's it is only in **No Longer at Ease** and **A Man of the People** that the theme of love is introduced.

The Love theme in Rand's earlier novels is not very successful because the protagonists in **We The Living**, Kira Argounova and Leo Kovalensky loved and lost. In **Anthem** the beginnings of a successful love are seen when Liberty 7-2521 elopes with Equality 5-3000 into the Uncharted Forests. But in **The Fountainhead**, Howard Roark's relationship with Dominique Francon ultimately triumphs. Initially Dominique Francon believes that a man like Roark is too good for the world and hence seeks every opportunity to destroy him by marrying his worst enemies, Peter Keating and Gail Wynand. But in the end of the novel, Dominique is convinced that however powerful and detestable a world, it cannot destroy a man with Roark's integrity and finally becomes his wife. There is not much of a love theme in Achebe's novel except for the Obi-Clara relationship which ends tragically. Obi's individually is always in conflict with his individual desire and his society's demand. He loves Clara but his parental opposition to her because she is an 'Osu' causes him to reject her. Odili of **A Man of the People** is too timid to check an assault on his mistress. Odili is ready to exploit any compliant girl. His sudden love for Edna, the girl he wins from Nanga and Plans to marry makes him out to be quite an inconsistent being. But unlike Obi, Odili's love triumphs in the end.

While Roark is attached only to things and persons who matter to him and for whom he will make exceptions, Obi experiences a gulf between what he learns and his practical life in this world. He is an aesthete but is attached to things of no importance. Though Roark, Obi and Odili are thrown in a very materialistic, commercialized, fragmentary world. Roark of **The Fountainhead** is neither influenced nor corrupted by the world around him. But Obi of **No Longer at Ease** and Odili of **A Man of the people** suffer the consequences of the values of Umuofia and Europe being synthesized in them. Roark exemplifies Hubert Bonner's Hellentic view of man where the individual tries to live the perfect idealistic life, while Achebe's exemplifies Hubert Bonner's Hebraic view of man, where the individual experiences a life of discipline and responsibility-a life shared, like Obi and Odili. Roark stands apart as a distinct breed by itself as he lives so idealistically a life that he becomes to

Dominique "worthy of worship" (**TFH** 95). While Roark tries to redeem his society by his art and integrity Obi and Odili try to eradicate all forms of corruption from their society. But the society is too strong for them and does not release its hold on these individuals. Gradually one observes in this phase that Obi, unlike Odili, takes to bribes himself and becomes one with his society, corrupt. Odili is the only protagonist who manages to swim against the tide of materialism and has moral integrity. But unlike Roark Obi and Odili are inconsistent characters-unstable moral beings in an unstable immoral society.

There is most positively an emergence of the autonomous individual to a large degree in this phase. Compared to the protagonists discussed in the two phases so far, Rand's Howard Roark and Achebe's Odili manages to show tremendous growth as characters. Roark is pictured as an ideal-man, worthy of worship and Odili manages to emerge from his struggle body and soul intact, uncorrupted by Westernization, and never cringes before injustice, bends under pressure, nor resorts to bribes.

Rand and Achebe's social satire in this phase is sharper than in the previous one. In phase I, Rand satirizes the policy of man living for the State, instead of the State living and functioning for the benefit of man. This is what Rand scorns in her two novels **We the Living** and **Anthem**. The individuals in Phase II emerges more autonomous than the first phase but there is still room for the parasites like Toohey's and Keating's who are all still secure in their comfortable positions in the world of **The Fountainhead**. Achebe satirizes the impact of the white man on Ibo Society and things fall apart at the socio-cultural and religious levels. In Phase II Achebe satirizes the political corruption and power that comes as a consequence of Western Education and Economic advancement this Achebe observes has replaced religious beliefs and traditions of the first place. Values here are vague and changing, aims and objectives are complex and not clearly defined.

There are also new stylistics innovations in this phase in both the writers. Rand is an innovator in the literary and philosophic field. On intellectual issues she said what no one else did, she voiced it so simply, logically, factually, persuasively that they seemed to be self-evident. It's no surprise that Loraine Pruette in "Battle Against Evil" observes: "Ayn Rand is a writer of great power. She has a subtle and ingenious mind and the capacity of writing brilliantly, beautifully and bitterly (Pruette 1943:9). Such a stylistic skill was found lacking in Phase I. But there are a few demerits in her literary writings. There is a contradiction at times in the events of her story. The events are conventional but their meaning and motivation are utterly unconventional. Dominique's passionate love for Roark is, on the surface, a very conventional event, but her decision to destroy him and marry the men she despises is rather unconventional, because her decision to marry these other men is not self-sacrifice but self-preservation and the reaffirmation of her values. This is what transforms an otherwise ordinary tale.

Achebe's criticism of Nigerian Society is sharper in this novel than in any of the others. Achebe not only laughs at corrupt politicians but also at these political leaders who imagine that since they were involved with the political struggle they had a right to eat the national cake. There is an extensive use of Pidgin in this novel, an apt mood and setting is captured, a well-knit structure which makes Achebe's work an impressive artistic work.

In this phase, both Rand and Achebe reach the end of the road they have been traveling so far; the individual's struggle to emerge autonomous; and in the next phase written after a long span of fifteen to twenty years, Rand and Achebe offer solutions and suggestions for the problems facing their respective countries. The next phase is a movement towards the creation of the 'demi-gods' in a Utopian Society of **Atlas Shrugged.** In this phase the parasites are completely eliminated and there is place only for the creative brains of society. Achebe also presents his suggestions and solution for an ideal Society through his concept of an ideal leadership in **Anthills of Savannah.**

IV

Towards Utopia

Phase III comprises of the last novels of Rand and Achebe's **Atlas Shrugged** (1957) and **Anthills of the Savannahs** (1987) respectively. Both **Atlas Shrugged** and **Anthills of the Savannahs**, besides the fact that they are political novels, can be called their philosophical treatise. Written after a span of fourteen and twenty-one years respectively, profound thoughts and introspection have gone into the making of these novels. All the questions and problems posed by these authors in their previous novels have been answered and solved in this phase. These novelists have a lot of suggestions to offer for the betterment of the individual and the society in their socio-cultural dimensions. While Rand's **Atlas Shrugged** is a consciously philosophic action. In this phase, the 'Man-Child' of **The Fountainhead** evolves into the ideal 'Demi-God' of **Atlas Shrugged**, worthy of worship. Achebe in **Anthills of the Savannahs** suggests that individuals, if they must exist should function as leaders and shepherd their flock to form a better society. Rand also seeks to portray the concept of an ideal society and hence finds the need to venture into Utopia-an 'Atlantis', an exquisite example of an ideal communal life, where the individual is still the priority and yet promotes and sustains society. This novel also displays a highly calculated literary style, so far invisible in the previous novels. In **Anthills of the Savannahs** Achebe, like Rand, offers solutions to the problems demonstrated in his previous novels. Both Rand and Achebe believe that the moral integrity of an individual in relation to his society will bring about an ideal, healthy society. Achebe's solutions for his society's problems are many-a new concept of leadership, gender transfiguration, the importance of the place of women in society, the class struggle, the method to combat corruption in politics, and a kind of 'spiritualism' as a substitute for the materialistic pursuits of independent Nigeria, to mention a few.

Rand's **Atlas Shrugged** and Achebe's **Anthills of the Savannahs** is a sequel to Rand's **The Fountainhead** and Achebe's **A Man of the People**. The ideal 'man-child' of **The Fountainhead** grows into the 'demigods' of **Atlas Shrugged** and Rand's pursuit of the individual consciousness reaches culmination point, where Rand creates her protagonists as "man ought to be", in the image and likeness of God himself. Achebe's **A Man of the People** explores the moral relations of an individual with his society and this is further developed in Achebe's **Ant-**

hills of the Savannahs. As in the previous phase, Achebe is also concerned with the question of who shall be the guardian of the public conscience.

The theme of **Atlas Shrugged** is, Rand tells us in **For the New intellectual**: 'the role of the mind in man's existence' and as corollary, "the demonstration of a new moral philosophy: the morality of rational self-interest" (Rand 1961:88). It demonstrates the application of the theme of **The Fountainhead** – 'Individualism', to the political-economic arena. It demonstrates that Capitalism rests on the mind and the freedom of the mind. "My most important job" wrote Ayn Rand, in her notes, quoted by Barbara Branden in her book, **The Passion of Ayn Rand**, is the formulation of a rational morality of and for man, of and for his life, of and for this earth" (Branden 521).

The plot portrays what happens to a world when the mind goes on strike; when the men of creative ability in every profession, quit and disappear. To quote John Galt, the leader and initiator of the strike:

> *There is only one kind of men who have never been on strike in human history. Every other kind and class have stopped when they so wished, and have presented demands to the world, claiming to be indispensable- except the men who have carried the world on their shoulders, have kept it alive, have endured torture as sole payment, but have never walked out on the human race. Well, their turn has come. Let the world discover who they are, what they do and what happens when they refuse to function. This is rule strike of the men of the mind (**AS** 981).*

The theme of the 'Producers versus the Parasites' reaches its climax here in this phase. In one of her notes, quoted in **Capitalism: The Unknown Ideal**, Rand states:

> *Reverse the process of expansion that goes on in a society of producers: Henry Ford's automobile opened the way for the expansion of many industries; oil, roads, glass, rubber, plastics etc. Now, in a society of parasites, the opposite takes place: a shrinking of industries and productive activities. A James Taggart at the head of a big concern would have exactly the opposite effect from that of a Henry Ford (Rand 1967:187).*

Since the essence of the creator's power is ability of independent rational judgement, and since this is precisely what the parasite is incapable of – the key to every disaster in the story, to the whole disintegration of the world, is in each case (big or small) a situation where independent, rational judgement is needed and cannot be produced, ('cannot' in the case of the parasites, 'will not' in the case of the creators) observes Rand (Ibidem: 189).

Atlas Shrugged, is an action story on a grand scale, but it is a consciously philosophical action story, just as its heroes are consciously philosophical men of action. It moves effortlessly and ingeniously from economics to epistemology to morality to metaphysics to psychology to the theory of sex, on the one hand, and on the other, it has a playboy crusader who blows up a multi-billion-dollar industry; a philosopher-turned-pirate who attacks government relief ships, and a climax that involves the rescue of the hero from a torture chamber.

John Galt is Rand's full and final statement of 'the ideal man' the statement towards which the whole of her life was moving her. Galt was to be the apotheosis of the human-potential, the man of theoretical genius, of practical efficacy, and who lives joyously, courageously, productively, rationally, and triumphantly-the man who belongs on earth. The person of John Galt dominates all the events of **Atlas Shrugged**. He is the man who conceives the strike, who initiates it, who seeks out the men of the mind to join it and who brings it to its final climax and triumph. He is the man who said he would stop the motor of the world and did. In the radio talk John Galt gives to the world of parasites, Galt describes himself thus:

*I am the man who loves his life. I am the man who does not sacrifice his love or his values. I am the man who has deprived you of victims and thus has destroyed your world, and if you wish to know why you are perishing-you who dread knowledge-I am the man who will now tell you (**AS** 960).*

John Galt is the man who discovers 'Atlantis', who gives his strikers their banner, the solemn oath that binds them together and their rallying cry in the form of the statement: "I swear by my life and my love of it that I will never live for the sake of another man, nor ask another man to live for mine" (**AS** 1003).

When Rand had devised the character and role of John Galt, Rand turned to her heroine, Dagny Taggart, the women who was to be worthy of loving Galt and being loved by him. "I had always been in awe of woman", Rand said. Dagny is Rand's first portrait of 'ideal woman'. Kira was still a young girl at the end of **We the Living**; Dominique was paralyzed by a profound inner conflict in **The Fountainhead**. But Dagny was to be free of psychological conflict, serene in her basic relationship to existence, passionately ambitious and creative. Rand wished to project her as the woman thought to be impossible by the conventional view of life and of sex; the woman engineer, dealing with the material world of metal rails and freight cars and diesel engineers, who is, simultaneously, a consummately feminine hero worshipper.

Dagny is myself, with any possible flaws eliminated, She is myself without my tiredness, without my chronic, slightly anti-material feeling, without that which I consider the ivory tower element in me, or the theoretician versus the man of action. ....Dagny is myself without a moment of exhaustion.

She said, in an "Interview with Rand ". Dagny first meets John Galt-after her plane crashes in Atlantis. Rand describes Dagny's reactions in one of the most exalted tributes to her ideal in all of her writing: When Dagny Taggart opened her eyes, she looked up into a man's face and she knew that in all the years behind her, this face was what she would have given her life to see-a face that bore no mark of pain or fear or guilt. It had a look of serene determination, with nothing to hide or to escape. This is Rand's way of introducing John Galt-the way men were meant to be.

In the above paragraph two women are in love: Dagny Taggart, the woman protagonist of **Atlas Shrugged** and Ayn Rand. What Dagny experiences with John Galt would come to an end through the living reality of John Galt, but they were not to end for Rand. Rand had never found the man whose "eyes imparted a superlative value to himself and to the world" (AS 981). But she would give him reality in a work of art; "and he would never disappoint her nor betray her, like the men Rand loved-like Frontz, like Leo, like Frank, like Nathaniel Branden, who had sentenced her to a life time of unrequited love" (Branden 1986:357).

The attributes most sharply emphasized in Galt's portrait are rationality, realism, serenity, self-esteem. An essential characteristic of Galt illustrates Rand's view of what she calls "the importance of evil", a concept of great importance in her philosophy and in the structure of all her novels. Galt has a profound contempt for evil, a contempt based on the conviction that evil is the irrational and therefore, the blind, the aberrated, the impotent. Evil is to be fought when necessary, but not to be taken seriously in one's own view of life, not to be granted metaphysical power or significance; evil is to be despised, not hated or feared. One may observe this premise in the plot-structure of **Atlas Shrugged**. The central lines of dramatic conflict are not between the good and the evil, but between the good and the good; between Galt and Francisco, the strikers on the one hand; and between Dagny and Rearden who will not join the strike, on the other. The errors that set Dagny and Rearden in conflict with Galt and Francisco are what Rand defined as "errors of knowledge, not breaches of morality" (Ibidem). This same pattern is also apparent in **The Fountainhead**. The central conflict is Roark versus Dominique and Wynand. In the both novels, the villains merely cash-in on the consequences of the hero's conflicts, but are not the initiators, the sources of the motive power of the story's events. In the novels, and in actual life, Rand said in 'An interview with Rand'.

The alleged victories of evil are made possible only by the flaws of the errors of those who are essentially good. Evil, left to its own devices, is impotent and self-defeating. To make my central conflicts a struggle between heroes and villains, would be to grant to evil an honour it doesn't deserve (An Interview with Rand, p. 35).

Francisco d'Anconia a copper industrialist, heir to an enormous fortune, Galt's closest friend and the first man to join him in the strike, becomes one of Rand's most colourful and dramatic figures; the man of ruthless purposefulness who assumes the role of a playboy in order to destroy his fortune in plain sight of the whole world. Francisco's leitmotif is a light-hearted gaiety: he is the man with a superlative capacity for the enjoyment of life, and an iron-disciplined worker of unsurpassed productive energy and achievement. It is Francisco who would explain the meaning of the novel's title and its theme, to Rearden and to the reader:

*"Mr. Rearden", said Franciso, his voice solemnly calm, "if you saw Atlas, the giant, who holds the world on his shoulders, if you saw that he stood, blood running down his chest, his knees buckling, his arms trembling but still trying to hold the world aloft with the last of his strength, and the greater his effort the heavier the world bore down upon his shoulders-what would you tell him to do?" "I...don't know. What... could he do? What would you tell him?" "To shrug" (**AS** 616).*

In her philosophical treatise, **Atlas Shrugged**, Rand uses each of the heroic characters of demonstrate in concrete philosophical terms, her very important theories for life on this earth. Francisco D'Anconia expresses one of the most essential concepts of Rand's innovative thinking on money. It is not the root of all evil and can't exist unless there are goods produced and men able to produce them. "Money is the material shape of the principle that men who wish to deal with one another must deal by trade and give value for value" (**AS** 714). The root of money, the root of all production and wealth is man's mind. Money is made by the effort of every honest man, each to the extent of his ability. Money rests on the axiom that every man is the owner of his mind and his effort. But money is only a tool. It will take you wherever you wish but it will not replace you as the driver. Money will not purchase happiness for the man who has no knowledge of what he wants: Money will not give him a code of values, "if he's evaded the knowledge of what to value," and it will not provide him with a purpose, "if he's evaded the choice of what to seek." Money does not corrupt man, man corrupts money. Money is a living power that will serve a mind that can match it. Francisco gives Galt a clue to men's characters: "The man who damns money has obtained it dishonourably; the man who respects it has earned it" (**AS** 715). "Franciso", Rand tells us in her notes, "is the philosophical expression, the concretization in a human character...of Minerva" (Branden 1986:414). To Rand, Francisco's name-Francisco Domingo Carlos Andres Sebastian D'Anconia, symbolized the whole character. "He us the other axis of my type of man", she once said. "There are two types of men in my novels", Rand wrote in her notes, quoted by Barbara Branden, in The Passion of Ayn Rand;

> *Roark, Gult, and Rearden are one line, Wynand, Bjorn Faulkner, Leo, and Francisco are the other. The Francisco type are the men who symbolize the enjoyment of life on earth. In my early attempts in Russia, the Francisco type was very prominent-so in devising the character of Francisco, I was cashing-in on an enormous store of ideas (Branden 1986:371).*

The leitmotif of Francisco was to be an indestructible, gaiety, the leitmotif of Ragnar Danneskjold, the philosopher who becomes a pirate was to be an implacable sense of justice. Ragnar tells Rearden:

> *...my only love, the only value I care to live for is that which has never been loved by the world, has never won recognition or friends, or defenders-human ability. That is the love I am serving, and if I should lose my life, to what better purpose could I give it? (AS 315).*

Ragnar is the symbol of the good man's helpless indignation against evil. That was Rand's lead to his character, the indignation that any victim feels against evil. That was the justification for a superior type of man choosing a career of violence. He was to be the avenging angel (Branden 1986:651).

Hanger Rearden is the key means of dramatizing the martyrdom of the men of the mind. He is the martyred industrialist, the concrete "Atlas' who carries the world on his shoulders and receives only torture in return. The characterization of Rearden, a leading industrialist and the chief victim of the novel was to be unique in Rand's work. He is a hero, the most attractive and memorable, a man whom one admires intensely for his education, his uncomplaining struggle, his achievement, his austere honour, the magnanimity of his personality. But he is a man torn by conflict-not only the conflict with the outside world that characterizes Rand's other heroes, but by inner conflict. The conflict between his sexual passion for Dagny and his conviction that sex is a degradation; the conflict between his love for Dagny and his sense of duty towards a wife he despises; the conflict between his love for Franciso and his conviction that the face of the playboy which Francisco presents to the world is the proof of depravity. It is Rearden's intense battle with himself and the unflinching honesty with which he fights it, that engages the readers. He is a man who, within the context of his understanding, will not deceive himself. After his first sexual encounter with Dagny, he tells her:

*I held it as my honour what I would never need anyone. I need you. It had been my pride that I had always acted on my convictions. I've given into a desire which I despise. It is a desire that has reduced my mind, my will, my being, my power to exist into and object dependence upon you-not even upon the Dagny Taggart whom I admired. Whatever I wanted I was free to proclaim it aloud and achieve it in the sight of the whole world. Now my only desire is one I loathe to name even to myself. I want no pretence, no evasion, no silent indulgence, with the nature of our actions left unnamed ... It's depravity-and I accept it as such... and there is no height of virtue that I couldn't give up for it (**AS** 640).*

In the end, Rearden comes to understand the nature of his mistake, and the reader understands the means by which a man of spiritual mobility faces his internal conflicts.

Hank Rearden is a self-made man who has risen to the position of the country's greatest steel industrialist. In the novel, Hank Rearden is on trial by the government, for an illegal sale of a metal alloy which he had created and which had been placed under government rationing and control. In this context, Rand uses Rearden to philosophize on the moral meaning of capitalism. Rearden tells the jury at his trial that he works for nothing but his own profits which he makes by selling a product to men who need it and are willing and able to buy it. The producer and the customer deal as equals by mutual consent to mutual advantage. Rearden further tells the jury that he is not willing to pay his workers more than their services are worth to him and he is not prepared to sell his product for less than his customers are willing to pay him. Rearden acknowledges his ability and his success and his money and he will not apologize for it. Rearden believes, if one individual's rights are violated, it will lead to universal devastation. The moral premise of achieving good by turning men into sacrificial animals is the most contemptible evil, which he is prepared to fight in the full confidence of the justice of his battle and of a living being's right to exist.

If Hank Rearden joins the strike as he refuses to compromise with Government controls, Dr. Hendricks, a distinguished brain surgeon quits and joins the strikers when medicine is placed under state control. Dr. Hendricks is not prepared to permit "the passionate devotion that goes into acquiring that skill to be placed at the disposal of men whose sole qualification to rule me was to dictate to me at the point of a gun" (AS 757). Men consider only the welfare of the patients, with no thought for those who are to provide it. Dr. Hendricks could not accept that people asserted their right to enslave him, to control him, to force his will, to violate his conscience, to stifle his mind. Their moral code has taught them to believe that it is safe to rely on the virtue of their victims. Richard Halley, a great composer and musician also joins the strike, because the world is not worthy of his music.

Having dealt with Rand's major protagonists, the researcher enumerates a number of secondary characters. Dagny's brother James Taggart who 'hides in mystical nonsense to avoid moral judgement' (**AS** 536); Lillian Rearden, Hank Rearden's wife, 'the archetype of the humanitarian liberal pseudo-intellectual who despises and hates the industrialist' (**AS** 641); Cheryl, the young girl who marries James Taggart believing his pretence of greatness, and is destroyed when she grasps the horror of the truth; Robert Stadler, the great scientist destroyed by his own cynicism; Ellis Wyatt and Ken Danagger, industrialists who abandon the work they live and join Galt's strike. In her outline, Rand does not determine the relative importance of the secondary characters, says Branden. She plans to use them as the plot requires, when it required them (Branden 1986:535). 'One character is an exception in my whole writing career' (Ibidem), she later says, shaking her head as if still startled by the exception and by how it came about:

He is a character who, without my intention seemed to write himself. He came out of the material inspirationally, as I was writing. All I had intended was to describe in one brief mention a modern young college boy bureaucrat (Ibidem:540).

The character is the young man nicknamed 'The Wet Nurse', in **Atlas shrugged** , sent by Washington to direct the 'fair' distribution of the new metal, Rearden had created. He is to be a boy who 'had no inkling of any concept of morality. It had been bred out of him by his college. This had left him with an odd frankness, naïve and cynical at once, like the innocence of a savage' (**AS** 31). The character began to interest Rand.

Rand realizes that through this type of innocent savage, not corrupt enough to know how corrupt his actions are, innocent enough to admire Rearden, a boy who really accepted what he had been taught in college, Rand could show the tragic representative of the good average young people. He would be a boy brought up as amoral, then awakening to moral understanding. 'The Wet Nurse' was to become the most endearing and touching of all Rand's characters. In his last scene, during a riot, Rearden Steel staged an order from Washington, he would be shot in a last desperate effort to save Rearden's Mills. Reardem takes the dying boy in his arms, to carry him to safety. But it is too late:

*The boy's features had no power to form a smile, but it was a smile that spoke in his glance, as he looked at Rearden's face, as he looked at that which he had not known he had been seeking through the brief span of his life, seeking as the image of that which he had not known to be his values (**AS** 316).*

One of the minor characters, 'fishwife', a woman striker in the valley, has a particular personal meaning to Rand, Her work is to provide the fish for the grocery market. As Dagny and Galt drive through the valley, Dagny sees "a young woman, stretched on the sun flooded planks, watching a battery of fishing rods. She glances up at the sound of the car, then leaps to her feet in a single swift movement and runs to the road. Dagny…sees the glance with which the young woman stood looking after Galt…hopelessness, serenely accepted was part of the worship in that glance. Galt says;' She's a writer. The kind of writer who wouldn't be published outside. She believes that when one deals with words, one deals with the mind" (**AS** 417). "The fishwife" is Rand's Hitchcock-like appearance in **Atlas Shrugged.**

While projecting what happens if the men of the mind go on strike, and defining how and why civilization collapses, Rand is led to a crucial question: If it is the men of the mind who carry the world on their shoulders and make civilization possible—why have they never recognized their own power, and why have they never challenged their torturers and expropriators? When she grasped the answer, she knew it was to be one of the most important moral concepts in the novel: the concept of 'the sanction of the victim'. Rand realizes that it is the victims, the men of virtue and ability, who make the triumph of evil possible by their willingness to let their virtues be sued against them; their willingness to bear injustice, to sacrifice their own interest, to concede moral validity to the claims of their own destroyers.

The parasitical society portrayed in this novel reaches its heights. The society is perishing because it fears knowledge. The society here 'sacrifices justice to mercy, independence to unity, reason to faith, wealth to need, self-esteem to self-denial, and happiness to duty' (**AS** 963). John Galt deprives this society of man's and is dragging to sacrificial altars the creators, producers, thinkers, industrialists, scientists-the men of justice, of independence, of reason, of wealth, of self-esteem. But John Galt beats the 'moochers' and the 'looters' to it. He reaches these men of genius and rescues them to 'Atlantis'.

The individuals in this phase alienate themselves from self-immolation. They decide they will not sanction society to victimize them, nor allow themselves to be swallowed by the herd. The individuals are striking against unearned rewards, unrewarded duties and the dogma that the pursuit of one's happiness is evil. They are on strike against the doctrine that life is guilt. The society here condemns these creators as 'evil', 'useless' 'dangerous and to be shackled' and to be shackled' and 'only an illusion' (**AS** 970), and so they remove themselves to a Utopian land, leaving the world as they saw it: 'a world without mind' (**AS** 973).

John Galt in his radio talk to the world: 'This is John Galt Speaking', says that neither of the demi-gods were to return until the American Society realized that 'a country's political system is based on its code of morality' (Rand 1974 182). America's moral system must be built on its foundation, on the premise that Rand advocates in **The Virtue of Selfishness**, that 'man's is an end in himself, not the means to the ends of others, that man's life, his freedom, his happiness are his by inalienable right' (Rand 1964:16) when it falls to a level of impotent chaos, when the advocates of the morality of sacrifice perish, when those hatred-eaten mystics are swept aside- 'then and on that day we will return' (**AS** 1008), promises John Galt.

And when they are called back, Galt promises to build and 'Atlantis' here on earth:

a city of smokestacks, pipelines, orchards, markets and inviolate homes, with the sign of the dollar as our symbol, the sign of free trade and free minds-and this country will become once more a sanctuary for the vanishing species: the rational being... In this world you will be able to rise in the morning with the spirit you had known in your childhood: that spirit of eagerness adventure and certainty. You will live in a world of responsibility being... your virtues will be given protection, your vices *and weaknesses will not...And when you look at men and at yourself, you will feel, not disgust, suspicion and guilt, but a single constant respect (**AS** 965-966).*

Rand in a dramatic and stunning finale makes her last plea to the American:

*In the name of the best within you...In the name of the values that keep you alive, do not let your vision of man be distorted by the ugly, the cowardly, the mindless in those who have never achieved his title... Do not let your fire go out , spark by irreplaceable spark... Do not let the hero in your soul perish in lonely frustration for the life you deserved but have never been able to reach. Check your road and the nature of your battle. The world you desired can be won, it exists, it is real, it is possible, it is yours (**AS** 1012).*

Rand's identification of the disastrous sequences of 'the soul-body dichotomy', the theory of 'from each according to his ability to each according to his need', and the meaning of love and sex are some of the other contributing elements to the growth of the novel's scale. They become central philosophical issues. In her notes quoted by Branden in **The Passion of Ayn Rand**, Rand describes the way in which this soul-body dichotomy serves as sanction and excuse for the persecution of industrialists and for the scorn directed against those who create physical means of man's survival. Rand observes:

Show that the real sources, key spots, spark plugs of material production (the inventors and industrialists) are creators in the same way, in the same sense, with the same heroic virtues, of the same high spiritual order, as the men usually thought of as creators, as artistic (Branden 1986:750).

The policy from each according to his ability to each according to his need had been taught to mankind from times immemorial, by parents, teachers and ministers, that it would achieve a noble ideal, that it was righteous and just. But in **Atlas Shrugged** Rand considers this policy evil, disastrous and dangerous for man's survival on this earth. Galt observes that this policy is equivalent to:

Pouring water into a tank where there's a pipe at the bottom draining it out faster than you pour it, and each bucket you bring breaks that pipe an inch wider, and the harder you work the more is demanded of you, and you stand slinging buckets forty hours a week, then fifty-six for your neighbours supper-for his wife's operation, for his mother's wheel *chair, for the baby to be born, for anyone anywhere around you-it's their to receive –from diapers to dentures, and yours to work without rest, without hope... From each according to his ability to each according to his need (**AS** 945).*

In **For the New Intellectual**, Rand scornfully observes that the premise 'we are all one big family' (Rand 1961:104) is absurd because 'you don't all get a belly ache together' (Ibidem:105). 'From each according to his ability to each according to his need is unjust as a man might claim he needs a yacht, and is it right, asks Rand, for him to need a yacht when he has not worked for it. Naturally, a man would hide every ability he had, and slow down and watch like hawks that we never worked any faster or better than the next fellow' (Ibidem) because the best would only go to 'the family' (Ibidem) whenever any man failed anywhere, another man had to make up for it in this policy. Rand observes the following:

*To work with no chance for an extra ration, till the Cambodians have been fed and the Protagonists have been sent through college, to work on a blank check held by every creature born, by men whom you'll never see, whose needs you'll never know, whose ability; or laziness or sloppiness or fraud you have no way to learn to right to question is no moral law to accept (**FTNI** 47).*

The meaning of love and sex takes on a very different interpretation in the works of Ayn Rand, just as money and the work ethics did. Rand believes that 'sex is not the cause, but an effect and an expression of a man's sense of his own value' (Rand 1961:99), Galt observes:

*The men who thinks that wealth comes from material resources, and has no intellectual root or meaning are the men who think for the same reason that sex is a physical capacity which functions independently of one's mind, choice or code of values (**AS** 965).*

A man's sexual choice is the result and the sum of the fundamental convictions, Rand challenges the reader in **Atlas Shrugged** when she says: 'Tell me what a man finds sexually attractive and I will tell you his entire philosophy of life. Show me the woman he sleeps with and I will tell you his valuation of himself' (**AS** p.972). A man according to Rand will always be attracted to the woman who reflects his deepest vision of himself. There is no conflict between the standards of his mind and the desires of his body. What glory can there be in the conquest of a mindless body, Rand asks in her comment on **Atlas Shrugged** quoted in **For the New Intellectual** (Rand 1961:101).

"Love" she says, "is a response to our highest values-and can be nothing else" (AS 963) Rand continues:

*Let a man corrupt his values and his existence, let him profess that love is not self-enjoyment but self-denial, that virtue consists, not of pride, but of pity or pain of weakness or sacrifice that the noblest love is born, not of admiration but of charity not in response to values, but, in response to flaws-and be will have cut himself in two (**AS** 987).*

Rand's full power of dramatic integration is visible in her masterpiece **Atlas Shrugged**. Each key event carries and illustrates her philosophic themes and simultaneously contributes it to the economic disintegration of the country, advances the personal relationships among the characters and heightens the element of mystery and suspense created by the disappearance of one man of ability after another.

In **Atlas Shrugged**, Dagny Taggart asks John Galt what he had told the inventors, the artist, the industrialists, the scientists the men of the mind in every field of activity who had joined his strike, to convince them to abandon everything and to join him. Galt answers:

*I told them they were right. I gave them the pride they did not know they had. I gave them the words to identify it. I gave them that priceless possession which they had missed, had longed for, yet had not known they needed: a moral sanction (**AS** 986).*

This was to be Rand's gift to America. 'A moral sanction'. The philosophical demonstration that to live for one's own rational self-interest, to pursue one's own selfish, personal goals, to use one's mind in the service of one's own life and happiness, is the greatest, the noblest, the highest, the most moral of human activities. Speaking of his strikers, Galt would say:

I have given them the weapon they had lacked: the knowledge of their own moral value. They, the great victims who had produced all the wonders of humanity's brief summer ... had not discovered the nature of their right. They had known that theirs was the power. I taught them that theirs was the glory (Ibidem 990).

Speaking to the unnamed, un-championed beating heart of her new land, Rand was to say: 'Yours is the glory' (Branden 1986:416).

America had given her life, and hope, and freedom, and the possibility of achieving everything denied to her in Soviet Russia. But Ayn Rand was a trader. She would write that '...the moral symbol of respect for human beings, is the trader. We, who live by values, not by loot, are traders, both in matter and in spirit. A trader is a man who earns what he gets and does not give or take the underserved' (**VOS** 96). She was to repay her adopted country for the gifts if offered her. She was to repay it by giving America its voice.

The researcher will now analyse the final stage of individualism as seen in the last works of Chinua Achebe. In this phase Achebe projects, the concept of ideal leadership as one of the very important solution to his society's problems. C. L. Innes in his book **Chinua Achebe** observes that **Anthills of Savannah** (1987) is Achebe's most complex and wisest book of date. It's a sequel to **A Man of the People** (1966), written almost twenty-one years later and shows a marked change in Chinua Achebe's novelistic interests, his political philosophy and his artistic vision (Innes 1990:46). The novel deals with the cynical calculations of Africa's latter-day power elite, and the bankruptcy of the sixties and seventies nepotistic politics, and in this sense it is a sequel to **A Man of the People**. But Achebe's view of that elite and its politics in the wider context has become more compromising and at least theoretically more attuned to gender a populist ideas. The elite, in **Anthills of the Savannah**, unlike in **A Man of the People** can no longer be expected to engage in a dramatic defence and its understanding of leadership and open its doors to traditionally excluded groups. Achebe signals this change in attitude by admitting to his narrative representative, members of 'the people': taxi drivers, or shop assistant, the urban poor and towards the end a market woman. This view of including the people is reinforced by the rather determined development of the novel's two main hero's: Ikem Osodi and Chris Oriko.

Osodi, the poet-journalist, comes to realise the importance of establishing "vital inner links with the poor and dispossessed … the bruised heart that throbs painfully at the core of the nation's being" (**AOS** 141), and Chris Oriko, carrying Ikem's light, forges contacts outside his elite group. The charge of deliberateness, however, should not disparage what is Achebe's obvious commitment to imagining a reformed national politics. Expressing at once mature disillusionment and heavily-qualified fresh hope, his tentative new vision is manifested (as David Maugham Brown observes in **Anthills of the Savannah** and the ideology of Leadership) in the strategic gender configurations of his central characters" **(Kunapipi 1990:142)**.

The novel opens with paranoid manoeuvres within a male elite determined to keep hold of power, it ends with a celebratory naming ritual involving three key female figures: Beatrice, Chris's old girlfriend, and a new priestess of the goddess Idemili, Elewa, and Elewa's child by Ikem, called Amaechina, 'May-the-path-never-close' (**AOS** 222). Headed by the powerful Idemili 'taliswoman' and together with its affiliates from various classes, urban and rural, this life-affirming sisterhood signifies a new conception of rulership, the beginning perhaps of a new era for Kangan and signals a new moment in Achebe's work, according to David Maugham Brown (Ibidem:140). The new moment indeed represents a revision of ideas of power and leadership – in Ikem's terms, a 'new radicalism' – or whether it remains in the main emblematic, a public enshrining of a canonized and perhaps stereotyped 'womanly' authority set up as a last resort in the face of a depraved political situation. Even in the case of a so-called radical revision, 'it may be that gender in Achebe remains a vehicle. Women is the ground of change but not the subject of transformation' (Ibidem:141).

In a pamphlet entitled: 'The trouble with Nigeria' (Achebe 1987:21), which Achebe wrote as an injunction to Nigeria just before the 1983 election scandal, Achebe bluntly admits that the 'indiscipline of leaders', a national condition of 'lawlessness' and 'selfishness' (Ibidem :27) was the trouble with Nigeria. Achebe throws light on the political conception behind **Anthills of the Savannah** and observes that the cure of the disease is "not to be found in society at large but in the nation's leaders" (Ibidem). Leaders combine and so compound their lawlessness with influence and power. 'They are in the language of psychologists 'role models'. People look up to them and copy their actions.... Therefore, if a leader lacks discipline, the effect is apt to spread automatically down to his followers (**TN**, p.31). Africa's national leaders have become its curse-but, he believes, they might be its salvation. Addressing Nigeria's elite as himself a self-conscious member of that group, Achebe is unambivalent in his view of leadership as the chief pivot of political and also of economic transformation. Though he believes that the advent of a new leader should be followed by 'a radical programme of social and economic re-organization or at least a well-conceived and consistent agenda of reform' (Ibidem 1), he sees the first step in any process of change as being new rulership, in effect, the intervention of personality.

Interviewed after the publication of, Achebe made it clear that one of his intentions in the novel has been to take up issues raised in The Trouble with Nigeria and to use his novel to propose solutions. What will save Nigeria's future progeny is, for Achebe, better leadership. Achebe interviewer, Anna Rutherford, says:

I had the feeling that what you were suggesting was that the society reflected the quality of the leadership; if the leadership was corrupt, the society would also then turn to corruption – in other words, the negative aspects in the society would be directly related back to the negative aspects of the leadership (Rutherford 1987:3).

Achebe agrees with this interpretation but adds: ... 'but what I'm really interested in is how you could begin to solve this problem. If you're going to do that, you have to pin-point the responsibility, specifically before you can even begin to break out of the vicious circle. And it is at the level of the leadership that this break must occur (Ibidem:3).

So, **Anthills of the Savannah** sets out to solve this problem. The solution proposed by the novel is couched in terms of 'leadership', a preoccupation carried over into the fiction from Achebe's non-fictional statements. The first sentence of 'The Trouble with Nigeria' states quite baldly: "The Trouble with Nigeria is simply and squarely a failure of leadership" (**TN**. p.1). Achebe then comments, The Nigerian problem is the unwillingness or inability of its leaders to rise to the responsibility, to the challenge of personal example which are the hallmarks of true leadership, and he concludes a few pages later that:

*Every single day of continued neglect brings (Nigeria) ever closer to the brink of the abyss. To pull her back and turn her around is clearly beyond the contrivance of mediocre leadership. It calls for greatness ... Nigerians are what they are only because their leaders are not what they should be (**TN**, p.10).*

In 1988, Achebe can be found interpreting the causes of the Biafran war in exactly the same terms: "The war resulted from the failure of the leadership of Nigeria to protect significant portions of the population from a pogrom, form destruction" (**TN**, p.1).

In pursuit of this leadership thesis Achebe goes as far as asserting that after two decades of bloodshed and military rule (**TN** p.7) in one of the most corrupt, insensitive, inefficient places under the sun (TN, p.9) what his "society craves today is not a style of leadership which projects and celebrates the violence of power but the sobriety of peace" (**TN**, p.34) what 'the wretched of the earth' crave as the solution to the 'gargantuan disparity of privilege' between the 'tiny class' of the elite and 'the vast multitudes of ordinary Nigerians' (**TN**, p.22) is, it is suggested, a change in leadership style. Achebe concludes that "if Nigeria is to avoid catastrophes of possibly greater dimensions than one has been through since Independence, one must take a hard and unsentimental look at the crucial question of leadership and political power" (**TN**, p.59). 'Leadership and political power, constitute a single 'question': Is it possible to separate the concept of 'political power' from that of 'leadership'.

When this concern with leadership finds direct expression in Anthills of the Savannah one finds reference to "leaders who openly looted our treasury, whose effrontery soiled our national soul" (**AOS** 42). Ikem comes to the conclusion that the 'prime failure' of leadership in Kangan, the novel's fictionalized version of Nigeria, can be seen as "the failure of our rulers to re-establish vital inner links with the poor and dispossessed of this country, with the bruised heart that throbs painfully at the core of the nation's being" (**AOS** 141).

The key to the ideological thrust of the novel lies in the usage Achebe makes of Ikem as the primary vehicle for his message, of leadership and reform, rather than revolution, in whose service Ikem lives, dies as fictional character. Achebe makes a point of trying in a variety of ways to signal a distance between himself as author and Ikem. The most obvious of these are:

i) The criticism which Ikem comes in for in front of the other characters, most notably Beatrice's criticism of his attitude to women (**AOS** 65).
ii) Potentially and more tellingly, the omniscient narrator's comment: By nature, he is never on the same side as his audience. Whatever his audience is, he must try not to be. If they fancy themselves radical, he fancies himself conservative; if they propound right-wing tenets he unleashes revolution (**AOS** 154).

This would suggest that Ikem's adherence to any political position can never be taken at face value and might seem to serve as insurance against the possibility of his being identified as an authorial spokesperson. But it is, nevertheless, Ikem, who is made responsible for expounding the central tenets of the political philosophy on which Achebe's central message about leadership is hung:

i) In the 'strange love-letter' (**AOS** 97-101) he reads to 'Beatrice'
ii) In his seminal speech at the students' union (**AOS** 152-161).

Ikem's credentials as an authorial voice are established so clearly that the distancing devices carry very little conviction. Beatrice, who can be taken as a reliable witness throughout, describes Ikem's treatment of women as 'about the only chink in his revolutionary armour' (**AOS** 65). The reader's sympathy is clearly sought for such statements as Ikem's: "While we do our good works let us not forget that the real solution lies in a world in which charity will have become unnecessary" (**AOS** 155).

Key scenes like the public executions on the beach are described through Ikem's eyes, and Ikem's perceptions are subsequently authorially endorsed in interview: "So you find a leader like the editor of the 'National Gazette' setting himself up to correct the situation. It is people like him who must initiate the action. It cannot be done by the group on the beach who are delirious and obscenely happy and enjoying the execution" (Rutherford, p.2). It enables Achebe to provide a continuous and favourable assessment to Ikem's performance in the crucial speech to the students. He develops a device whereby description of the audience response serves as an index to the incisiveness and accuracy of what Ikem is saying. Thus, for example, the statement that 'the laughter had died all of a sudden' (**AOS** 160) indicates that Ikem has scored a telling point at the students' expense. This is a device which readers first had the opportunity to familiarize themselves with the wholly uncontentious context of the long speech given by the Old Man of Abazon at the Harmony Hotel (**AOS** 122-128). Apart from canvassing support for resistance to 'catchy, half-baked orthodoxy' (**AOS** 158), 'modish radicals' (**AOS** 159) and 'half-digested radical rhetoric' (**AOS** 161), the main burden of Ikem's political message in the novel lies with his elevation of reform over revolution: This is obviously a very far cry from Achebe's earlier endorsement of 'a revolution that aims toward true independence' with its apparent recognition that neo-colonialism and mere 'flag' independence are not susceptible to 'reform'.

In "The Trouble with Nigeria" Achebe castigates a corrupt African, elite, in **Anthills of Savannah** he sets about deposing one. In the process, developing some of the concepts he introduces in the pamphlet, he begins to suggest what sort of leadership it is that might come in its place. Chris Oriko dies with the phrase 'the last green (bottle)' on his lips (**AOS** 216,231) – it is a cryptic reference to his own description of the increasingly more inward-looking and alienated rulers of the nation, Kangan. In her revelatory conversation with Ikem, Beatrice comments that, from the point of view of the three men trained for power at Lord Lugard College, 'The story of this country, as far as you are concerned, is the story of the three of you', that is, Sam, the present military chief of state, Chris, his commissioner for information and Ikem himself, the editor of the 'National Gazette' (**AOS** 66). During what will be the last days of his life, Chris comes to the same realisation, as mentioned below:

> *We? Who are we? The trinity who thought they owned Kangan as BB once unkindly said? Three green bottles. One has accidentally fallen; one is tilting. Going, going, bang! Then 'we' becomes 'I' becomes imperial 'We' (**AOS** 191).*

In a review titled 'Betrayal', Neal Ascherson observes 'it parts a joke about Sam being left alone in power, the 'imperial We' reference is also Chris's final comment on the obsession with power that, in different ways motivated and so also undermined each member of the trinity' (Ascherson 1988:4). Ironically, however, after the demise of the troika, a highly exclusive elite will still remain in place and in force. The group that coheres around Beatrice is to be the catalyst of the future, Rutherford observes the ultimate responsibility for getting us out of this bad patch is with the small group of people who, in one way or another, find themselves in positions of leadership' (Rutherford, p.2). In this small group, the tendencies to nepotism and corruption which have compromised elite rulers in the past, will presumably be mitigated by the advent of women's salubrious force.

Elleke Boehner in his article, 'Of Goddesses and Stories: **Anthills of the Savannahs** observes that Achebe believes that woman must be included in the new elite because she is uncorrupted by power and once native female rule depends on the stereotypical image of woman as inspirer and spiritual guide; but whether the practical application of the idea has much hope is another question. Achebe seems to be confused about (**Kunapipi**, 1990:128). On the one hand, Achebe portrays a pessimistic political system, which dominates the greater part of the novel, and which Ikem gives expression to, and, on the other, an apparent commitment to gender reform and to the redemptive power of myth which comes into its own towards the end.

An exponent of the present politics and the herald of a future vision, Ikem gives us a clearer sense of these ambiguities. In the incendiary speech to the University which is the immediate cause of his arrest and murder, Ikem resolutely rejects text-book revolutionary specific African or Kanganian contexts (**AOS** 158). The abstractions of such theories have permitted every sort of misinterpretation and licence on the part of their proponents. However, as he has already enjoined Beatrice, '(n)one of this is a valid excuse for political inactivity of apathy … the knowledge of it (is) the only protective inoculation we can have against false hopes' (**AOS** 100). His proposal, which recalls assertions of Achebe in 'The Trouble with Nigeria' is to re-form society around … its core or reality' (**AOS** 100) that is, to develop its inner strength, which in **Anthills of the Savannahs** includes the power of womanhood. In typically metaphysical terms, Ikem wishes to connect his essence with earth and earth's people' (**AOS** 140-141) yet is also aware of the classic dilemma of radical intellectuals, namely, that the knowledge and experience which constitute their power, also isolate them. Ironically, it is precisely his belief in indigenous sources of healing that tags his status as outsider, one who appreciates rituals as an observer but does not live them. The same cultural distance marks off Beatrice's position as one removed from custom. Being a bearer of redemptive vision does not transform Beatrice, into a representative member of the earth's core: significantly, her status is that of special icon, not people's goddess. Ikem's meditations lead to the point of resolution which is captured in Achebe's idea of broadening from the top – as opposed to, say, democratisation or widening from the base: 'You have to broaden out so that when you are talking for the people, you are not only talking for a section or a group interest' (Rutherford, p.3). Given the need for an elite and therefore for hierarchy, the main possibility of reconciliation lies in building and extending person-to-person connections across class, gender and political hierarchies. The intention is to maintain an elite leadership within a national framework, but to change its style: to develop responsibility, a newly-gendered image of power, not a little scepticism and a broader support base-in general to 'widen the scope' (**AOS** 158). The leaders approach the 'owners' of the country in order to embrace and take into their bosom certain of their number. So, Beatrice, leader, inspirer and new seer, becomes the informing centre of a new select group drawn from various social sectors. David Maugham Brown observes that according to the leitmotif of the novel, in the anthill that survives after the fires of the harmattan, Beatrice is queen, keeping the colony together. As with Yeat's interlocking gyres, though things threaten to fall apart, though old vortices collapse, centres – stable 'cores of reality (leaders, elites, women as dispensers of succour) – are needed, if there is to be movement and change" (**Kunapipi** 1990:142).

In terms of the revolutionary of Marxist theory 'orthodoxies of deliverance' (AOS 99) Ikem derides, the cop-out is patently obvious: existing economic and political structures remain firmly entrenched, class hierarchies (such as outlined in The Trouble) are endorsed; a soft-core middle-class moralism is reinforced. From the gender perspective, by implicitly presenting the sisterhood's investiture as, in the main, metaphoric redemption, the danger is that woman's conventional position as inspirational symbol –the mentor who is never a full political actor is entrenched.

Yet Achebe has prepared for his caveat by eulogizing the power and importance of myth and story – telling in the novel – in the particular through the rhetoric of the Old Man from Abazon (**AOS** 122-128), in the hymns and the poetic role Ikem, and in the apotheosis of Beatrice. For the present, the national is to be redeemed metaphorically – or perhaps metaphysically – only: that is, by London-educated civil servants turning into Ibo priestesses, by syncretic ritual ad emblematic cross-class and cross-ethnic alliances. Achebe's general idea seems to be that, in the African context, where much theory has already been uselessly imposed, political postulates, such as those set out in **The Trouble with Nigeria** do not of themselves offer hope of regeneration. Not by way of clichés from other histories and struggles, but in the figures of gods and rituals drawn from its own local cultures, can the nation, whether Kangan or Nigeria interpret present confusion conceptualise a new future, or as Beatrice puts it, '(subvert) the very sounds and legends of day-break to make straight the way' (**AOS** 109). This is related to Ikem's idea that humanity be re-formed around what lies within it; that, where 'times' will always 'come around again out of story-land' (**AOS** 33), one should draw on history and story as it is and has been lived.

The metaphoric and allusive images of a future dispensation give primary colour to the hope of **Anthills of the Savannah** and to Achebe's own hope for the African nation. His idea of the relation between symbolic transcendence and the presence of women should be more clearly defined. Significant emblematic elements appear in Ikem's two dense prose poems (the 'Hymn to the sun' (**AOS** 30-33) and the Meditation on Idemili's owner' (**AOS** 102-105). 'Masculine' images of power and agency are juxtaposed with 'feminine' evocations of peace and reconciliation. It is clear that old dichotomous gender distinctions run deep. However, the final scene at Beatrice's flat, in dramatizing and unifying Achebe's central symbolic meanings, demands the focus of attention. It is here that Beatrice, pre-figurement of a 'gynocentric' spiritual way, stands forward as the harbinger of a new order. From the initial act of having pointed Ikem in the direction of his vision of woman (**AOS** 96), through being flippantly called a 'prophetess' by Chris, we find Beatrice metamorphosed through sorrow (her suffering is stated not dramatized) into a priestess of Idemili, 'the unknown god (sic)' (**AOS** 224); and also a leader of the naming ceremony (replacing the traditional position of father or male family head (**AOS** 222). Whether the cross-reference is intentional of not, Achebe rather appropriately draws on the same redemptive Ibo tradition of female devotion and worship (as did Nwapa in Efuru, as Ifi Amadiume tells us in "Class and Gender in **Anthills of the Savannah**) with her moral authority, godless-like carriage and capacity for mediation and inspiration, Beatrice has recognizably become a daughter of the Idemili described in the myth earlier told by Ikem.

The incarnation of Idemili is a redemption of the present political situation, as it is of the neglect of the goddess in the past. Ikem's observation, that myth has been used to marginalise women (p.89) is also echoed by Achebe in the Rutherford interview. Attended by Elewa, child of the people and bearer of the seed of a poet, and a new child, a girl with a male name – Beatrice's spiritual power as a blessed woman thus represents the fulfilment of Ikem's final vision of Woman as adopting a new and yet-to-be-imagined role, as signifying new hope (**AOS** 98). To quote Achebe himself, Beatrice and her entourage represent women in their place 'in the forefront of history' (Rutherford:4).

The potential of woman as celebrated at the end of **Anthills of the Savannah** represents a significant advance in the African novel, being most distinguished perhaps by Achebe's refusal to dictate exactly how that potential will be fulfilled. Space is made for woman to be herself, the prefiguring subject of a new social and political vision. Yet at the same time, despite the efforts at 'rescheduling' power, it is also true that the way in which Achebe privileges woman continues to bear familiar markings for gender, and that this must, to a certain extent compromise his re-imaged hope. Symptomatic of Achebe's difficulties is Elewa's transmogrification through the implantation of Ikem's seed (**AOS** 184). As part of the same symbolic logic, Amaechina's name – "May the path never close is translated as the 'Shining path of Ikem' (**AOS** 222). The implicit idea of inheritance along a male line – of masculine influence as life-giving, and of man as passing the rod of leadership on to woman – can of course be justified in terms of Achebe's belief in continuity: 'The remnant-shall-return' (**AOS** 222). Yet it equally signifies that maleness remains potently generative: as Beatrice discovers the day she dances with His Excellency, 'the royal python' still stirs '(gigantically)' in the 'shrubbery' of Idemili's shrine (**AOS** 81).

Certain traditional gender-specific spheres of influence appear to remain in force. In their time-honoured way, women in **Anthills of the Savannah** especially the heroine who lacks 'book', wield power through sex and their bodies, whereas man continues to control the word (Ikem's poetry) and also, one presumes the rule of the word that is politics. As in earlier nationalist writing, Ifi Amadiume tells us in "Class Gender in **Anthills of Savannah**" 'the artist, the one who defines first the vision of the future and transmits the myths of the people, is male' (Amadiume 1989:9). Towards the end of the novel, it is true, a woman does decisively obtain control of vatic power. However, in that her transfiguration is, almost by definition, symbolic, she remains trapped in a role that women have occupied many times before in the mythologies of nations, states and politics, she incarnates 'the ideals and the desire of men'. On the same point, one might ask to what extent Beatrice's induction into the cult of Idemili is in part a specific development of a stereotype; the inverse of the image of woman as unclean, or as body? As in more traditional evocations of Mother of Africa, woman in **Anthills of the Savannah** is represented as mystical, in touch with the unknown, as mentor or genius of the renewed nation.

As problematic as cross-gender filiation are relationships within 'the sex'. In this case, differences of class complicate gender status, returning us to the question of the constitution of the ideal elite. In another representative scene, Beatrice plays the central role, Elewa – or perhaps Ikem – is the main Catalyst of the situation. Conflict arises during the time of crisis after Ikem's death when Agatha, Beatrice then treats Agatha roughly, pushing her aside to do the job herself. At this point Achebe equips his chief heroine with a fair amount of defensive rationalization: she is concerned to repeat that Elewa's emergent consciousness' has acted with transfiguring power, singling her out from the mass represented by Agatha. It is this special 'almost godlike' touch which, in addition to being 'Ikem's girl', Beatrice concludes, has "transformed a half-literate ... girl into an object of veneration" (**AOS** 184), and someone she is able to befriend. Beatrice makes quite clear that the 'complaining millions of men, who darken in labour a and pain' are to be saved, not by their own efforts, but by those with inner light – a capacity which would further separate the elite from the mass. Yet given this chasm of consciousness, how are the enlightened humans, even if female (asks Brown) to interact with the masses, like Agatha, who do not have the gift of 'luminosity' (unless this is sympathetically transfused), or, with class barriers still in place, do not come into contact with those who have light? The apotheosis of women figures, impelled by the need to save the elite from itself, finally brings us back to the original problem of how to form an enlarged caucus, a problem now compounded by the distancing effect of the canonization of woman.

Achebe wants his novel, **Anthills of the Savannahs** to give hints of a new and regendered order. There are inconsistencies and contradictions or moments of insight in his art of narration. The problems of elite politics remain insoluble but symbol provides a powerful means of thinking forward. Beatrice asks: "what must a people do to appease an embittered history?" The answer is there in the eyes of her guests: they recognise in her act of articulation, 'the return of utterance to the sceptical priest struck dumb for a season by the Almighty for presuming to set limits to his competence (**AOS** 220). 'Truth is Beauty', Beatrice explains at the very end of the novel – it is the truth that lies in the last image of Chris withstanding his assailants like Kunene's Emperor Shaka' (**AOS** 233) and the truth contained in the prominent image of the anthills holding their own truth of the past. Implanted in the 'truth (is) beauty' postulate, is an evitable suggestion of abstraction from real, material life: it is in keeping with this that Beatrice's new vocation, if we are to believe Nwapa, demands retreat from everyday life. Yet Beatrice's assertion is also a practical adaption of the doctrine of aesthetic appreciation to a context, where, as Soyinka has also held, myth and ritual continue to thrive as living presences; Achebe in **Girls at War** makes Gladys program from 'girl' to sanctified object as much as for their beauties of ceremony to be redeemed, for their truth, their lived reality, as much as for their patterned form (Achebe 1972:103-23).

Achebe appears to want to hold the two ideals truth and beauty, in balance, the one intimating the other: So, just as a relatively ordinary woman may become, through her spiritual understanding, an example or 'shining path' to her companions, in the same way an ordinary stick in the sand is transformed through ritual into a pillar of Idemili, the connection with 'earth and earth's people'. The real functions as index to the beautiful. In this way too, random collection of individuals can come to represent the ritual passage into the future of another Kangan. In 'serious' politics, symbols and supernatural signs such as these might seem superficial and, certainly from a gender point of view, compromising. Yet, where other options and modes of recompense are unsteady of have failed, symbols stand for points of intersection with, as Achebe would have it, the very present divine: as interjections of spirit, 'transactions' between the market place and goddesses.

Anthills of the Savannah reveals that Achebe has risen to new heights in both artistic excellence and social vision. A writer who is continually coming to grips with the problems of society and art is likely to develop to higher levels of social consciousness and as a consequence to strive for new forms of artistic representation, forms which match his or her quest for democracy and social transformation.

When writers make their debut with a classic of the quality of **Things Fall Apart** it is often not easy to match that first performance in later works. **Things Fall Apart** stands head and shoulders above the other three novels. Emmanuel Ngara in **Stylistic Criticism and the African Novel : A Study of the Language and Content of African Fiction** says : With regard to the use of the language it may be argued that although he over-played the importance of proverbs in **Arrow of God**, his skill in that particular aspect has become so perfect that the language of the third novel is superior to that of any of the other novels, **Things Fall Apart** included. But when one reads **Anthills of the Savannah** one is struck by a new and refreshing quality in the use of language, a quality that is perhaps discernible in **No Longer At Ease** and **A Man of the People,** but not in the same degree of excellence (Ngara 1985:59). Achebe's basic philosophy regarding the use of the English language by the African writer has not changed. There is, for instance, a clear distinction between the language of relatively uneducated people like Agnes, Beatrice's housemaid, and Elewa, Ikem Osodi's girlfriend. These consistently speak Pidgin, unlike Beatrice, Chris, Ikem and His Excellency, all of whom belong to the educated elite and would normally use standard English. It is also clear that the bearded old man who is one of the leaders of the Abazon delegation that meets Ikem at Harmony Hotel in Chapter 9 is reminiscent of the like of Ezeulu, those who represent traditional wisdom and are blessed with the gift of eloquence. His English is meant to be Achebe's rendering of the Ibo he would have spoken. This is all familiar to Achebe's readers, but there are some new elements now. George Lukas in **The Historical Novel** tells us that Achebe is such a master of the English language that he is able to skilfully combine what sounds like conventional English spoken and written by linguistically talented mother tongue speakers with a local educated variety of the language and the idiom of non-English speaking characters, to produce a style which is almost classical but almost with an underlying informal touch that saves it from being stilted (Lukas 1981:331-332). Consider, for example, these two passages from **Anthills of the Savannah**:

*On my right sat the Honourable Commissioner for Education. He is by far the most frightened of the lot. As soon as he had sniffed peril in the air he had begun to disappear into his hole, as some animals and insects do, backwards. Instinctively he had gathered his papers together and was in the very act of lifting the file-cover over them and dragging them into his hole after him when his entire body suddenly went rigid (**AOS** 3).*

*I was determined from the very beginning to put my career first and, if need be, last. That every woman wants a man to complete her is a piece of male chauvinist bullshit I had completely rejected before I knew there was anything like Women's Lib. You often hear people say: But that's something you picked up in England. Absolute rubbish! There was enough male chauvinism in my father's house to last me seven reincarnations! (**AOS** 880)*

The first passage represents Chris Oriko's language and the second Beatrice's. The features which are clearly noticeable in the two passages are the conventional style, the natural flow of the language and how easily readable the extracts are. It is also worth noting that in these and many other passages Achebe is able to maintain a fine balance between informality and formality. This is partly because he employs the first-person narrator point of view. At the same time, he does not lose the opportunity to exploit the use of local idioms which even highly educated people like Professor Reginald Okong are wont to use in appropriate situations, as in the passage were Professor Okong is attempting to curry favour with His Excellency, the President (AOS 18).

It is amazing how Achebe manages to combine a wide variety of stylistic features and to slide into different moods with great ease. The style is on the whole light-hearted. The novel deals with very serious matters but the tenor of discourse is relaxed and sufficiently informal to allow the reader to reflect and digest the ideas without being overburdened by a heavy style. This is also true of **A Man of the People**, but it is more difficult to achieve in **Anthills** because in the former novel the principal characters, Odili and Chief Nanga, are not portrayed as serious-minded characters, but **Anthills of the Savannah**, all the major characters are addressing what they believe to be grave matters but in a manner which is never so serious as to bring about a feeling of depression in the mind of the reader. On the contrary there is even irresistible humour in many a passage when Professor Okong refers to overthrow of the civilian regime as 'a historic fall from grace to the grass' (**AOS** 12), and in passages depicting His Excellency, the President's wit and wry humour.

In **Anthills of the Savannah** the use of language is intricately bound up with the author's narrative technique. The story is told from the point of view of three characters – Chris Oriko, the Commissioner for Information in the Republic of Kangan; Ikem Osodi, editor of the **National Gazette**; and Beatrice Okoh, Chris's girlfriend and a Senior Secretary in the Ministry of Finance. In addition to these three narrators there is the omniscient narrator who takes over from each one of them at a convenient point. For example, the event that take place in Chapter I are narrated by Chris Oriko who, like Beatrice, puts his observations in writing. But in Chapter 2 the omniscient narrator takes over again, and this goes on and on. An important consequence of the technique is that the author is able to explore in depth wide variety of issues from different angles. Instead of seeing the events through the eyes of one storyteller as in **A Man of the People**, one is presented with the versions of at least four major narrators. Take the character of His Excellency, the President, for example, one gets to know him from what Chris says about him, from what Ikem says, from Beatrice's internal monologues as well as her conversations with Chris, and also from the events described by the omniscient narrator. As a result, His Excellency emerges as a rounded character who does not only have distinctive features and qualities, but also gives us a genuine insight into the behaviour and ideology of some African Heads of State and into their relations with their ministers and other senior government officials. Through the omniscient narrator one gets an insight into the President's capacity to keep his ministers on their toes by playing them off against one another, and through Beatrice's narrative one begins to see a sharp contrast between his ability to control his own ministers and the ease with which Westerners, even mere Journalists, can dominate his thinking and behaviour, as in the case of Lou Crauford, the American journalist one meets in Chapter 6. The upshot of this multiple narrator technique is that Achebe creates four main characters each of whom gives us a view of society and the political set-up depicted in the novel.

As if the multiple narrator technique is not sufficiently complicating in itself, Achebe adds to the complexity of the plot by making generous use of the flashback and other modes of narration. For example, one gets to know about the past lives of His Excellency and of other characters through the recollections of Chris and Beatrice. For instance, one meets His Excellency exercising his power as Head of State at the beginning of Chapter 1 and only at the end of the same chapter does Chris explain how Sam came to be President and how his education and military training prepared him for the position. What is more, one only gets a clear account of the relationship between Sam, Chris and Ikem at the end of Chapter V.

There are other features which add to the complexity of the narrative structure of **Anthills of the Savannah**. One of these is the use of symbolism in conjunction with myth and allusion. A supreme example of this feature is Ikem's 'Hymn to the Sun' (**AOS** 30-33) which foreshadows the disaster that follows in the novel and is probably a comment on the self-destructive tactics of His Excellency who, in an attempt to preserve his own power, resorts to destroying his former friends and is himself destroyed in the process. There is also the reference to David Diop's poem, 'Africa', whose last lines encapsulate one of Achebe's suggestions about the way forward for Africa – that what is at issue, is not so much a political system, as the patience to develop, through experience and over a long period of time, a viable political and economic system (**AOS** 23-128). Finally, there is the naming ceremony for Elewa's daughter which symbolizes a new major development that the world of **Things Fall Apart** and **Arrow of God** has now gone and has been replaced by new social values in that, contrary to custom, the naming has been done collectively by young people and the old man from the village who was supposed to perform the task realises that social values have changed and so accepts and blesses what the young people have done.

It is thereby evident that new developments in Achebe as an artist have taken place, but the development in social consciousness and artistic vision, and in authorial and aesthetic ideology, and from the point of view of dialectical criticism i.e., from nationalist consciousness to revolutionary consciousness and from the point of view of critical realism, the aesthetic ideology that characterize his first four novels to socialist realism, is not significant enough, because Achebe has not become a Marxist. Dialectal criticism maintains that the vision of a non-Marxist writer like Achebe is constrained by the limitations of the writers' 'false consciousness' and so he or she will display a limited world view with regard to the place of various classes in society'. Achebe's analysis of African society, is presented from the point of view of one class – the petit bourgeois or to be more precise, the political and intelligent elite, to which he himself belongs. Achebe thereby portrays only a partial view of the social fabric of the Republic of Kangan.

All his major characters- Chris, Ikem, Beatrice and Sam (His Excellency) are members of the educated elite class. The intelligentsia occupies the entire of the stage in Achebe's world while the other classes are either pushed to the periphery or relegated to oblivion. The two major classes of oppressed and deprived people, the peasants and the workers, are given a place in the world of **Anthills,** but they are given minor roles to play in the drama of that world. The peasantry is represented by the delegation from Abazon and by Elewa's mother and uncle who visit Bassa for the naming ceremony. The working class is represented by the taxi-drivers who form an alliance with Ikem. These are minor characters and Achebe does not give us sufficient insight into their lives and into their response to the events and problems that plague the Republic of Kangan. Indeed the peasants to Abazon Province come to Bassa in an effort to reach an accommodation with 'the big Chief' with a view to persuading the Government to continue with the work on bore-holes which stopped because of the people of Abazon's refusal to support His Excellency's claim to life presidency, and indeed Chris Oriko ultimately flees to drought-stricken Abazon and dies there in the company of Emmanuel Obete, the President of the Students' Union, and Braimoh, one of the taxi-drivers; but the readers do not have first-hand information about the living conditions, life style and predicament of the inhabitants of rural Abazon. As for the most privileged class, the class of rich people who own the means of production, one's only encounter with it is through a brief reference to Alhaji Abdul Mohamoud, Chairman of the Kangan/American Chamber of Commerce who wallows in the filth of wealth and corruption (**AOS** 177).

One of the major indications of Achebe's development in social consciousness is his portrayal of women. In the earlier novels women are given minor roles and all the major parts are taken by male characters. There is one significant exception to this and that is Clara in **No Longer**

at Ease, but while she is a fully developed character, she finds herself acting in a world dominated by men, and while Obi genuinely loves her, he tends to patronise her and is portrayed as her intellectual superior. Beatrice, on the other hand, is neither intellectually inferior to Chris nor dominated and patronized by him. Their relationship is a relationship of equals who have a natural attraction for each other. While she rejects the Western concept of Women's Lib, she is certainly of the view that woman is equal to man and a woman can live a complete life without a man. It is indeed significant that Beatrice is the only government official who is brave enough to tell His Excellency off. Disgusted by the excessive deference His excellency shows to Lou, a mere journalist, because she is an American, Beatrice is bold enough to accost the Head of State who normally reduces his ministers to the status of mere boys: "If I went to America today, to Washington DC, would I, could I, walk into a White House private dinner and take the American President hostage. And his Defence Chief and his Director of CIA?" (**AOS** 81)

It is also significant that Beatrice is closely connected with Ikem's daughter, who symbolizes hope for a better future, and worthy of note that Ikem's child is girl. It is Beatrice who names the child and the symbolic significance of the child is captured in the name Beatrice chooses for her. 'We have our own version of hope that springs eternal. We shall call this child AMAECHINA: May-the-path-never-close. Ama for short' (**AOS** 222). So the struggle for justice and democracy continues and the seed of revolution Ikem Osodi has planted, shall grow again patiently and obstinately, until its fruit gradually acquires the bitter taste of liberty, as David Diop says in his great poem which is quoted as an epigraph at the beginning of Chapter 10.

Ikem Osodi's views on art and politics are observed to be closely related to Achebe's. Through Ikem, Achebe persuades the reader to reflect on a number of topical issues in **Anthills of the Savannah** the place of women in society, issues relating to class struggle and theories of revolution, the African predicament, as well as issues relating to literary theory and the role of the writer in society. As a novelist and a journalist and also as one who is not directly part of His Excellency's government machinery, Ikem appears to be the most appropriate character to raise some of these questions and to reflect on them.

With regard to the question of women, his views are deeply influenced by his interaction with Beatrice who has definite ideas about the place of women in society. Among other things, Beatrice holds the view that 'giving women today the same role which traditional society gave them, of intervening only when everything else has failed is not enough' (**AOS**

91), and she sees this as weakness in Ikem's original political position, as a fact which blurs his vision as a writer, it is her discussions with him on questions such as these that lead him to formulate his new theory on women and other oppressed social groups. His reflections on the problem of women result in the formulation of a radical theory of social class. "The women … are the biggest single group of oppressed people in the world", says Ikem,…"but they are" not the only such group. There are others –rural peasants in every land, the urban poor in industrialized countries, Black people everywhere, including their own continent, ethnic and religious minorities and castes in all countries" (**AOS** 98). Using Ikem as a mouthpiece, Achebe comments on the theory of class and class struggle and calls to question some of the fundamental tenets of historical Marxism, including the idea of a millennium in which there is no oppression of one social group by another after the establishment of communism. Ikem believes that the orthodox Marxist position proposes a simplistic remedy to the problem of oppression. For his part, he does not believe that once a socialist and communist revolution has taken place, all the social problems of society are bound to disappear.

*The sweeping, majestic visions of people rising victorious like a tidal wave against their oppressors and transforming their world with theories and slogans into a new heaven and a new earth of brotherhood, justice and freedom are at best grand illusions. The rising, conquering tide, yes, but the millennium afterwards, no! New oppressors will have been readying themselves secretly in the undertow long before the tidal wave got really going (**AOS** 99).*

In his lecture to university students in Chapter 13 Ikem addresses the all-important question of the function of the writer. The writer does not provide solutions to problems, he argues. The most important function of the writer is to include people to reflect upon the condition of their lives to raise their consciousness so that they can begin to ask why things are as they are, why things are going wrong:

*No, I cannot give you the answer you are clamouring for. Go home and think! I cannot decree your pet, text-book revolution. I want instead to excite general enlightenment by forcing all the people to examine the condition of their lives because, as the saying goes, the unexamined life is not worth living ... As a writer I aspire only to widen the scope of that self-examination (**AOS** 158).*

Ikem's point about all certitude being suspect (**AOS** 99) and his scepticism about a millennium has been vindicated before our very eyes in this decade. In Eastern Europe and Asia socialist countries have come to the realization that the mere adoption of socialism as a political ideology is not in itself a panacea that resents ready solutions to all problems of social and economic development. After going through a fervent cultural revolution China abandoned the approach in 1978 and adopted an open-door policy and a form of socialism that is suited to Chinese conditions. In the Soviet Union, Gorbachev had followed suit with his Perestroika, while one of the former leaders of the German Democratic Republic, Mr. Krenz, recently called for a redefinition of socialism, observes David Maugham brown. This is not to say that there is necessarily something inherently wrong with socialism, but simply to emphasise the point Achebe makes that simplistic remedies like the 'dictatorship of the proletariat' are likely to fail. One observes in Achebe's works more specifically **Anthills of the Savannah** that he is both socially and morally a revolutionary thinker and consequently a social reformer.

Thus, is Phase III, both Ayn Rand and Chinua Achebe's last two novels, which have been called their philosophic treatise, have been discussed. In **Atlas Shrugged** and **Anthills of the Savannah**, Rand and Achebe, have offered suggestions to solve their society's problems, versus society, in this phase, takes on a new dimension. Rand in her novel **Atlas Shrugged** depicts the growth of the 'man-child' into the 'demi-gods' of **Atlas Shrugged**. Rand creates a Utopian society in the mountains where all the demi-gods who go on strike reside. The society, if one can call it so, is pictured as an ideal society where each man lives for himself and never expects another to sacrifice himself for another. Every man's creativity, integrity and freedom are respected, and though each man is alone, they are not alienated or lonely but enjoy a kind of creative bliss in their aloneness.

Chinua Achebe's book **Anthills of the Savannah** depicts two protagonists Ikem and Chris who are trying to carry the torch of leadership. Achebe believes that a society's success depends on its individual leaders. It is the responsibility of the leaders to lead their people to a better life. It is also the responsibility of the led to inform their leader of their responsibility, says Achebe.

This phase is considered their philosophic treatise because in **Atlas Shrugged,** Rand combines Metaphysics, Morality, Economics and also discusses concept like love, Money, Politics, Sex, Woman's issues along with Rand's notion of the ideal men who consequently will form an ideal society. Achebe also in this phase, offers solutions to the problems demonstrated in the previous novels. For example, Achebe discusses the kind of leadership necessary for Nigeria, gender transfiguration, the place of women in society, class struggle, the method to combat corruption on Politics, and spiritualism that is necessary for a better society.

Both Rand and Achebe are social and mora revolutionaries in the sense that they are concerned with the socio-moral problems that affect their respective societies and are keen to offer suggestions and solutions for the same. While Rand believes that man, if he exists, must live as he 'ought to be' like a God himself, Achebe believes that a certain degree of individuality is necessary for the growth and development of an ideal society.

The theme of **Atlas Shrugged** is "the role of the mind in man's existence". In this phase, Rand applies the theme of **The Fountainhead** to the political and economic arena in Atlas Shrugged. It demonstrates that capitalism rests on the mind and the freedom of the mind. Achebe's **Anthills of the Savannah** depicts a number of themes; to mention a few: the ideology of leadership, gender transfiguration class struggle, corruption and women's place in society.

In Rand's **Atlas Shrugged** the central lines of conflict in this phase in further developed, not between Good and Evil as in phase II, but between 'Good' and 'Good'; between Galt, Francisco and the strikers on the one hand, and between Dagny and Rearden who will not join the strike on the other. The errors which set these protagonists in conflict are errors of knowledge, not because of morality. 'Good versus Evil' means to grant to evil an honour it doesn't deserve.

In this phase, women play a very important part. One observes there is a progression even in the woman characters of Rand's novel. Rand has always been enthusiastic about presenting her kind of woman. Here in phase III, Dagny is Rand's first portrait of the ideal woman. In **The Fountainhead** Dominique Francon was paralyzed by a profound inner conflict, and Kira of **We The Living** was still a young girl. But here, in Atlas shrugged one observes Dagny is free of any psychological conflict, serene in her basic relationship to existence, ambitions and creations. Rand wanted to present a woman thought to be impossible by any unconventional standard of life and sex. Dagny is a woman engineer, dealing with the material world of metal rails and diesel engines, who is simultaneously a consummately feminine hero worshipper.

One of Achebe's remarkable developments in social awareness is his attitude towards women. In the earlier phases women are used functionally as mere objects and no major role was attributed to them except for Clara in **No Longer at Ease**. Though Clara is a fully developed character, she exists in a male dominated world, and though Obi loves her, he patronizes her and is portrayed as her superior, intellectually. But in this final phase, Beatrice is neither intellectually superior to Chris, nor is she dominated by him. They function on an equal plane and are naturally attracted to each other. Beatrice like Dagny is induced with qualities of courage and ability, integrity and grit. She tells off His Excellency, accosts the Head of the State, who reduces his ministers to the status of mere boys. Beatrice is also given important duties to perform like naming Ikem's daughter.

Both Rand and Achebe deal with topical issues like the place of woman in society, political anarchy, theories of revolution and the American and African predicament respectively. While Rand projects women as autonomous individuals strong intellectually oriented, principled women of integrity who yet believe in hero-worship; Achebe in **Anthills of the Savannah** is of the opinion that women are the biggest single group of oppressed people in the world, besides the rural peasants, religious minorities and castes in all countries.

In this phase, the 'second-handers' or the parasites of **The Fountainhead** (in phase II) become the 'moochers' and 'looters' of **Atlas Shrugged** (Branden 1986:211).
In the previous phases the second handers are not productive and litter the cultural world with mediocre works; there is still room in the world of Howard Roark and Dominique Francon for genuine geniuses to function. In the world of **Atlas Shrugged** of phase III the 'moochers' and 'looters' not only hamper the 'producer's' or 'First-handers' ability to function, they pass laws and directives which confiscate both the means and the ends of their efforts. One of John Galt's rationales for the 'strike of the mind' is that if the weak have harnessed the strong to their service (as they claim the strong have exploited the weak in the past), then the strong should use the same means that the weak have used-a strike. When the productive withdraw their talents and abilities, the looter's economy crumbles. When there is no host to feed on, a parasite cannot exist. This is the lesson that Rand teaches in **Atlas Shrugged**. In one of Francisco's speeches to Rearden he explains that Rearden is helping those who torment and hobble him because he still tries to produce even with all of the 'looters' restrictions. Francisco suggests that the only way to defeat looters is by not giving them anything to loot.

Phase III evolves into the most successful and most optimistic ending in **Atlas Shrugged.** Although Howard Roark (the good) succeeds in **The Fountainhead**, Ellsworth Toohey and Peter Keating are still holding fort. But in phase III, the strike of the 'men of the mind' vanquishes the looters, leeches and the second handers of the previous phase, leaving the world firmly in the hands of the demi-gods – the creative and the productive. So, one notices through the four novels of Ayn Rand, the individual develops from the 'foetus' of **We the Living** in the first stage to the ideal 'demi-god' of **Atlas Shrugged** in the last phase. The corrupt society in Rand's fiction gradually deteriorates and a Utopian society-a kind of heaven on earth atmosphere is created in her chapter titled: 'Atlantis' This could be Rand's concept of an ideal society. As far as Rand is concerned, the existence of ideal men would result in an ideal society and the world will be the richer by it.

Achebe in this final phase depicts the individual emerging as leader trying to lead his society out of its present state of anarchy and corruption. Achebe also suggests that the role of government could also be handed over to women, as they are less corrupt and better transforming agents.

In his five novels, Achebe oscillates between the past and present alternatively, mainly to show the strength, validity and beauty of Ibo life and culture. The first is the anthropological background of the Ibo community and the second the impact of Colonialism on the above community, its teething problems and the process of its readjustment for a new order. The theme therefore is the conflict and tension generated by the clash of cultures and religion and so in these novels, the emphasis is not so much on the individual as on the whole community.

Achebe's heroes are not mere victims of a social change; their fall as he sees it is an inevitable outcome of their own suppression of their gentler of feminine impulses. Thus, the novels are not an elegy to a lost world, but a tribute paid to the dignity of a people and their ancestors. He does not see the white man's intrusion into Africa as 'the white death'. Maintaining an ambivalent stand on this issue, he agrees that Christian intrusion to a certain extent was the disruptive force that force asunder the clan and undermined its solidarity, but he also points out that the Ibo clan at that time was ripe for this cultural onslaught. Viewing both traditional and modern values in a mild, comic irony, Achebe sees the inability to adapt to new demands as the major weakness that destroyed the Ibo anxiety. In his book **Chinua Achebe**, Ravenscroft tells us that it is a communal culture, which allows a considerable measure of individuality but not quite flexible to survive the appearance of the white man" (Ravenscroft 1969:30).

In the course of the five novels Achebe shows that change is inevitable and logical. He "accepts mutability as an ineluctable factor in human civilization and progress" (Peters 1978:130). Achebe believes in the brotherhood of man, in the importance of the collective consciousness, but he also admits that a certain degree of creative individuality is necessary for the progress of civilization. Both Rand and Achebe philosophize on a number of issues necessary for the individual and his fulfilment in the society.

In the next chapter the researcher purposes to discuss Rand as a 'Novelist-Philosopher' and Achebe as a 'Philosopher Priest', and also brings to light some of the tensions and contradictions in their philosophic thinking.

V

'Novelist-Philosopher' and 'Philosopher-Priest'

Ayn Rand and Chinua Achebe are novelists and philosophers with a difference. Barbara Branden, describing the death of the novelist in **The Passion of Ayn Rand** refers to Rand's dream being realized when the world acclaimed her a famous 'Novelist-Philosopher' at her death and Bernth Linfors tells us that Achebe is concerned with "serious moral issues" in all his novels and never "abandons his usual role as Philosopher Priest" (Branden 1986:311).

Ayn Rand is a Novelist Philosopher as she declares in the 'Preface' to For the New Intellectual. In a certain sense, Rand observes, every novelist is a philosopher, as one cannot present a picture of human existence without a philosophical framework. The novelist's only choice is whether that framework is presented in his story explicitly or implicitly; whether his work is the individual projection of existing philosophical ideas or whether he originates a philosophical frame work of his own (Rand 1974:vii). While Rand did the second, Achebe did the first. Rand observes:

This is not the specific task of a novelist I had to do it, because my basic view of man and existence was in conflict with most of the existing philosophical theories. In order to define, explain and present my concept of man, I had to become a philosopher in the specific meaning of the term (Ibidem:vii).

This then becomes one of the major contrasts between Ayn Rand the Novelist-philosopher, originating a philosophy of her own titled 'Objectivism'; and Achebe, the novelist presenting a picture of human existence against an already existing philosophical framework. In this chapter, Ayn Rand's theory of Individualism as a central component of the Objectivist philosophy is juxtaposed along with Achebe's Altruist- Collectivist doctrine of the Brotherhood of Man. The aim of this chapter is the following:

i) to introduce the main premises in Ayn Rand's Objectivist philosophy and Achebe's Altruist-Collectivist philosophy and
ii) to highlight certain contradictions in Ayn Rand's and Achebe's philosophy and to prove invalid certain fundamental premises on which Rand's theories are based.

This is attempted in two parts of this chapter. Part I introduces Ayn Rand's Objectivist philosophy and Achebe's philosophy. The major factors responsible for its growth and popularity are also highlighted.

Part II demonstrates a few of Rand's and Achebe's philosophic contradictions:

i) It shows how Ayn Rand's Objectivist movement is reminiscent of a religious cult, much as Ayn Rand may have laboured to denounce, not only herself as an atheist, but also all forms of mysticism and religion.
ii) It exemplifies that Ayn Rand's Objectivist standard of value, 'man's life', does not and cannot logically include pleasure and happiness as even aspects of 'man's life', thus accounting for the suffering of Objectivists. It portrays why 'man's life' is an invalid standard of value.
iii) It shows that contrary to the Objectivist dogma, happiness is not just a concrete subjective experience, not merely a "psychosomatic" response", but that it is both an objective cognitive 'tool' and a valid moral primary-that it is in fact, the objective standard of value.
iv) It will be seen, that not only are Ayn Rand's ethical premises invalid, but that a crucial aspect of her metaphysical-epistemological view is incorrect as well.

Since Achebe does not have a theory of philosophy like Rand does, his contradictions, tensions and anxieties are specifically related to his last book Anthills of the Savannah. It depicts:

i. Achebe's portrayal of the students as highly sensitive and reliable sounding boards in one moment, and immature adolescents in the next.
ii. Ikem's concluding speech, where he ascribes "a heavy weight of responsibility to the leaders" and simultaneously confuses the matter by also expecting 'the led' to hold 'their leaders' to responsible performance". There is tension between the content of the message to be conveyed and aesthetic demands of the form used.
iii. Achebe thinks leadership to be the preserve of the 'elite' and yet it must also represent the people – ("the taxi driver, the market woman and the peasants") so as to broaden out, but the question asked is, how one retains one's leadership and yet broaden out.
iv. Anxiety exists between the role of the intellectual and the role of the artist in revolutionary politics.

Ayn Rand is not only a novelist and philosopher, she is, in the words of Loraine Pruette in "The Battle Against-Evil" the greatest salesman philosophy had ever had" (Pruette 1943:16). Only Ayn Rand could write a philosophic treatise like **Atlas Shrugged** in which the protagonist and villains are differentiated fundamentally by their metaphysics; in which the wrong epistemology is shown to lead to damnation and the right ethics to an indispensable rebuilding of man's soul (Branden 1986:411).

While the major theme in Achebe's fiction is the primacy of the collective consciousness, the major theme of Rand's fiction is the primacy of the individual. The unique and precious individual human life is the standard by which good is judged. All of the secondary themes in Rand's fiction develop as the logical consequence of her major theme. If individual human life is the standard by which good is judged, then it follows that political, economic and ethical systems and institutions which encourage and protect individual freedom and happiness, are the proper systems to develop and sustain. While her major theme is explicitly developed in all of her novels, it is not until **Atlas Shrugged** that she works out all of the political, economic, and metaphysical implications of that theme.

Rand repeatedly articulates her respect for America's Founding Fathers and the premises upon which this country is based. If there is a phrase in the Constitution which synthesizes her philosophy, it is the statement that each individual is endowed with certain inalienable rights: the rights to life, liberty and the pursuit of happiness. As Rand worked out her interpretation of what those rights entailed, she saw three areas of conflict in which those rights were held in balance.

i. Individualism versus Collectivism
ii. Egoism versus Altruism
iii. Reason versus Mysticism

In Rand's philosophy all of these areas are interconnected. Reason is the tool by which the individual discerns that which is life-sustaining and ego-nourishing. Collectivism, altruism, and mysticism work against the individual freedom, a healthy ego, and rationality.

In all of Rand's works, the individual human is the most important being in the universe. Not God, nor country, nor cause, proceeds the individual in Rand's hierarchy of values. In her first novel, **s**, she pointedly illustrates how, putting one's state or political cause above the self, is detrimental to human happiness and ultimately creates a destructive and poorly functioning state. The value that Rand places on the individual is clearly seen in Kira's affection for Andrei. Though she hates the Communist, she sees Andrei's worth as an individual and worries about him, expressing fear for his safety when he fights the rebellious farmers. **The Fountainhead** is Rand's fullest explication of the primary of the individual. One of her stated purposes in writing it was to develop a defense of egoism, which Rand has also called selfishness and rational self-interest. Howard Roark explains the virtue of selfishness in his defense at the Cortlandt trial. In his explanation of how independent creators have benefited human kind he says, "The creators were not selfless. It is the whole secret to their power that it was self-sufficient, self-motivated, self-generated (**TFH** 430). He goes on to explain that only by living for oneself can one accomplish those things which are the crown of human achievement. The mind, in which great creations are conceived, is an individual thing. "There is no such thing as a collective brain" (Ibidem). The much-quoted rule of living in Mulligan's Valley-the Utopia of **Atlas Shrugged** is another of the specific articulations of Rand's belief in the primacy of the individual. Carved in granite on the door to the structure which holds the motor, the product of one mind that could power the world, is the oath: "I swear by my life and my love of it that I will never live for the sake of another man, nor ask another man to live for mine" (**AS** 921).

Parallel to Rand's development of the dichotomy of the individual versus the collective is her working out of the analogous situation of the productive versus the parasitical. In Rand's fictional world, the elite are the able, the doers. The ability to create, to produce, to do is a primary virtue. For Rand, "you are what you do" (Branden 1986:431). This is not as evident in her early works as it was to become in the novels that were the hallmarks of her philosophy. Achebe's emphasis is not so much on the individual as on the highly communal way of life, which itself becomes a character in his novels. The individual in Ibo society exists in a cosmic totality, and hence his understanding of reality, is a collectively shared vision.

Achebe portrays this 'collective consciousness' in all his works and shows a "clan which once thought like one, spoke like one, shared a common awareness and acted like one" (**TFA**, p.6). The life of the individuals like Okonkwo and Ezeulu, and the beliefs, rituals, ceremonies of the community are merged into an order and significance. Though the individuals exist, they are deeply aware of the communal aspect of their very existence and no individual can think of detaching himself from the way of life or religion of his clan, for to do so is to be severed from his roots. Okonkwo, declares the value of kinship in a proverbial statement: An animal rubs its itching flank against a tree, a man asks his kinsmen to scratch him (**TFA** 151). According to Hume, this close association between members of the family teaches them the value of mutual support, giving them internal satisfaction of the mind and providing them with extended power of labour which in turn results in the prosperity of the clan. But it is a community that also values individual achievement. The clan judges a man according to his worth, and not his father's. Okonkwo, at eighteen, is declared the greatest wrestler in the nine villages, the owner of two barns of yam, three wives, two titles and has shown incredible prowess in two intertribal wars. But whatever be the individual's achievement, even if he is the chief priest, they must accommodate themselves to communal morality. This explains why Achebe's characters, while being individuals, collectively symbolize a way of life. It is this folk consciousness that allows Achebe to create fiction out of the trivialities of life. Ezeulu's remark that "a man must dance the dance prevalent in his time" (**AOG** 189) can be regarded as the basic metaphor, for this dance symbolizes the cohesion and orchestration of a united communal life. This cohesiveness of the village is maintained thought its unwritten laws. Though laws are nor written, there is no lawlessness. The Ibo community acts as a unit and purifies itself. For instance, the excommunication of Okonkwo is a very significant communal action of the village cleansing itself of the sin Okonkwo commits by spilling the blood of a clansman. Thus, in this society where even an individual conflict acquires communal dimension, the belief is that the individual's sin can affect the entire clan for "as the elders said, if one finger brought oil it soiled the others" (**TFA** 114).

The primary contrast of the 'individualistic' American society and the 'communal' African society is often linked to the contrast between the 'traditional ' and the 'modern', the 'rural' and the 'urban', and often closely associated with a distinction between a 'mystical' attitude towards nature that does not separate the individual from the cosmos (as seen in Chinua Achebe's works; and an 'empirical' or 'rational'; attitude towards nature (as seen in the works of Ayn Rand).

Metaphysically, Rand believed in objective reality. Reality exists as an objective absolute; that facts are facts; and Reason (the faculty which identifies and integrates the materials provided by man's senses) is man's only means of perceiving reality, his only source of knowledge, his only guide to action, and his basic means of survival (**VOS** 31).

Rand's and Achebe's attitude to nature is typical of the accidentalist and orientalist respectively. While Rand's is a rational and utilitarian attitude, Achebe demonstrates a more mythical closeness to nature, thus, marking the difference in their nature.

In **The Fountainhead**, Ayn Rand's protagonist, Howard Roark, not only looks at nature in the face but also conquers it. He looks at the world around him and transforms nature as it were:

*He looked at the granite. To be cut, he thought and made into walls. He looked at a tree. To be split and made into rafters, He looked at a streak of rust on the stone and thought of iron ore under the ground. To be melted and emerge as girders against the sky (**TFH** 1).*

To Ayn Rand, nature is to be commanded. Rand emphasizes the productive, commercial and materialistic response to nature. Nature is an integral part of the Ibo world, not an independent phenomenon, as in Ayn Rand. Emmanuel Obiechina observes: "Nature is so intricately woven into the social, economic and metaphysical realities" (Obiechina 1975:214) that this explains why there is an absence of scenic description in Achebe's novels. The people in Achebe's fiction are closely linked with the soil and highly dependent on the weather and so nature does serve a utilitarian purpose too. At the same time, trees, birds, animals and natural phenomenon are treated with awe and reverence. Nature Gods dominate their lives and so the names of these pagan Gods are usually the names of natural or divine powers – Ani, the Earth Goddess; Idemili, the god of water; Amadiora, the Ibo God of thunder and other spirits associated with groves, streams, market, etc. shape their destiny. The Evil Forest is filled with mystery and terror. The moon is also associated with abnormal psychic conditions and lunacy, while the sun is associated with mixed feelings of life and death. Ibo attitude to nature is not one of romance and aesthetics, rather it is connected with the fundamental question of survival. Further in their ritualistic and collectively shared vision of nature, they also explore nature's vast potential occult energy. This is because of their belief that "every act of creation is a personified and unique manifestation of the creative essence.

Thus, religion in the works of Chinua Achebe unlike in the works of Ayn Rand is rooted in a primal vision of the oneness of the universe, and according to J.V. Taylor, such a mind believes that all things:

share the same nature and the same interaction one upon another – rocks and waves upon a ship, the power of a drum over a dancer's body, the power in the mysterious waves of Kokola, the living, the dead and the first ancestors; from the stone to the divinities of hierarchy of power, but not of being, for all are one, all are here, all are now (Taylor 1963:21).

In Achebe's works, the religion is so much part of the people lives. The experience of the world permeates the very consciousness of the African mind for as John. S. Mbiti says "wherever the African is there is his religion" (Mbiti 1967:17) since there is an absence of a well-derived theological basis, distinction between the 'sacred' and 'secular' does not exist and their attitude to their Gods is ambivalent. Thus, a God can be overthrown of he and his priest do not satisfy the demands of the clan; and thus, the lesser Gods are not above jealousy and spite. Ezeulu's fall at the end of the novel is regarded as a just punishment from Ulu for a proud and ambitious priest.

Religion, finds no place in Rand's fiction, but her protagonists radiate a new kind of religion, the belief in man or "the cult of Man-Worship" (Branden 1986 :416). Rand's philosophy is called 'The Bible of Objectivism', her word was the final word and her lectures referred to as: 'The Gospel according to Ayn Rand's, and Rand loved being the Deity (Ibidem) unlike Achebe. Rand declared herself of be an Atheist. In an article titled: "Theologians call 'God Talk' Irrelevant", Rand expresses her shock at God being considered as a process of creative social intercourse. She observed in her article "Faith and Force': I who am an Atheist am shocked by so brazen an attempt to rob religion possessed". 9Rand 1982:76) Rand believed that even if there was a God, He is no longer part of the human experience and hence "God Talk' is both meaningless, and irrelevant in the contemporary situation and religion is an outmoded ideology. It involves a certain kind of outlook on the world and a consequent way of life. In other words, the term 'religion' denotes a precursor of philosophy. As such it should include a view of knowledge. Religion, Rand felt was not a solution to man's problems; it is the problem. Religions must be left free, no philosophic view point, right or wrong should be interfered with by the state (Ibidem). Rand's concept of God is similar to Feurbach which is a reversal of the Genesis Man created God in his own image. Rand advocates Reason as man's tool of survival and not blind belief. But ironically, Rand laments, before a man learns to think, he is ordered by faith to believe. 'Faith", "She says", is the worst curse of mankind, the exact antithesis and enemy of thought" (ibidem). All Rand's protagonists are religiously alienated beings, while the archvillains are considered religious. Rand believes that an individual's human life should be the standard by which his religious, moral and ethical life is judged

Such a religious concept was considered by the objectivists to be the most practical, comforting and progressive religion. What Ayn Rand termed 'man-worship' was her feeling for the ideal man to whom she associated concepts such as 'worship', 'reverence' 'exaltation'- epithets oriented to the supernatural or mystical or religious, when these values are actualized and embodied in a specific man, man-worship becomes romantic love. Thus, the special quality of the Ayn Rand romantic love is the union of the abstract and the concrete, of ideal and reality, of mind and body, of uplifted spirituality and violent passion, of reverence and sexuality. Throughout the early years, female protagonists predominate in Ayn Rand's fiction and one of their essential traits is this kind of man-worship. The early heroes are merely suggested, they are not fully realized until Roark in **The Fountainhead**. But whatever the language and literary problems may be, the motif of the woman's feeling for a hero is realised. Henry, in the **The Husband I Bought** (1926) is the earliest ancestor of Leo (in **We The Living**), of Roark, of Francisco in **The Fountainhead** and of Rearden (in **Atlas Shrugged**). These heroes foreshadow the later heroes.

It may be wondered why Ayn Rand chose to present man-worship first of all, in the form of a story of unrequited love. It is only that this aspect of the story was autobiographical. Ayn Rand as a college student was in love with a young man in Russia who was the real-life source of the character of Leo. She remembered this young man, and her feeling for him, all her life. The relationship between them, however, was never fulfilled – whether for personal reasons or political ones (he was exiled to Siberia). But either way, it is easy to imagine that alone in a new country, on the threshold of a new life, she should be drawn to focus as a kind of farewell to the man she loved and had now last forever - or, more exactly, to focus on her own feeling for that man and loss. This concept of man-worship does not feature in Achebe's novels.
In Chinua Achebe's fiction, one finds there is quest for a return to morality, a return to their own specific sense of African religions or African ethics or African morality. It is a thirst to return to their ancestral worship, their gods, their beliefs, rituals and customs, their divine life: "With Rand it is not a 'return' to morality but a discovery of it" (**AS** 987). The Ethical theory of Objectivism is a morality to love, as against the other major schools of ethical theory – the mystic, the social and the subjective, which according to Rand have brought the world to its present state and which represent the morality of death. All the three schools are variants of realism, and anti-life, not merely in content but also in their method of approach.

Rand's work portrays a matchless delineation of the morality of survival and mental health and a projection and concretization of the self-esteem possible to men who choose to live by the judgement of their mind. Rand affirms that there is "a morality of reason, a morality proper to man" (**VOS** 16) and that man cannot function effectively without it. It relates good and evil directly to man's volition – the choice to think or not to think, that is the manner in which one uses ones consciousness. There can be no universal and objective standard of moral values.

The two most important features of Rand's moral view are

i. her defence of rational selfishness and
ii. her insistence on the existence of, and respect for human rights.

Rand contrasts these doctrines with all varieties of self-negating ethics, (i.e.) Altruism. It consists in contrasting depictions of self-respecting self-loving, and independent people and self-sacrificing, self-loathing and dependent people, and accounts of the long-run; psychological, sociological, and economic accompaniments of self-abnegation.

The dichotomy between good and evil is another of Rand's philosophical themes, which finds a place in all her works. Rand observes, in her article "The Objectivist Ethics" :

> *Since reason is man's basic means of survival that which is proper to the life of a rational being is the good; that which negates, opposes or destroys it is the evil. Since everything man needs, has to be discovered by his own mind and produced by his own mind and produced by his own efforts, the two essentials of the methods of survival proper to a rational being are: thinking and productive work (**VOS** 23).*

Rand's rationality and productivity are welcomed as essential traits for the life and happiness they bring. Rand seems to behave like an ethical hedonist here, declaring that pleasure, and pleasure alone is the good, and also feels uneasy about judging all else by its tendency to maximize pleasure. The hedonist talks about higher, 'refined' pleasure and 'lower', 'swinish' pleasure, Rand also talks about 'subhuman survival' versus "man's survival qua man" (Ibidem). Rand seems to advocate Hubert Bonner's "Hellenic view of man." Quoting Bonner, Singh defines such a man as, "the full actualization of human potentialities, of a life individually perfected, a life of aspiration and freedom; while Achebe advocates Hubert Bonner's Hebraic idea of man – a man of responsibility and duty. This stresses a life shared, a life of discipline and self-control" (Singh 1979:31). Rand tries to depict man proving his existence or validating his individuality by means of the courage to be himself. This self-validation through actualization of one's being is matter of moral integrity, but Achebe tries to tell us that in the final analysis, while man is potentially the author of his own history, no existence and most particularly no personal existence, is possible in the absence of man's regard for and commitment to other human beings. Contrary to the

Randian philosophy that every individual fulfils his purpose in the attainment of happiness, Achebe believes, that the men who have left a mark upon their fellow beings, have been individuals with the passion to leave the world different from what it was before they were thrust into it. Being thus free from the compulsive search for happiness, the proactive individual can lend himself freely in the service of others. Freedom without commitment is licentiousness. Yet all the conditions of contemporary experience point unequivocally to the fact that man's most desperate longing is not group-relatedness but self-fulfilment. Man does not seek merely the happiness that a group can provide, but more profoundly the dedicated search for himself. Man is truly his own foundation.

It is one of the characteristic traits of human nature that man finds his fulfilment and happiness only in relatedness to and solidarity with his fellowmen. Hence Achebe's ethics, morals and justice are socially oriented. There are powerful individuals in Achebe's world. For instance, Okonkwo thinks he can make his 'chi' obey him, and Uzowulu who listens to no lesser a voice of judgement than the 'egwugwu'. However, their individuality, while not repressed or denied, is held in check by communal solidarities. After accidentally killing a fellow villager, Okonkwo must go into exile because the earth would take revenge upon the whole community; the chief concern of the egwugwu in their settling of the Odukwe-Uzowulu dispute is not that the truth should be unearthed or that justice should be done, but that the disputants should be reconciled in a way that makes for the peaceful continuation of the tribe, for this in the end, is the supreme and only criterion.

Corruption is a vital moral concern in Achebe's fiction especially in the last two novels: **A Man of the People** and **Anthills of the Savannah**. Issues especially connected with politics are raised, like the question of popular representation in government. Achebe questions, observes David Maugham Brown, not only the honesty of politicians but also the kind of leadership that prevails in society (Brown 1990:62).

Achebe focuses on the moral dilemma of the protagonist, the way in which his ideals conflict with the community ethics, and the extent to which he is true to his own beliefs. From the first scene, Odili wonders over the proper standards to follow:

*I knew I ought to be angry with myself but I wasn't. I found myself wondering whether, perhaps, I had been applying to politics stringent standards that didn't belong to it (**AMOP** 9).*

Any crime is accepted and the criminal admired for his villainy. People see nothing wrong with the politicians making money, as long as they too have some share in the wealth: As a policeman states: "We know they are eating", he said, "we are eating too. They are bringing us water and they promise to bring us electricity. We did not have these things before; that is why I say we are eating too" (**AMOP** 139). Achebe criticizes this commercial spirit in his society which measures good only by the immediate benefits it acquires. Odili's father joins them in approving Odili's political activities as long as they bring him money and a car, his tacit assumptions being that one enters politics in order to make money. To this extent these novels display a more immediate social engagement than the earlier three.

Unlike in Ayn Rand's fiction, life in Ibo society is replete with cultural and religious activities which follow a rhythmical pattern from the womb to the tomb. The Ibo tribe has its own anthropological pattern which includes birth, puberty, initiation, marriage, procreation, old age, death and entering into the community of the dead. Such patterns do not exist in Rand's anthropological perspective. While in Rand's fiction concepts like love, sex and marriage are purely personal happenings, in Achebe's world, every stage can be regarded as a renewed incorporation of the individual into the clan with highly symbolic ritualistic ceremonies. Of all the ceremonies, the most protracted ceremony is marriage, for it is this which ensures the continuity of the tribe. Marriage, which is missing in Rand's fiction, is a complex affair involving various economic social and religious implications.

It is the concern of the whole tribe and not just of the couple or their families.

The love theme is not given much room in Achebe's fiction except for the Obi-Clara relationship in **No Longer At Ease**, but it plays a major role in Rand's works. Obi, a young man of the 1930's and 1940's, falls in love on the boat coming home, with Clara: Clara has been to England too and is a nurse. Innocent, she yet belongs to an 'Osu' family. By obscure, stupid and surely unjust village reckoning, she is an outcast, and hence Obi is not permitted to marry her. Love is an important philosophical theme, in Ayn Rand's fiction. Love is not only a response to values but a representation of all that one holds dear. Hence when Rand's characters love they love without reservation. This is demonstrated in each of Rand's work of fiction. Leo's health is so important to Kira in **We The Living that** she becomes Andrei's mistress so that she will have the money to send Leo to a sanatorium in the Crimea. Prior to that she has risked her life attempting to escape with Leo, although she doesn't even know his name. Kira, who never lies, lies to both Andrei and Leo in order to save Leo's life and pride. She pretends that she loves Andrei and she lies to Leo regarding the source of her money. Roark in **The Fountainhead** who is fiercely independent, openly acknowledges to Dominique how much she controls him. When she attempts to play power games with him, he shows her immediately that she owns him "all … that can be owned". His love for her is so great that he will not ask her to be his wife because he knows that she cannot be whole until she comes to him with a healthy ego. He stands by when she marries, first Peter Keating and then Gail Wynand, enduring the pain while she first goes through her perverse penance. Gail Wynand explains to Dominique in Atlas Shrugged that "love is exception-making". He has broken every person of supposed integrity that he can find in order to prove his power, but he doesn't want to break her, although he tells her that she is in love with integrity and in his eyes is a person who has it, a 'person who matches inside and out" (**TFH** 510). John Galt puts his life in danger in order to be with Dagny. Eventually his association with her results in his capture and torture. Before the government agents arrive, he tells her that he does not regret his action. Dagny exclaims, "I didn't care whether either one of us lived afterwards, just to see you this once!" The life-worshipping Galt tells Dagny that he will kill himself rather than allow her to be tortured.

Rand's and Achebe's attitudes to sex are equally contrasting. Alfred Kinsley points out in **Sexual Behaviour in The Human Male** that there are three different interpretations of sex in social and religious philosophies:

i. the hedonistic doctrine that sexual activity is justifiable for it immediate and pleasurable return,
ii. sex as the necessary means of procreation to be enjoyed only in marriage and then only of reproduction is the goal of the acts, and
iii. sex as the normal and biological function acceptable in whatever form it is manifested (Kinsley 1948:4)

While Rand belongs to the Hedonistic school, Achebe belongs to Kinsley's second and third interpretation of sex.

In most of Rand's stories the first meeting of the hero and heroine is accompanied by a rape-like encounter, which rather than distancing the couple, cements their relationship. In **We The Living**, though Kira has never seen Leo before, she is willing to let him believe she is a prostitute rather than let him go out of her life. In **The Fountainhead**, Howard Roark's rape of Dominique establishes an unspoken bond as neither speaks during the entire episode. In **Atlas Shrugged,** John Galt's first sexual experience with Dagny is a ritualized rape in the tunnels of Taggart Transcontinental. For Ayn Rand, these romanticized rapes are symbolic of the head-on clash is. The rapist is conquered just as his victim is. This symbolism of her rape scenes may be condemned by those who have a raised consciousness about the nature of rape.

The basic socio-political principle of Rand's Objectivist ethics is Capitalism, while Achebe is a left-wing anti-capitalist. Laissez-faire capitalism is Rand's political system where men deal with one another, not as victims and executioners, not as masters and slaves but as traders, by free, voluntary exchange to mutual benefit. The government Rand believed in **Capitalism; The Unknown Ideal** should act only as a policeman to protect man's rights. In a system of full capitalism, there should be (but, historically, has not yet been) a complete separation of State and Economics, in the same way and for the same reasons as the separation of State and Church (Rand 1967:54).

Achebe's socio-political principle is Altruism. Altruism holds that an individual has no right to exist for his own sake, that service to others, is the only moral justification of his existence, and that self-sacrifice is his highest moral duty. The political expression of Altruism is Collectivism or Statism, which holds that man's life and work belong to the state, to the society, to the group, the gang, the race, the nation and that the society may dispose of him in any way it pleases, for the sake of whatever it deems to be its own tribal, collective good. Hence an Okonkwo is exiled, and an Ezeulu dethroned so that the tribe may continue. Philosophically, tribalism is the product of irrationalism and collectivism, according to Rand. It is a logical consequence of modern philosophy. She argues that if men accept that reason is invalid and that the individual is intellectually and morally helpless, and the group is all , and his only moral significance lies in selfless service to the group – they will be forced to join a group which claims the ability to lead them by some sort of unspecified means.

In Capitalism: The Unknown Ideal, Rand tells us capitalism has been called "a system of selfishness and greed, nationalistic and cruel" (Rand 1967:73). But strangely enough it is the only system that has enables men to unite on a large scale, into great countries and thereby raise the standard of living. It is the only system that has been able to banish ethnicity and bring hope, progress and good-will among all, while collectivism according to Rand has split the world into Balkanized tribes. On the other, the practical results of altruism and statism have seen slave labour camps, gas chambers, mass slaughters, starvations, sale of human lives and reigns of horror and terror.

These atrocities, would never be possible had man not accepted the idea that man is a sacrificial animal to be immolated for the sake of the 'public good' and if the word 'sacrifice' was regarded not as a moral ideal, but as the anti-human evil which it is. In her famous non-fictional work For The New Intellectual, Rand observes: Capitalism and altruism are incompatible; they cannot coexist in the same man or in the same society. Today, the conflict has reached its ultimate climax; the choice is clear-cut: either a new morality of rational self-interest, with its consequences of freedom, justice, progress and the individuals happiness on earth – or the primordial morality of altruism, with its consequences of slavery, brute force, stagnant terror, and sacrificial furnace (FTNI 65).

Achebe is an altruist, in the sense that he believes in the brother-hood of man. The ambiguous politics of Achebe's works pertains to his known identification with left-wing, anti-capitalist groups, and intellectuals in his native Nigeria, and more broadly in Africa, at the same time that this identification has been fraught with problems and controversies. Achebe is, in this sense, very much in the company of other post-colonial writers like Wole Soyinka, Gabriel Garcia Marquez, Salman Rushdie, Nadine Gordimer and Carlos Fuentes, whose left identified politics sit very uneasily with the orthodox Left and its set revolutionary perspectives and objectives. In Achebe's novels, one sees the Ibos as a people without kings or chiefs, yet they operate highly efficient democratic government. The government functions through the cultural and traditional Council of Elders (Ndichie), Council of Masquerades (Egwugwu), the Oracles and their Chief Priests who were the liaison between the people and the gods. The traditional government has a set of rules and laws which must be obeyed by all. The Council of Masquerades is presided over by the 'Evil Forest', the leaders of Umuofia. They try cases and inflict punishments. The law of the land is no respecter of persons as is the case with Okonkwo who, himself a titles man, is fined for beating his wife during the week of Peace. The following verdict by Ezeani, the priest of the earth goddess, on Okonkwo's crime is an example. "You will bring to the shrine of Ani tomorrow one she-goat, one hen, a length of cloth and a hundred cowries" (**TFA** 22). These are for appeasing the gods. For more serious offences like murder, the offender is required to go into exile for a period of seven years, as in the case of Okonkwo who fled to Mbanta.

The coming of the white man with his government disrupts this age-long tradition and there is a great conflict between the new and the old order. The white man establishes his own court which is presided over by the

District Commissioner. The District Commissioners are said to have judged cases in ignorance because they are foreigners and do not know the customs of the people especially in land disputes. The Court Messengers, who are agents of the District Commissioners, are disliked also because they are strangers. They come from Umuru which is regarded as a foreign land. Obierika describes them as 'arrogant and high-handed'. The white man has no regard for Umuofia titled men and they, in turn, do not recognize the white man's brutal government. The white man has two major types of punishment. For minor offences the people are flogged and in murder cases the offenders are hanged. In the traditional system these require only sacrifices to appease the gods or exile in cases involving killing or spilling of human blood. On the new judicial system Obierika tells Okonkwo, "I told you on my last visit to Mbanta how they hanged Aneto" (**TFA** 124). Aneto had killed Oduche and fled the village as required by custom. The court Messengers, however, arrest him and he is hung at Umuru. Hanging is seen as an abomination and is abhorred by the people, while the white man regards it as a legal act.

While Rand conceives of property rights as necessary for the individual's happiness, Achebe conceives of property rights as a communal concept. African societies have communal ownership of land – that is, the 'lineage' not the individual owns the land. Ownership involving rights of alienation on the part of the individual, as conceived by Rand, is an inapplicable concept here. However, individuals do matter as well, they do have 'use rights' which they inherit and sometimes may procure in other ways.

The intellectual history of these familiar contrasts might begin with a distinction in nineteenth century German social theory, between 'Gemeinschaft' and 'Gesellschaft', originally found in Tonnies, but also present in Max Weber, and anticipated in Marx, who is certainly an influential figure in modern African thought. Such contrasts serve to highlight the absolute difference between African and American psyches. While the African writer deals with societal problems, the American writer deals with purely personal ones. The absence of 'introspection' is so far as it exists, is more related to the absence of a developed literary tradition of introspection than to the external feature of the 'African Mind'.

Having introduced the major premises, in Rand's Objectivist Epistemology and Achebe's philosophic thinking, the following section will discuss the major tensions and contradictions in Rand's and Achebe's thinking.

Rand believes it is only through the rejection of 'subjective standards' and a total commitment instead to reason or objectivity that one can be a good person and have a chance of happiness. Ironically, despite Rand's explicit rejection of all forms of mysticism, subjectivism, supernaturalism and religion and their attendant political ramifications like statist collectivism, perhaps the most distinctive quality of the objectivist movement in general was one reminiscent of a religious cult. The very name 'Objectivism' is one suggesting dogmatism (Branden 1986:341).

Though Rand stated that she based her philosophy on the basis of her metaphysical epistemological view, that 'reality' is objective, that reality exists as it is, independent of what consciousness may want, wish or fear it to be. She nevertheless applied the name 'Objectivism' to everything she had written or approved. Given that objectivity in effect means 'validity', Rand's philosophy might well have been named 'Truth' which suggests an 'infallibility' and thus takes on a religious-like orientation, inherent in its very name. Moreover, the main thrust of Rand's philosophy was not concerned only with ideas. Rand and her 'chosen apostles' – 'the class of 43', as Barbara Branden tells us in **The Passion of Ayn Rand**, acted as 'spiritual leaders' whose writings and preaching in every area were laden with endless 'good and evil polemical moralizing" (Branden 1986:364).

Students and adherents of her philosophy were asked not to describe themselves as 'Objectivists' but rather 'students of Objectivism', on the premise that only Rand and those chosen by her, could decide who did and did not understand her philosophy and approach, which suggests not only articles of faith but articles of subjectivity known only through personal revelation. Nathaniel Branden Institute and lecturers had an atmosphere similar to church masses, an air of hushed sepulchres, solemnity and a sense of worshipful reverence and awe for the leaders and preachers of the philosophy. Those who questioned were sometimes chastised for irrationally; and feared not only condemnation but also excommunication. These students, like Rand's protagonists in her fiction, radiated a strange de-personalized intensity, a preoccupation which gave them the appearance, not of life loving, self-interested pursuers of happiness, but of austere, stiff, self-denying, ascetic styles, more closely associated with persons involved in and dedicated to unearthly, mystical, and other self-sacrificial religious beliefs which these same advocates of objectivism professed to despise. This 'ecclesiasticism' became a way of life. Outwardly much time was spent in pious, moralistic proselytizing. Inwardly mental life was occupied significantly with tense, anxious, guilt-ridden soul searching trying to expunge their immortal souls of all earthly thoughts and desires. There was constant self-monitoring (checking) of one's emotions, to see if these feelings were founded on rational or irrational principles or if they were being as responsible as one must to achieve 'man's life qua man'. Nathaniel Branden, Ayn Rand, Frank O'Connor, Leonard Peikoff, Alan Greenspan and other disciples of Rand, like the class of 43, were all supposed to be living practical substantiations of the validity of 'man's life qua man', as a standard of value and proof of the 'realisticness' of Rand's fictional characteristics. These colossal giants of character would pardon errors of knowledge but never breaches of morality. They adopted an attitude of being morally and psychologically perfect. Never was heard a public reference by the leaders to any sort of personal, psychological or moral difficulty. The students had no other alternative but to follow their leaders. None of them were prepared for the shock they received with the sudden notification in The Objectivist (1980, May) that Rand had totally and irrevocably repudiated Nathaniel Branden for behaviour which included a lessening of his interest in philosophical issues and in the Objectivist Movement – the deliberate deception of a certain person over a period of years; and his intellectual, professional, and dishonest financial exploitation of her- as well as certain other unnamed moral transgression, rumoured in Objectivist circles including Branden's rejection of Rand in romance (Rand 1980:94).

Branden was condemned and excommunicated for action on the basis of his emotions, a transgression which students of Objectivism found absolutely un-integrable in the light of Branden's all-encompassing knowledge and implicitly suggested success in achieving happiness through rationality and objectivity (Rand, The Objectivist, May 1980).

However, the significant result of this schism (the Object schism) was the first suggestion of the remotest possibility of Rand herself not being the monument to absolute intellectual integration and moral perfection that her moral and professional attitudes seemed to suggest. Branden himself, in his published reply to Rand's repudiation of him, had subtly suggested certain irrationalities on Rand's part, in his book **Who is Ayn Rand?** All those who supported Branden and even those who purchased Branden's books were repudiated by Rand and her inner circles.

It is surprising that Rand herself should subscribe to such contradictions, given that Rand's foremost principle of rationality demands that moral judgements be made only upon first hand evidence. There were also rumours of 'Ayn Rand's Loyalty Oaths' having been administered by inner circle members. That Rand should practice such things, let alone tolerate them, is appalling. Rand's own ethics is irrational, in the sense, that 'her sense of life' (a gut-feeling basis of judgement) comes closer to being subjective rather than objective.

These apparent contradictions in Rand, disillusioned, angered and confused many students of Objectivism and relieved them from trying to emulate Rand, her fictional characters or Branden or to seek their future in 'man's life' through Objectivists rationality. This marked the beginning of the end of the 'Objectivist Movement' (Nathaniel Branden, **Who is Ayn Rand?**). Just as there are hangovers from the Christian ethic in the minds of those who reject the religion but accept its moral premises, so are there hangovers among many thousands of former Objectivists, who feel that the ethics of Objectivism should have been presented in a more benevolent fashion. They feel that Objectivist ethics are, for the same reasons as Christian ethics are, false, incorrect, invalid, illogical, non-objective and that it should be made clear, 'rational'. The ethics presented in **The Virtue of Selfishness** is an example of its non-objectivity and invalidity and is similar to the ethics of religion which Rand herself condemned and for the same reasons. This is the reason why the Objectivist movement resembles a religious movement. It is not only a doctrine based on articles of faith; it exhorts man to accept as their standard of value, a floating abstraction, which in principle is, as divorced as the concept of 'Heaven', as from the meaning of their own existence.

While repudiating all forms of mysticism and denouncing all moral standard, Objectivism's very own standard, 'man's life qua man' – is itself little less than a platonic ideal. It is little less than platonic as it isolates the good, as related exclusively to the individual human being as must be the case in a fully consistent, fully rational and objective standard such as 'Happiness'. Further it was the invalid basic premises of the ethics of Objectivism which doomed the Objectivist movement.

What is good for him personally will depend on what gives him the most pleasure. But pleasure is a feeling, an emotion. "And an emotion is not, according to Objectivist ethics, a rational or Objective standard of value". Pleasure and Happiness are in no way destructive to 'man's life' and their co-existence as values implies no neurosis. The only basic difference between them as values is the level of pleasure involved. Pleasure in thus the only intelligible criterion of action here, yet according to Objectivism, it is "irrational to guide oneself on the basis of pleasure or happiness". Rand holds that happiness by its nature is such that it can 'never' be considered a valid standard. To her it is subjective concrete, and unlike the concept of man's life, cannot be used as a tool of cognition. Sid Greensberg in his book titled: **Ayn Rand and Alienation : The Platonic Idealism of the Objectivist Ethics and Rational Alter-**

native argues that Objectivism is thus not logically entitled to consider pleasure and happiness as rational guides to action in any context, including the context in which one is confronted with the two 'pro-life' alternatives. To use pleasure or happiness as guides is according to Rand, to act irrationally and destructively. Herein lies that characterized the Objectivist movement ; the premise that acting on the basis of emotions is to be guilty of evil. The only alternative guide to action offered by Objectivism is 'man's life'. This includes countless life preserving things, but without an objective standard of personal selection (which is what Happiness is, but which Objectivism denies) one has nothing to go on, except abstract forms of the good forms of life. Objectivism fundamentally and logically rejects happiness as being important yet holds happiness to be "man's highest moral purpose". Rand does not state that since Happiness is the purpose of life, action based on the greater of the two 'pro-life' pleasures is justified. If she did so, it would imply two distinct types of objectivist standards.

i) Man's life as an objective standard
ii) Pleasure i.e. (action based on the greater of the two "pro-life" alternatives) as an objective standard.

But to Rand, there was only one objective standard – 'man's life'.

That "Happiness is man's highest purpose" is, as far as Rand's premises and logic are concerned, absolutely nothing but an empty claim, an unproved assertion. Rand labours through two specious arguments which enables her to integrate happiness with 'man's life'. The first involves a dichotomy of the meaning of 'standard of value' and 'highest of purpose'. Rand cannot admit that happiness is a valid, objective standard of value. She cannot define it in non-circular terms, thereby making it to her, a subjective concrete and therefore an invalid and unreasonable standard of value. Yet she undeniably feels the profound and fundamental significance of happiness. She writes: "In psychological terms, the issue of man's survival does not confront his consciousness as an issue of 'life or death', but as an issue of 'happiness or suffering'. Rand feels, that she must get happiness integrated with her standard somehow. Rand attempts to switch from 'life' to 'happiness' as the purpose.

The maintenance of life and the pursuit of happiness are not two separate issues. To hold one's own life as one's ultimate, and one's own happiness as one's highest purpose are two aspects of the same achievement. Existentially, the activity of pursuing rational goals is the activity of maintaining one's life: psychological its result, reward and concomitant is an emotional state of happiness. It is by experiencing *happiness that one lives one's life in an hour, year or the whole (**VOS** 19).*

The fact is that this is merely an assertion and in no way proves that happiness has anything to do with an ultimate purpose. It is literally false, that by experiencing happiness one lives… "Happiness is not literally equivalent to living. Man's life may include happiness but does not 'mean' happiness. Rand also states above, that "existentially, the activity of pursuing rational goals is the activity of maintaining one's life'. This means that by pursuing rational goals, one lives. No doubt the pursuit of rational goals is the 'psychological reward' and its reward of happiness does not make the experience of happiness the same thing as the process of living. Pleasure and Happiness are somehow significant, and happiness is 'for life', it aids men in living, it is a value 'because' of life. One is subordinate to the other.

If 'life' is identical to 'happiness', it invalidates Rand's assertion that happiness can properly be the 'purpose' of ethics but not the "standard", because then the standard 'becomes' happiness, and happiness is a standard which Rand explicitly and categorically rejects as non-objective. Then if she literally means to equate happiness with 'life', then by Rand's own premises 'man's life' is also a non-objective standard. Rand states that "metaphysically, life is the only phenomenon that is an end in itself"; then how can 'happiness' also be 'an end in itself'. And if "the experience of pure happiness is worth living for", how can life be the ultimate value against which the worth of all else is measured; if happiness is worth living for, it is happiness that is the standard against which the worth of life is measured. In fact, what one greets and affirms in emotional and metaphysical terms upon experiencing happiness is the fact, that happiness, not life, is an end in itself.

Rand, thus, fails to prove that happiness is man's ultimate or 'highest' purpose. But Rand senses that without happiness, there is in fact no concrete experiential end for man to achieve, except life which has no end to achieve except more life. And life is not even a concrete that can literally have something 'for' it, so that to view life as man's ultimate purpose or highest value is to view the preservation or achievement of an abstraction as an ultimate purpose, which again is plutonism. Rand believes one must never choose anything on the basis of the pleasure it gives, even if they are needs to life, as that ultimately implies action guided by emotion. This is the reason that Rand announced that sports and games are 'purposeless activities' (An Open Letter to Comrade Spassky 'The Ayn Rand Letter, date unavailable). To consciously chose to gain pleasure at play is not productive of life support, according to the implications of her standard. This is to say that objectivist ethics are designed to make men into automations. Happiness and pleasure are not standards of good reasons for action and therefore must be considered as side-issues in human affairs, even if Objectivism views them as 'needs' and 'purposes'.

One can therefore say that just as Christianity and its variants illogically promise that through denial of pleasure, man will reach happiness in the floating abstraction of 'Heaven', so Objectivism illogically promises that through implicit rejection of pleasure, man will reach happiness in the floating abstraction of 'Man's life'. It is interesting to note, that on examination of the implications of Rand's writing, Rand views all value alternatives in terms of good or evil; in other words, her approach and premises completely ignore a context in which all of one's values are abstractly good. Emotions, to Rand represent real anti-life values. This constant struggle of good versus evil as a way of life, no matter what it cost in terms of personal suffering has been the chief characteristics of those in religious circles.

In Rand's arguments the masterpiece of confusion is presented as a proof of 'man's life' as the metaphysical root of value considerations, Rand first establishes her basic premise: that there is only one fundamental alternative in the universe: existence or non-existence, and it pertains to a single class of entitles i.e. living organism' (Rand, **IOE** 15). On the basis of this, one supposes that when one such 'entity' is 'destroyed' something 'concrete' goes out of existence. However, Rand, in her very next statement, implicitly denies this: 'The existence of inanimate matter' is unconditional, the existence of life is not… (Rand **VOS** p.12). Rand in the first statement suggests that the alternative of existence or non-existence is to apply to some concrete 'entity', then changes in her second statement to the position that it is 'life' which faces this alternative. In Rand's equivocation between 'entity' and 'life', she attempts to make an abstraction the equivalent of a concrete entity. The transformation of 'life' from and abstraction to a concrete, enabled Rand to find something the 'faces' non-existence. When a process ends, it means that a concrete goes out of existence. Rand does not actually tell us what goes out of existence. It can't be life; that's not 'concrete'. It can't be master; that's indestructible: There Rand was forced to use the terms 'life' and 'death', instead of using the terms 'existence' or 'non-existence'.

*Matter is indestructible, it changes its forms, but it cannot cease to exist. It is only a living organism that faces a constant alternative: the issue of life or death (**VOS** 35).*

But 'life' and 'death' do not mean the same thing as 'existence' and 'non-existence': Life refers to action, death refers to cessation of action.

Thus, by reference to living organism, Rand is giving equal status to 'life' and 'matter', which then enables her to create the impression that something concrete goes out of existence when 'life' ends'. Though Rand refers to the concreteness of 'life' she also refers to life as an abstraction. 'It is only the concept of 'life' that makes the concept of 'value' possible' (**VOS** 39). It turns out that Rand has 'need' of such a view that life in itself is precious and even holy, that it is some sort of metaphysical thing. The foregoing identifies the most immediate roots of the plutonism in the Objectivist standard of value, 'man's life qua man'. To hold this as one's standard of value and ultimate goal, is to hold on to an abstraction as that goal. To deny that 'something' went out of existence, after something goes out of existence just because that which 'goes out' cannot be perceived, is to say that 'nothing' existed in the first place. That is the contradiction.

The answer to the objection will prove an explanation of the fallacies in Rand's epistemological premises. The above objection is given the validity of what Rand here considers an entity to be. However, such validity is being denied here. For Rand's 'entity', her 'primary existent' (that which exists as such) refers only to the which can be perceived (Objects). Even Rand is not willing to deny absolutely the existence of 'sensory concretes' as she admits parenthetically in her '**Introduction to Objectivist Epistemology**': It may be supposed that the concept 'existent' is implicit even on the level of sensations. A sensation does not tell man what exists, but only that it exists (**IOE** 15). Rand, in her arguments on the metaphysical foundation of ethics implicitly but contradictorily makes reference to the existence of existents more fundamental than that which can be perceived. Rand was ultimately forced to refer implicitly to such entities so as to enable her to claim that 'life' (living organisms) is the only thing facing the fundamental alternative of existence or non-existence and that such things have the exclusive claim to value considerations. Rand would have had to conclude that value considerations apply to all 'entities', living or not, since all can be 'destroyed' or she would have had to deny the concrete existence of the processes of 'inanimate entities' (which she did, by not acknowledging the indestructibility. This of course would have left her in a theoretical limbo. Indeed, she would have to deny the existence of anything that faced a fundamental alternative of existence or non-existence (the very foundation of her ethics). She could not have logically held in either of the above cases, that it is only the concept of 'life' that makes the concept of 'value' possible.

The main point is to explicitly establish the fact that Rand has not proved 'life living organisms' as that exclusively facing the fundamental alternative of existence of non-existence. A process (such as life) does not exist as such, is not a concrete existence in the fundamental sense, and therefore cannot face in the first place the above alternative.

It is, thus, only awareness or consciousness, that in any sense faces the fundamental metaphysical alternative of existence or non-existence. It is thus only with respect to consciousness that things can be regarded as 'for' or 'against' as 'good' or 'evil'. It is only the concept of 'consciousness' that gives rise to the concept of 'value'. Life as such is not only not concrete, it is, as such, valueless. True, life is necessary for consciousness, and in that respect could be considered a value-but not life as such. That life is necessary for consciousness in no way makes life a more fundamental value than consciousness. If it were, existence would be a more fundamental value than life.

Rand's implicit but disguised reliance on consciousness as a base for her ethics is explicit here. In order to justify the discussion on the objectivity of values, Rand refers to the requirement of human consciousness. Rand states : The concept of value is not a primary: it presupposes an answer to the question – of value to whom? A 'whom' means a consciousness. But 'if the concept of value' presupposes an answer to the question of 'whom' and also presupposes an entity capable of an alternative, why does 'value' apply to plants? A goal implies an end, a 'what for', a design. And though Rand may qualify as she does in her footnotes that she:

> *Uses the term 'goal-directed', in the context to designate the fact that the automatic functions of living organisms are actions whose nature is such that they result in the preservation of an organism's life (**IOE** 63).*

It is irrelevant and misleading because it does not make plants 'goal directed', nor a 'whom' nor does it create a 'design', nor have a 'purpose' or a 'what for'. Rand is forced to ascribe goals to plants in some sense, otherwise she cannot generalise that 'an organism's life is it's standard of value' or that 'metaphysically, life is the only phenomenon which is an end in 'itself'. There is no 'standard of value' directing a plant's actions. What 'directs' a 'plant's actions' is its chemical, mechanical activity. This activity has no 'goal' or 'end'. Each chemical, mechanical action and reaction occurs as a result of the nature of the individual material components of the plant. They don't design their interaction. They do not 'seek life'. They do not act 'for life', they merely act as their identity demands in conjunction with other material components.

Rand nowhere presents a dichotomy between sentient and insentient living things in regard to their facing fundamental alternatives; 'There is', she writes, 'only one fundamental alternative in the universe: existence or non-existence and it pertains to a single class of entities: to living organisms'. All 'perceptual entities' are 'destructible' including life. Life is merely the process of indestructible matter, From the foregoing, one can merely isolate 'consciousness' as the only aspect of existence which metaphysically faces the alternative of existence of non-existence. i.e. which faces good and bad, the nature of consciousness is such that it experiences itself at times in a partially deprived state. This deprivation is pain. Every instance of pain is fundamentally some sort of loss. There is only one alternative to pain, that is pleasure. The primary root of the notion of 'value' is thus to be found in the experience of pleasure. The complete restoration of awareness is the complete final good, that is to say, the ultimate value. The complete restoration of awareness is the entity of consciousness, or in other words 'consciousness qua consciousness'. Taking into consideration the above and given that the sum total of possible pleasure is none other than 'happiness', then one can conclude that 'consciousness qua consciousness' is happiness. Happiness is thus the standard of value because an ultimate value is the standard of value. Happiness is thus, that by which value should be judged. That which serves to achieve it is the good, that which serves to destroy it is the bad, the evil. When a particular goal does not contribute to the achievement or maintenance of one's happiness (one's consciousness qua consciousness), then it is not a value to one. Since consciousness has identity, happiness cannot be achieved or maintained in any arbitrary fashion. Its achievements have definite requirements.

It should be stressed that the standard of value being positioned here is not consciousness can be aware of its own parallel destruction that it comes to value itself and its restoration (pleasure). The ultimate, final, complete end or value is complete restoration from pain, which is happiness, which is 'consciousness qua consciousness', not consciousness in any condition or state; not consciousness as a 'faculty' even though, consciousness as a state is identical to 'consciousness qua consciousness' as a 'faculty'. Happiness is a means to an end, not an end in itself. However, observe that they are identical in a fundamental sense in that they both refer to the same entity, thus demonstrating that consciousness is both the means and the end of value, as well as an end in itself. To name happiness as the standard is to name one's own 'consciousness qua consciousness' as the standard: between means and the end (Consciousness is the means and the end); and especially, the dichotomy – the psychologically disastrous dichotomy between happiness and the good, which dichotomy exists in the ethical premises of Objectivism.

It is important here to make explicit that the present theory of value also eliminates any traces of the 'mind-body', or soul-body dichotomy, which dichotomy is fundamental to the Objectivist ethics though that is what Objectivism claims to have eliminated through its premises.

The mind-body dichotomy exists in the Objectivist ethics by virtue of the fact that one is, under it, not supposed to consider happiness, pleasure, feelings, and emotions (i.e., 'psychosomatic concretes' which, in effect, represents the body) as having anything fundamentally to do with what is good (i.e., as being moral primaries). What is 'good', according to Objectivism, is fundamentally related only to the mind, i.e., to abstractions. Pleasure and happiness or emotions (the body) must not be issues of primary focus, but rather 'results' or 'responses'. To consider them as fundamentally significant, is to be irrational, immoral. The antagonism to emotions as moral primaries versus abstractions as primaries, represents the implicit mind-body dichotomy of Objectivism's ethics. Implicitly, there is in those ethics a fundamental split between the goodness of the mind versus the body.

Observe, on the other hand, that 'Happiness' as a standard of value eliminates this dichotomy forever: 'Happiness' refers simultaneously to both the mind and the body (i.e., emotions, feelings, and thoughts). The mind is significant 'only' to the extent that 'it' contributes to 'consciousness qua consciousness'. In 'Happiness as the standard of value', the mind and the body are clearly, 'perpetually' united. Another controversy about values is also solved by reference to 'consciousness qua consciousness' as the standard of value; the controversy over whether values are objective, subjective, or 'intrinsic'. The values involve all the three.

Despite the fact that pleasure and pain are primary to one's existence on earth as a human being, one is to view them as secondary, or 'subordinate' them to something else. This something else, again, is an abstraction. This is the mind-body dichotomy of Objectivism.

However, pleasure, and happiness are not just the 'psychological base' of valuation: They are the 'metaphysical' base. One experiences pleasure in all forms as a primary because consciousness, awareness (happiness, pleasure) is a metaphysical primary. One needn't (indeed, shouldn't) refer to an abstraction such as 'life' to justify metaphysically the value of pleasure. Indeed, 'life' is not metaphysical, it is epistemological. Only consciousness and matter are metaphysical. One does not 'justify' metaphysical axioms and primaries by reference to abstractions. The primaries are the justification for the abstractions.

There is no 'biological' basis for value. 'Life' does not face good and bad. Only consciousness does. Pleasure is a conscious enhancing state, while pain is the destruction of consciousness. Thus, the basis of 'value' is not to be switched from concrete reality to abstractions. If pleasure is experienced obviously as a value, pain as a disvalue, then one should accept them for what they are, as awareness and its destruction. One should not go searching for 'floating abstraction' as a means of 'saving the phenomena', of pleasure and pain or changing epistemological things into metaphysical things, metaphysical ones into psychological ones. And so contrary to Rand's claim that:

> *Epistemologically, the concept of 'value' is genetically dependent upon the derived from the concept of 'Life'. To speak of 'value' as apart from 'Life' is worse than a contradiction in terms. It is only the concept of 'Life' that makes the concept of 'value' possible... (**VOS** 36).*

The truth is that the concept of 'value' is not genetically dependent upon any other concept. 'Value' is dependent upon the existence of consciousness. To speak of 'Value' as apart from consciousness is really worse than a contradiction in terms: 'Value' means Consciousness.

Having dealt with the contradictions, tensions, anxieties in Ayn Rand's theory of Objectivism, the researcher moves on to analyse the contradictions and tensions in Achebe's thinking, very specifically in **Anthills of the Savannahs**. Achebe is not primarily a philosopher, like Rand. He does not evolve a philosophic framework of his own, and so the contradictions and tensions are not seen in a theoretical frame work as in Rand's, but there are certain contradictions and anxieties in his thinking process which are brought to light very obviously in his last novel, **Anthills of the Savannahs.**

In a number of interviews and essays published, Achebe reveals a slant towards 'radical populism' and a 'commitment' on the part of writers of fiction. Achebe believes the masses own the nation as they have the numbers. Incisiveness is seriously weakened by the students' being raised to the status of the characters in terms of Ibo mythology becomes relevant. For example, Beatrice's role as priestess makes a significant contribution to the novel's examination of the political leadership and, in the process, sheds light on the ideology of leadership informing the novel.

Achebe's contradictions, tensions, anxieties, discrepancies seem to arise mainly from Achebe's attempt to use the novel, a fictional product, as a vehicle for proposing solutions to the socio-political problems of Nigeria. Achebe seems to be convinced of the functional obligations of literature and of the writer's duties to teach and lead his people.

In his article, "**Anthills of the Savannah**" and the Ideology of Leadership, "David Maugham Brown believes that:

*Contradictions derive unavoidably from the conflicting determinations acting on an author: from, for example the discrepancies between the events of history and conflicting class-based readings of those events; from anxieties about the role of the intellectual and artist in oppositional and, in particular, revolutionary politics; from a discordance between the class-based ideological perspectives of writers and their assumptions about the perspectives of their putative audiences; from the tensions between the content of the message to be conveyed and the aesthetic demands of the form being used (**Kunapipi**, 144).*

It is one of the functions of criticism to attempt to identify and account for tensions and contradictions in an author's work. Be highly sensitive and reliable sounding boards one moment and immature adolescents in dire need of Ikem's political bullying in the next. The assembled students are described as a "ticklish humorous crowd" (**AOS** 156) whose applause "redoubled laughter"(**AOS** 160), "explosion of laughter" (**AOS** 160), "mixed noises" (**AOS** 159) and "uproarious laughter" (**AOS** 161). Ikem can manipulate at will. The students appear as a bunch of politically naïve buffoons out for a laugh. Yet Achebe uses the same audience earlier as the sounding board for a speech (**AOS** 153) "so well-crafted and so powerfully spoken it took on the nature and scope of an epic prose-poem". The same audience, which needs to be told "not to swallow every piece of superstition you are told by witch doctors (sic) and professors" (**AOS** 161), which is apparently prone to "too much parroting, too much of half-digested radical rhetoric" (**AOS** 161) is said to have "sat or stood silently entranced" (**AOS** 154) in appreciation of the epic prose-poem. Ikem's concluding injunction, towards which the whole speech to the students leads, is itself contradictory, given Achebe's apparent ascription of all responsibility for social ills to 'leaders'. Ikem tells the students:

*I have no desire to belittle your role in putting this nation finally on the road to self-redemption. But you cannot do that unless you first set about to purge yourselves, to clean up your act. You must learn for a start to hold your own student leaders to responsible performance; only after you have done that can you have the moral authority to lecture the national leadership (**AOS** 160).*

This confuses matters considerably. If so heavy a weight of responsibility lies with the leaders, it cannot also lie with the led. The whole leadership thesis obviously falls down if it is the responsibility of those who are led to hold… (their) leaders to responsible performance", irresponsible performance then becomes the responsibility of those who failed to keep an adequate hold on their leaders according to David Brown.

The novel's concluding message, as explicated in an interview by Achebe, seems equally problematic:

> *I think this group around Beatrice has learnt a lot in the course of the story. They have learnt, for instance, that the little clique that saw themselves as leaders was not big enough, that it had no perception of incorporating others. You have to incorporate the taxi drivers, the market women, the peasants, the workers, the students. You have to broaden out so that when you're talking, you are talking for the people, you are not only talking for a section or a group interest (Rutherford, p.3).*

What is needed is not a little clique of leaders but a larger group of leaders, the group must broaden out to enable it to talk 'for the people' who, crucially, are still presumed to be unable to talk for themselves. But as you broaden out, asks David Maugham Brown how do you retain your concept of 'leadership? If, as Achebe maintains, the role of leadership is "to create the circumstances in which the people begin to act with awareness" (Rutherford, p.3), do the incorporated taxi drivers market women and peasants then represent the "people" beginning to act with awareness, or are they now 'leaders'? It would seem from the distinction Achebe draws elsewhere between the elite and the people that leadership is probably, in fact, the preserve of the elite. "The elite are important because they have been given special training and education and qualifications and their duty is to use it to initiate the upward movement of the people" (Rutherford, p.5). But it is quite awkward, at the very least, for a political analysis so dependent on a concept of 'leadership' to have the boundary between the leaders and the led becoming completely blurred.

For all Achebe's sympathy for "the wretched of the earth" and his recognition that when politicians give hand-outs to the people what they are 'giving' the people already, in fact, belongs to the people, some of Achebe's formulations suggest that he is putting some distance between himself and 'the people'. Thus, for example, one finds him asserting in the context of manifestly vicious, incompetent and corrupt leaders, that "the people get the leadership they deserve up to a point" (Rutherford, p.2). More tellingly, he denies 'the people' any capacity to think: "leaders" are defined by virtue of their being "the few thinking people" (Rutherford, p.2).

Where Anthills of the Savannah is concerned, the obvious question to ask is why Achebe should choose as the central scene, representative of the essence of 'the people', the public execution on the beach. "The fact (is) that the people are prone to this kind of behaviours (Rutherford, p.2). But the people are also prone to other kinds of behaviour. Ikem, through whose eyes the execution scene is portrayed, is much taken by the Gelegele Market: "I never pass up a chance of just sitting in my car, reading or pretending to read, surrounded by the vitality and thrill of these dramatic people. Of course, the whole of Gelegele market is one thousand live theatres going at once" (AOS 47). Yet Achebe does not choose to make any of the thousand live theatres of the Gelegele Market central to his depiction of 'the people'. That he does not do so can be attributed to the fact that the Gelegele Market offers no obvious occasion for demonstrating the need for leadership – which the execution scene, by contrast, clearly does.

> *The fact that the people are prone to this kind of behaviour, that they could come to a stage where they could relish this kind of scene, must make the leadership say to itself, "why is this possible? How can this happen? It is wrong. We must do something about it. So, you find a leader like the editor of the National Gazette setting himself up to correct the situation. It is people like him who must initiate the action (Rutherford, p.2).*

What Ikem does is to have the public executions stopped. This is obviously a good thing, but it in no way even begins to do something about the prior "fact that the people are prone to this kind of behaviour" (Ibidem).

The centrality given to the delirious and obscenely happy crowd at the execution scene, however accurate a depiction of such an event the scene may be, is not 'natural' or inevitable'; it is the product of ideologically determined selection on the part of the author, who had many other options open to him. It is clearly directed towards proving the necessity for 'leadership of the inherently brutish masses by the elite. As Achebe himself asserts: 'Stories ... are not innocent (Rutherford, p.5).

Achebe's overall view of human nature in this novel appears to be pessimistic. Ikem is allowed, for example, to reflect ... "I grab my torchlight and take her down our unswept and unlit stairs. Whenever I go up or down those stairs I remember the goat owned in common that dies of hunger" (**AOS** 36). Authorial approval of Ikem would appear undismayed by the fact that, as one of the common owners, he presumably bears part of the responsibility for the goat's death. It must be assumed to be this unenthusiastic view of "human nature" that underlies the undemocratic tendency of Achebe's preoccupation with "leadership". Chris's final message in the novel, a message uttered with his dying breath, is interpreted by Beatrice as a declaration that: "This world belongs to the people of the world not to any little caucus, no matter how talented…" (**AOS** 232). Yet now where in the novel, or in **The Trouble with Nigeria,** is the possibility ever entertained that 'rule' by an elite leadership might be replaced by genuinely democratic structures, whereby the people could become responsible for government of the world that is said to belong to them. The logic of Achebe's preoccupation with 'leadership', as embodied in this novel, would lead not to democracy but to enlightened dictatorship by the elite-an outcome very much at odds with the populist tendency of some of Achebe's views quoted earlier. Though it is not, of course, at odds with the role claimed for the intellectual and he writer in particular, through the award of the eagle-feather to the story-teller.

For a writer who aspires to a role that lies "more in determining than merely reporting", what Achebe provides by way of guidance for his society for the future is not perhaps as convincing as one might expect from some of the acclaim with which **Anthills of the Savannah** has been greeted.

There is a surprisingly passive acceptance of impotence as a price. One is told one must be prepared to pay for freedom of thought – articulated by the student leader Emmanuel, but derived from Ikem: …"We may accept a limitation on our action but never, under no circumstances, must we accept restriction on our thinking" (**AOS** 223). There is an assertion that the world belongs to the people of the world, but there is no suggestion as to how those people can become involved in the government of their world. Instead for us, is presented a view of the people sufficiently unflattering not to be particularly enthusiastic about encouraging their involvement in government. Achebe tells us that "experience and intelligence warn us that man's progress in freedom will be piecemeal, slow and undramatic" (**AOS** 99), but very little insight is given as to what should be demanded of that "freedom". Unsatisfactory relationships and attitudes of a group of leaders in depicted but this is done in a such a way as never to call 'rule' or 'leadership' into question. Although the head of state is a military officer who owes his position to a coup, the answer to the problems appear not to lie with political structures but to a matter of leadership style. Achebe does not tell us how a change in leadership style can solve the structural problems inherent in creating out of a society characterised by massive inequalities" a world in which charity, will have become unnecessary" (**AOS** 155). The recipe for an acceptable leadership style "the re-establishing of 'vital inner links...with the bruised heart that throb" painfully at the core of the nation's being' (**AOS** 141) – is not precise enough to be very helpful.

There are obviously many other facets to this profoundly engaging novel than are dealt with in this section but Anthills of the Savannah is an avowedly political novel and, among other possible responses, it accordingly invites critiques directed primarily at its political implications. David Maugham- Brown seems to think that the solutions Achebe's fiction here proposes to what he sees as the problems afflicting contemporary Nigeria, seem to be unlikely to have any durability.

The next chapter is the concluding chapter, where the researcher not only sums up the findings of the previous chapters, but also portrays the distinct patterns in the fiction of Rand and Achebe, that relates both to their vision and technique.

Conclusion

The concept of the individual versus society is not exclusively an American or African experience. It is as old as man and as pervasive and intractable as feelings of joy and sorrow. As and experience, it cuts across boundaries of place and time. **The Old Testament** is a haunting expression of human loneliness. This applies to Job, who is vanquished by 'the Voice out of the Whirlwind', to the wise men of Ecclesiastes who amid the uncertainties and vanities of life, have found certitude in the attitude of God and to Faustus whose quest for a richer and fuller life, ends in his alienation from man and God (Ch. 40:6).

There is overwhelming evidence from psychology, sociology and other branches of contemporary thought in support of the fact that man has lost his ancient moorings in nature, religion and simple human relationships. These changes have so affected man that he was become lonely and insignificant. The very titles of a number of provocative books on modern life suggest the anxiety concerning the state of man in our time: Caudwell's **Studies in a Dying Culture**, Rollo May's **Man in Search of Himself**, Eric Fromm's **The Sane Society,** Erich Heller's **The Disinherited Mind**, Erich and Maria Josephonson's **Man Alone**, and David Riesman's **The Lonely Crowd** are among a vast selection of books that read like the fever-chart of a sick society. Eric Fromm in his book **The Sane Society** says that "there is something fundamentally wrong with our way of life and the aims towards which we are striving" (Fromm 1965:19).

The problem of the individual versus society is the culmination of a long historical process. In primitive societies, the world was identical with the tribe and the individual was an integral part of the world or tribal community. In the medieval world, the concept of the universe was broadened to include the earth, and the elements. But it was seen with the earth as its centre and man as the purpose of creation. Everything was interrelated and secure in a fixed relationship just as everybody had a fixed position in the medieval society. But in course of time, new vistas were opened up. The earth became one of the satellites of the sum. Doubts began to crop up concerning the place and purpose of man. Yet until the end of the nineteenth century, nature and society had not lost their concreteness and definiteness, nor was the old framework of belier completely lost. But with the progress in scientific thought, technical discoveries and the dissolution of traditional bonds, the definiteness and concreteness are in the process of being lost. The decline of man, as reflected in contemporary thought and literature, is an expression of the awareness of his total loss, which is so upsetting because man has not been able to find new compensations and rationalizations. Eric Fromm observes in The Sane Society that:

> *We are not any more in the centre of the universe, we are not any more the purpose of the creation, we are not any more the masters of a manageable and recognizable world-we are a speck of dust, we are a nothing, somewhere in space without any concrete relatedness to anything (Fromm 1956:110).*

Nietzsche, Freud and Marx were the most powerful influence on the twentieth century mind and had different ways of looking at the individual's plight in society. Nietzsche saw that the individual was being swallowed by the herd, and that people were living by a 'slave morality'. But Freud saw alienation as a symptom of neurosis or the recurrent conflict between the individual nature and society. Marx saw alienation as a product of the compulsive dehumanization of man in the modern bourgeois society. All these three thinkers believed that the modern industrialized society robbed the individual of his actual worth and dignity.

In both Rand's and Achebe's novels, one notices a change that evolved from surface description to the invocations of the deep silent regions of the mind, from art as a means of social propaganda, to a powerful medium used for the expressions of a 'real' reality that is different from photographic representation.

The writings of Rand and Achebe are psychological in the sense that it projects action inside. Both writers operate from a dialectical experience of reality. Rand and Achebe are concerned with those paradoxical experiences of life, and the contradictory elements of the interior world of consciousness leads them to undertake an epistemological exploration of reality. With Rand, the dialectic can be seen operating from a thematic and a philosophical level; and with Achebe, from a structural, symbolic and thematic level. The sense of reality is presented as a matter of opposites held in dialectical relations.

The dialectic is given in the form of tensions and problems that have concerned mankind from the beginning :

i) Individualism versus Collectivism
ii) Good versus Evil
iii) Faith versus Reason
iv) Meaning versus Absurdity

v) Tradition versus Modernity
vi) Life versus Death
vii) Being versus Non-Being
viii) Myth versus Reality

The dialectic has been a perennial source of inspiration to the American artist, Ayn Rand and the African artist, Chinua Achebe. Both American and African Literature derive their alien quality from this tension.

The dialectic is seen operating in the form of the most fundamental experiences of life : order and chaos unity and dissolution, isolation and communion. The dialectic is also woven around the basic impulses, emotions and instincts that the human mind may be presumed to be experiencing continually: ecstasy and terror, hope and fear, love and hate, expansion and contraction of moods, like the 'dystole' and 'systole' movements of the heart.

This dialectic is seen operating in the form of the most fundamental experience of life : order and chaos unity and dissolution, isolation and communion. The dialectic is also woven around the basic impulses, emotions and instincts that the human mind may be presumed to be experiencing continually: ecstasy and terror, hope and fear, love and hate, expansion and contraction of moods, like the 'dystole" and 'systole' movements of the heart.

Since the Existentialists are much concerned with the plight of man in a mass society, with the threat to his freedom and identity and with man's loneliness, a case may easily be made in favour of the Existentialist influence on Rand and Achebe. It is true that loneliness exile, disaffiliation, nausea and the loss of self have become part of the Existentialist vocabulary in our time. The protagonists in Rand' and Achebe's fiction are estranged from their respective societies and are conscious of futility, absurdity, nothingness, falsity, emptiness and ugliness of life. As pioneers in some sense or other, these protagonists must have felt the problem of their identity.

Achebe in his article, 'The Nature and Fulfilment of the Individual' tells us that almost every human culture either now or in the past has been confronted with the two realities of social man – his individuality and his membership of a group. Differences between cultures may therefore be sought not in the presence of absence of this polarity but rather, on whether they place their emphasis nearer one pole or the other. Of course, the social and moral consequences of this apparently 'simple' choice of emphasis by society, Achebe says, may result in differences between cultures so great as a appear almost qualitive. Yet it is important to remember that however strongly one culture may seem to be dominated by either of these realities, the other is always present, if only in a recessive role (Achebe 1983:161).

Whether a man's individuality or his membership of a group is better, will depend on the goals which a particular society sets for itself, depending on its view of a good life. In America, the emphasis, on the supremacy of the individual seem to be the right one and is even a hallmark of civilization itself. One of the major sources could be the Judaic Tradition. In The Book of Ezekiel, there is a memorable prophetic insight when an older tribal, teaching on collective responsibility for sin, is superseded by a new morality based on individual accountability. "The soul that sinneth, it shall die", said the prophet. The old proverb: "The fathers have eaten sour grapes and the children teeth are set on edge", does not hold good anymore (Ch. 18:1-4).

When the West was ready to enthrone individualism, there was biblical authority ready at hand: but there were also assertions of the equality of man in the democratic revolutions of the eighteenth century in America and France. Ultimately, the sweeping success of Freud gave the seal of scientific approval, in a scientific oriented age, to the growing preoccupation with self. It was perhaps Ralph Waldo Emerson who first used the word 'individualism' as a contention for the way of life which upheld the privacy of the individual. His definition was imbued with an optimistic faith, peculiarly American. But in his book Democracy in America, the Frenchmen Alexis de Tocqueville was far less optimistic. He used individualism pejoratively as a threat to society, as akin to selfishness.

The critical inquiry into the nature of individualism in the novels of Ayn Rand and Chinua Achebe has been a fascinating voyage through a fictional locus of remarkable linear progression. The perception gained here reinforces our initial assumption that the understanding of individualism in invariably linked with non-conformism, as it challenges and repudiates existing norms. In a sense, this response to conventional modes is facilitated, as one sees in this study, under the substitute norms which appear more viable. What is triggered off and eventually promoted, is the search for a new self-identification where it becomes possible for the individual to be released from the corporative reality of social and tribal existence. Still it is possible that even such a novel ideology, when not challenged by new forces either in the form of opposition or increased awareness, tends to become submerged and for the most part go unrecognised. But this is certainly not what occurs in the case of the

American novelist Ayn Rand or the Nigerian Novelist Chinua Achebe. The theme of 'Man against the State' and the 'Producer versus the Parasite' in Rand's fiction and the successful emergence of the autonomous individuals as 'Demi-Gods' in 'Atlantis' in Atlas Shrugged covers a span of almost half a century as represented in the four novels analysed in this study.

In the fiction of Chinua Achebe, the theme of the Ibo tribe's contact with the West, & the consequential transition and the changes that resulted are neatly squeezed into a time span of over half a century as represented in the five novels the researcher has analysed. The conflict of the individual versus society sown in the fiction of Ayn Rand and Achebe, involving immense possibilities of a challenging nature, is developed steadily through their works, until it reaches a totally different milieu and value system. But this unhampered growth towards a new world view and mode of existence is worked out through overt statements, explicit commentaries, theories on the individual and social factors that are dovetailed into the thematic structure by the delicate handling of the human involvement in this crucial problem.

Ayn Rand believes in the individual self. In her view the creator, producer, artist, scientist, thinker never believes in a collective brain. All great creation and production are experienced in the silent solitary sanctuary of one's own mind. None of these creators are prompted by a desire to serve another but their own selves. The creator's truth is his only motive. He wants to achieve it his own way … be it a building, a book, an engine, a symphony, an air plane, a creation that is his whole goal and his life, his prime mover : The creation is important as an end in itself, not its users. In Randian terminology, this is what is called 'selfish' – to be concerned with the 'self' and its own interests. A man's spirit is his 'self'. The vision, strength, courage evolves from his own spirit … his own essence of being; the entity which is his whole consciousness. In **The Virtue of Selfishness** Rand defines a self. "To think, to feel, to judge, to act are the functions of the ego, the spirit" (**VOS**: 16). Man must live true to his own nature first and not negate the spirit that is within him. One that denies one's own self cannot be called whole of human and cannot be considered alive to relate to the selves outside it. It is a contradiction in terms.

Though Rand's protagonists, in all her fictional works advocate the glorification of the 'self', and this may appear to be in direct contrast to what the great religions of the world preach today; a closer and deeper study of the philosophy of the various religions can be capsulized to mean that man, in order to be termed morally sound or good, must be truthful and honest to himself first, only then can he be truthful and honest to those around him. This is precisely what Rand articulates and advocates. There should not be a dichotomy between the self within and the self without. It is within one's own conscience, observes Rand that one should seek God, not in outward forms and rituals.

In this respect, Rand's positive outsider are the most aesthetically sound, 'selfish' beings, which in Randian terms is directly opposite to those souls that denounce a 'self'. The word 'selfish' denote virtuous qualities of character for Ayn Rand, but this word has antagonized many people to whom the term does not signify the things Ayn Rand means. The semantic meaning and the dictionary definition ascribed to the word 'selfishness' is, 'concern with one's own interests'. In the popular usage of the term, the word has become synonymous with 'evil'. It conjures up an image of a 'dog eat dog' attitude; an individual who cares for no living being and pursues nothing beyond the gratification of the mindless whims of a given moment. But 'selfishness' entails two concepts, observes Rand in **The Virtue of Selfishness:**

1) a hierarchy of values set by the standards of one's self interests
2) the refusal to sacrifice a higher value to a lower one or to a non-value (Rand 1964:9).

The concept of being 'concerned with one's own interests' does not include a moral evaluation. It does not tell us whether 'concern with one's own interests' is good or evil. Nor does it tell us what constitutes man's actual interests. Interests are relative, it differs from individual to individual.

Altruists conclude that any action taken for the benefit of others is good, and any action taken for the benefit of one's own self is evil. If it is so, the beneficiary of the action is the only criterion for morality. According to Rand, it is the most immoral concept, and ultimately, she observes, even the altruist thinks only in terms of himself. Every man, even the most religious, seeks his own end first. Even in the 'selfless' process of being concerned and involved with 'the other', he is being gratified that he is concerned with and for others and that gratification is his selfish pleasure. He is concerned thereby with the 'self' – the concern with his own interest and pleasure. A dictator is regarded as amoral according to Rand, since the unspeakable and unquestionable atrocities he commits are intended to benefit the people and not himself. Rand says, the battle is only over the question of whose whim, one's own or society's or God's. Consequently, Rand's protagonists, be it a Roark, a Dominique, or a Galt, are not actually alien from society, as everyman, whether he accepts it or not, is to a certain extent caught in the raptures of their own individual selves, their own individual lives. This is what Nathaniel Branden in his book **The Psychology of Self-Esteem** terms "The Psychology of Pleasure" (Branden 1987: 41). And if these protagonists are condemned as selfish brutes, then every man, king and beggar will be and should be condemned because they too live for their own personal pleasure. As Branden says; "pleasure is not a luxury but a profound psychological need" (Ibidem).

Throughout the three phases, Rand brings to light the fact that the main focus in her society is on the individual consciousness while Achebe's focus is more on the communal consciousness. In each of their literary works, an individualistic hero battles the forces of collectivism and mediocrity, which are threatening to destroy the world.

In Phase I, Rand is not yet prepared to depict, her concept of the ideal man. Kira Argounova and Leo Kovalensky of We The Living are only suggestions of what they might have been, had they been born into a free country, instead of the Soviet Union. Here is this phase, Sobran in his article, "Mussoline Shrugged: Ayn Rand Revived" tells us that Rand's appeal seems to be to young people of Kira's age, for whom "Society is just parents writ large, and in whom the desire to be parents is still unborn" (Sobran 1989:54). Individualism and Collectivism are the only options; no network of affection and obligation has reality. When Rand includes parents in her picture, she shows them as they look to unhappy adolescents, kind but potentially tyrannical, and above all, uncomprehending. Kira's parents understand nothing, neither the nature of the Soviet State (they think it will pass quickly) nor her own desire to be independent (they disapprove of her living with Leo out of wedlock.) Kira's parents are ineffectual. They have no wisdom to impart. She has no debt to them. From early childhood she has rejected their religion, and they have long since given up taking her to church; it does not even seem to matter to them. Their speeches expose them as small, deluded people.

Though the protagonists Kira Argounova and Leo Kovalensky defy the social system (communism) and will not give in, **We The Living** ends on a pessimistic note. But in the next novel, **Anthem,** the seeds of an optimistic thinking are sown and the consequent triumph of the individuals (namely, Equality 7-2521 and Liberty 5-3000), over the collective is illustrated. Equality 7-2521 is considered a threat to the established order. But unlike Kira Argounova and Leo Kovalensky of **We The Living** who succumb to the collective mass, Equality 7-2521 and his lady love Liberty 5-3000, break free in happiness to rediscover their humanity and freedom. Howard Roark succeeds in evolving as the 'man-child' of **The Fountainhead**. He believes that the fountainhead of all human progress and happiness on earth is the Ego. Roark is seen triumphing over the Peter Keatings and the Ellsworth Tooheys, the social suckers of **The Fountainhead**, and for the first time the individual reigns supreme, steadfast in his goal, namely the pursuit of his own happiness. John Galt takes the concept of Individualism to its culmination point. The 'man-child' of **The Fountainhead** in this stage becomes "the demi-god; the self-created, without ancestors or blood-ties". John Galt stops the motor of the world, drains the brains from society and creates an Atlantis on the mountains of Colorado. This Utopian society of the demi-Gods serves as a refuge from the 'looters', 'moochers' and 'scraps' of society, who survive on the productivity of the demi-Gods, contributing nothing to society. The motto of the Utopian community strikes a strong contrast to the parasitical society where a man "will never live for the sake of another man, nor expect another man to live for mine" (AS 1003). Till the world of **The Fountainhead,** parasites like the Peter Keating and Ellsworth Toohey, still remain, but in the world of **Atlas Shrugged,** these parasites are totally annihilated, the men of the mind succeed, and the producers and creators are called back to recreate and rebuild.

The concept of the 'Individual versus Society' is dealt with quite differently in the fiction of Chinua Achebe. In the process of developing the concept of the emerging individual, Achebe articulates not only the destructive forces in the social system, but also describes the positive values against which they can be measured. Here each individual must accommodate himself to a broader social context, and undermining the social system is a moral order. But in spite of the fact that in Achebe's society much more emphasis is placed on community values than it does on the individual, Okonkwo, Ezeulu, Obi and Ikem Osidi and Chris Oriko and Beatrice Okoh are fully conceived characters. Nevertheless, the community has an equal status with the individual protagonists. But unlike in Rand's fiction where the individual triumphs and society fails, the protagonists in Achebe's works, while trying to evolve as individuals, meet with tragedy and consequent failure, and the community survives. As Okonkwo hangs from a tree, as Ezeulu retreats into madness, as Obi gets sucked into corruption and imprisonment, as the people fail to remove their concept leaders and as Chris Oriko falls victim to a rapacious police sergeant, one may feel that there is not much prospect of a better future for the individuals. The seeds of corrupt disintegration seem to be bearing fruit in all too fertile a way. The novels end not just with personal disaster for the protagonists (only Beatrice Okoh in '**Anthills' of the Savannah** is an exception), but with the passing of tribes, the hardening of colonial authority and the imposition of military rule.

The redeeming factor in Achebe's works is that, in spite of the corruption and brutality, there is an element of human goodness & moral sense inherent in humanity which cannot be eradicated, and which eventually must triumph.

In Achebe's works the first note of estrangement from tribal ethos is heard from Nwoye in **Things Fall Apart,** where due to his disillusionment with Ibo life as he found it, he sets out in quest of more human concerns. Achebe tells us later that he finds refuge in the new religion, Christianity and the knowledge it offers. In a more advanced stage of this pursuit of knowledge as an accepted way of life, Obi embodies within himself extreme idealism and an intense sense of alienation from his roots. Both attitudes: estrangement and alienation, reflect a deep-seated inability to conform, and lead to gradual withdrawal into the self: more of an escape into inescapable realities than a solution. This passivity implies a very individualised form of revolt in the face of a moral crisis. The narrative here is engaged in a sustained, very controlled working out of the conflict inherent in the situation of a cultural clash, aggravated by an increased awareness in the individuals. It is the uncommon sensitivity to the surroundings and a tendency towards introspection embodied in the characters of Nwoye and Obi that makes for a radical shift in their approach to life. In the case of Nwoye it is more of a personal anguish, but as one sees it in the wider perspective of the deep cultural interaction of Africa and the West, the issue is one of the irreconcilable nature of two warring ideals, one of synthesizing his traditional virtues with the new awareness he has acquired. The uncertainty and idealism of the moment is typified in Obi who faces the social impasse with its unresolved problems yet is explicitly representative of the emerging individual who is engaged in the dual task of severing himself from his tribal roots and integrating himself into a new social order.

A simultaneous growth towards an internalized perception of things and a reflective mode of existence, rather than the purely physical level is perceived even in the typically tribal characters of Okonkwo and Ezeulu. Initially, it is inconceivable for a society that had prided itself for centuries on its ancient wisdom, to permit any intrusive elements to create disruption in its confined world. And inevitably, when the change comes, it causes such violent hostility and frustration to Okonkwo, so much so, it costs him his life. Yet eventually, the tribe reveals itself vulnerable to the material promises that come to it in the form of intellectual pursuits and economic advancement and succumbs. But the next phase, encountered by Ezeulu suggests an explicit compromise with the alien forces, unlike the total rejection of the new order by Okonkwo; Ezeulu realizes that "the world is changing", and his adaptability and acceptance of the European presence on the continent marks a significant departure from the Umuofian ethic upheld by Okonkwo. Again, whereas the enraged Okonkwo expels his son Nwoye from the family for giving himself to the missionaries, Ezeulu, with an unprecedented sense of reality, sends his son, "Oduche, to the Whiteman's church to be his "eyes and ears" there (**AOG** : 151), lest he regrets later.

Achebe deploys a totally new technique of narration to capture this fresh awareness that results from Ezeulu's unconventional moves specifically probing into the nature of the disapproval of the clan. Very insidiously, the criteria for success is changed from physical prowess and skill in warfare to knowledge of the 'white man's magic' and response to the changing social reality. Tribal recognition and acclaim as the norm of judgement, so overtly pronounced in **Things Fall Apart**, very subtly gives way to a more inward-looking, personal kind of speculation, where individual claims and convictions supersede other preferences. Besides, through numerous instances of asserting his own worth and identity in a new perspective, the enigmatic character of Ezeulu himself stands poles apart from the world and values symbolised by Okonkwo.

The traits of individualism traced through Nwoye and Obi Okonkwo arises from the smouldering ashes of the dying Ibo clan. This new individual is caught in the collapse of values. Born in an `age which is slowly sacrificing its traditional values, to meet the demands of a new way of life, Obi feels helpless, for though he is aware of the old dignified order, he is thrust into the new. His problem is that he is not able to accommodate the contradictory ethical values of the two cultures. Obi's is a case of double alienation, for his missionary upbringing and education only serve to cut him away from his father's adopted religion, neither is he able to relate wholly to the complex living of the mid-twenties in Nigeria in spite of his modern education. Unlike the dignified and single-minded Okonkwo or Ezeulu, Obi is a naïve, selfish and vacillating character. This child of two worlds has a nostalgic memory of his noble ancestors which makes him impatient with the corruption and indignity of modern Nigeria. But Obi himself lacks the energy and will power to act competently about any crisis in his life, because his conviction about the justness of his position: …comes from the periphery and not the centre-like the jerk of the leg of a deal frog when a current is applied to it (**NLAE** 124). Obi's moral weakness and warped sense of morality, which finally make him accept bribes, is the outcome of his failure to reconcile two conflicting demands – his loyalty to his clan and his position as a senior civil servant. The Umuofia Progressive Union to which Obi is indebted for his education, sums him up as a person who wishes to be associated with wise men of the past - but without making any personal sacrifice of commitments to his present-day clansmen.

*You are very young, a child of yesterday. You know book. But book stands by itself and experience stands by itself. So, I am not afraid to talk to you (**NLAE** 74).*

In Obierika's questioning of the meaning of some of the traditional Ibo values in Things Fall Apart, Achebe shows that even traditional values have to be revalued and updated according to the need of the time. What Achebe advocates is not a superimposition, but a successful adaptation of the old to the new, if the old is to survive. Nwoye's conversion perhaps illustrates the author's conviction that the only way for the future is cultural cohesion. This view of Achebe's is best summed up in the words of Jonathan Peters in The Dance of Masks:

Ideally Achebe would have wished for a gratifying of the best elements of African tradition with desirable elements from other cultures as a guarantee against the eruption of hate and violence which proved ultimately to be his country's colonial legacy (Peters 1978:125).

There emerge certain distinct patterns in the fiction of these writers which relate both to their vision and technique. Though Rand was popularly known as a Philosopher, she was first and foremost a writer of fiction. In all of Rand's works, the individual human is the most important being in the universe.

Rand in her book : **Introduction to Objectivist Epistemology** states that reason is the tool by which the individual discerns that which is 'Life-sustaining' and 'Ego-nourishing' (Rand 1979:21). Objectivist Ethics holds that man's life is the standard of value, and his own life is the ethical purpose of every individual man (Ibidem).

It is interesting to find that Rand's major fictional works follow similar plot patterns. In each, an exceptionally able and individualistic protagonist, battles the power of collectivism and mediocrity, which are threatening to destroy the nation and the world. Of Rand's five protagonists, three are women and two men. Almost all of them are drawn from real life experiences. The other characters, major and minor are male, and her insight into the workings of the male chauvinistic psychology, mental and emotional make-up is astounding. Her main female characters share many characteristics. They have slender physiques, defiant stances, and inner calm. Rand's heroes are all tall, straight and strong. Like their feminine counter parts, defiance is a keystone to their characters. Fear is never a part of their demeanour.

Love is a response to value for Rand, and hence the object of one's love is a representation of all that one holds dear. When Rand's characters love, they love without reservation. Just as a Randian personality will battle for that which he or she considers precious, a Rand character will do anything for a loved one. In **The Night of January 16th**, Karen Andre is willing to do anything for Bjorn Faulkner. She defies the law, engages in criminal acts and even permits Bjorn Faulkner to wed Nancy Whitfield, since that is what Bjorn Faulkner thinks is necessary to buttress his otherwise failing financial empire. She allows herself to be tried for his murder because she thinks she is helping him engineer a fake suicide. Leo's health is so important to Kira Argounova that she becomes Andrei's mistress as seen in **We The Living**. She does this so that she will have the money to send Leo to a sanitorium in the Crimea. Kira, who never lies, lies to both Andre and Leo, in order to save Leo's life and pride. She pretends that she loves Andre and lies to Leo about where she gets the money. Roark (in **The Fountainhead**) who is fiercely independent, openly acknowledges to Dominique how much she controls him. When she attempts to play power games with him, he shows her immediately that "she owns him – all that can be owned" (**TFH** 231). His love for her is so great that he will not ask her to be his wife, because he knows that she cannot be whole until she comes to him with a healthy ego. He stands by when she marries Peter Keating and then Gail Wynand, enduring the pain, while she goes through her perverse penance. Gail Wynand explains to Dominique that "love is exception making" (**TFH** 321). He has broken every person of supposed integrity that he can find in order to prove his power. He tells her that she is in love with integrity and in his eyes is "a person who matches inside and out" (**TFH** 341). John Galt in **Atlas Shrugged** puts his life in danger to be with Dagny. Eventually his association with her results in his capture and consequent torture. Before the Government agents arrive, he tells her that he does not regret his action. Dagny claims : "I didn't care whether either one of us lived afterwards just to see you this once" (**AS** 865). The life worshipping Galt tells Dagny that he will kill himself rather than allow her to be tortured.

In the majority of Rand's fiction, another common occurrence is the trial scenes which act as a significant plot juncture. The most important trial in terms of plot structure, is towards Roark's arrangement for blowing up the Cortlandt Housing Project. His acquittal is evidence that justice can prevail and that the individual does not have to be destroyed. Hank Rearden's trial in **Atlas Shrugged** for defying an unfair government edict also results in his winning. In Rearden's case he contests the court's jurisdiction over him. In both of these trials, the accused act as their own defence attorneys, and both their summation speeches are important statements of Rand's philosophy of personal rights. Since the juries agree with the accused in each case, one could infer that Rand has faith that an average dozen citizens will respond to reason and appreciate greatness. **The Night of January 16th** is a court room drama. The trial is the plot of this play. But whereas the trials in **The Fountainhead** and **Atlas Shrugged** demonstrate the value of the jury system, the trials in the former works are travesties of justice. When Equality 7-2521 does not confess where he has been he is sent to the Palace of Corrective Detention. Without a trial, and on the instruction of two judges, he is lashed repeatedly. Later his actions and invention are condemned by the ignorance of the World Council of Scholars. When Kira and Leo go to the People's Court to protest the fact that one of their rooms is taken from them, they are judged not in accordance with the merits of their case, but upon their ancestry.

Instant recognition of the 'like-minded', is an ability shared by Rand's heroes and villains alike. Though Kira has never seen Leo before, she is willing to let him believe she is a prostitute rather than let him go out of her life. Equality 7-2521 and Liberty 5-3000 need only eye contact to establish a bond strong enough to make them defy their collective society. After minimal conversation she is sure enough of him to follow him into the Uncharted Forest.

In most of Rand's stories the first meeting of hero and heroine is accompanies by a rape-like encounter, which rather than distancing the couple, cements their relationship. Howard Roark's rape of Dominique establishes an unspoken bond, as neither speaks during the entire episode. Bjorn Faulkner rapes Karen Andre in **Night of January 16th**, when she comes for a job interview and she remains his business partner and mistress for the rest of his life. John Galt's first sexual experience with Dagny is a ritualized rape in the tunnels of Taggart Trans-Continental. For Rand, these romanticized rapes are symbolic of the head-on-clash of two strong personalities. The rapist is conquered just as his victim is. This symbolism of her rape scenes may by condemned by those who have a raised consciousness about the nature of rape.

Rand also uses a technique, traditional in Comedy and Allegory, by which character's names are indicators of their personalities. Such names as Wesley Mouch, Ellsworth Toohey, Homer Slottern carry strong suggestions of the bearer's offensive natures. There are, to be sure, many villains with neutral names such as Robert Stadler or James Taggart. However, even if the character has a handsome physical appearance and a neutral name, the reader is never left in doubt about Rand's attitude towards him or her. Rand's usual method of character introduction is a brief biographical sketch in which the individual's virtues or vices are clearly delineated. Though Pavel Syerov is described as nice looking, the reader is quickly informed that while he represents himself as a revolutionary hero, he actually stays at home during the war with a cold. Lillian Rearden, whose classic beauty fools Hank into thinking she is woman to strive for, turns empty eyes and a superficial gaiety on those who encounter her. Although she claims to love her husband, she does not appreciate his abilities.

Certain motifs recur in Rand's fiction. The flamboyant or extravagant gesture is one. Bjorn Faulkner gives Karen Andre a dress of platinum mesh; 'Guts' Regan sends her one pound of Orchids; Hank Rearden buys Dagny an exorbitantly priced pear-shaped ruby to wear for his eyes only; Dominique purchases a priceless sculpture of Helios from a museum and then destroys it because she considers it too beautiful for a world of 'second-handers'. For Rand's characters these gestures indicate freedom from monetary and mundane restraints.

Music also plays an important role in Rand's works. It symbolises the creative and inspirational capacity of man. **We The Living** and **Atlas Shrugged** have the strongest musical components. For Kira, 'The song of Broken Glass' a tune from an opera captures a sense of gaiety and joy, possible in life. It's promising notes echo in her brain as she dies. Richard Halley's unpublished fifth concerto echoes Dagny's search for the great minds that have vanished. Its triumphant strains reverberate in her head through much of the book. It is interesting to note that it is typical of Rand, she herself being a romantic realist. As Ayn Rand's body lay in state, light operetta music was played as the crowds paid her their last respects.

The setting of Rand's fiction needs a comment. Cities, especially those with a sky-scraper, skyline are the preferred settings for Rand's stories. Sky-scrapers serve as a positive symbol. They represent the potential of human conquest over nature. Rand is enamoured by technology and the urbane landscape. Kira's chosen profession is engineering. She keeps a picture of an American sky-scraper over her bed. Howard Roark's most important commission is the Wynand Building which towers over Hell's Kitchen in New York. When Dagny walks on the streets of New York, she is filled with reverence for the skyline. Rand is the antithesis of a primitivist. Her characters are not refreshed by interaction with nature. For them, nature is there to be harnessed.

In Rand's philosophy, the individual human is the most important being in the universe not God, Country, nor Cause precedes the Individual in

Rand's hierarchy of values. The value that Rand places on the individual is clearly seen in Kira's affection for Andre. Though she hates communism, she sees Andre's worth as an individual and worries about him, expressing fear for his safety when he fights the rebellious farmers.

Whitfield the villainous banker who kills Bjorn Faulkner in **The Night of January 16th** states his credo on the witness stand: "I believed in one's duty above all. Bjorn Faulkner believed in nothing but his own pleasure" (**NOJ** 61). One of Rand's favourite techniques is this kind of dramatic irony where the speaker is trying to explain what is wrong with the character by his standards, and actually explains what is right with that character by Randian standards.

In Achebe's novels too, a thematic order or pattern can be traced through the five novels. The theme of the song of the traders in **No Longer at Ease**, about the world turned upside down, has its first relevance in **Things Fall Apart.** It reaches its climax in **Arrow of God** when the free poetic and collective spirit is sapped and replaced by a selfish and corrupt system, which finds its full expression in Obi's acceptance of bribes in **No Longer at Ease**, which may be considered as the decline of the old way of life. The freezing death of the older order is seen in the shameless corruption and cynicism expressed in **A Man of the People** where Achebe depicts the anarchy that rules the Ibo society, it having lost all contact with the old ceremonious and ritualistic social order. The process of deterioration which begins with the breaking of communal life in **Things Fall Apart** reaches its final stage in **A Man of the People**, when a new government takes over, and the people see it as an alien institution to which they can cling as parasites, a far cry from the healthy communal life which created men like Okonkwo and Ezeulu. There is an absence of a centre which will hold. Speaking of the degeneration of moral and spiritual values in Ibo life, Achebe explains that in the ancient days, titles were not given but taken and each title had its own value. He comments on how in the modern times, spiritually which would have controlled excess is rejected and materialism is retained. G. D. Killiam, quoting Achebe in **The Novels of Chinua Achebe** says that Ibo Society,

> *... has always been materialistic. This may sound strange because Ibo life had at the same time a strong spiritual dimension controlled by Gods, ancestors, personal spirits or Chi and magic. The success of the culture depends on the balance between the material and the spiritual ... Today we have kept the materialism and thrown away the spirituality which should keep it in check (Killiam 1969:155).*

Disorientation is the price the modern Nigerian pays for rejecting the superstitions of his forefathers and embracing the rationalism of the new order. Quoting C.G. Jung, G.D. Killiam says the when spiritual values are exposed to the impact of the modern civilization in a primitive society, "it's people lose the meaning of their lives, their social organization disintegrates and they themselves morally decay" (Ibid: 157). It ends in isolation, alienation and lack of communication as in the case of the tragic heroes of Achebe.

If **A Man of the People** exposes the corrupting power of privilege and position and personal pleasure at the expense of the majority, **Anthills of the Savannah** reveals massive corruption, subservience to foreign manipulation, the problems of capitalism and

> *...the failure of our rulers to re-establish vital inner links with the poor and dispossessed of this country, with the bruised heart that throbs painfully at the core of the nation's being (**AOS** 141).*

The novel examines in an incisive way the fundamental issues relating to political leadership and also the position of women in modern African society. Using Ikem as his mouthpiece, Achebe gives his views on the theory of class and class struggle, and calls to question some of the basic tenets of Marxism, including the idea of a millennium in which there is no oppression of one social group by another, after the establishment of communism. Ikem sees the orthodox Marxist position as a simplistic remedy to the problem of oppression. A socialist and communistic revolution cannot solve all social problems of a society. Achebe strongly believes that the only way to reform a corrupt society is by changing the corrupt leadership. In this novel he offers a kind of solution for determining the course of Nigerian history. Beatrice's role as priestless makes a significant contribution to the novel's examination of political leadership and sheds light on the ideology of leadership in the novel.

Achebe in his article "The Trouble with Nigeria", feels that Nigeria's problem is the result of its leaders unwillingness or inability to rise to the responsibilities and challenges of leadership. The lack of the hallmark of true leadership, namely the challenge of personal example, has brought Nigeria to the brisk of disaster. Nigerians are what they are, only because their leaders are not what they should be (**TN** 10). Through Ikem, Achebe shows how all social ills stem from its 'leaders'. Addressing the students, he says:

> *I have no desire to belittle your role in putting this nation finally on the road to self-redemption. But you cannot do that unless you first set about to purge yourselves, to clean up your act. You must learn for a*

*start to hold your own student leaders to responsible performance; only after you have done that, can you have the moral authority to lecture the national leadership (**AOS** 160).*

To Achebe, leadership implies responsible performance on the part of the individual. A leader should be able to create the circumstances in which the people begin to act with awareness. Leadership may be a privilege of the elite, but the latter who have been specially trained and educated should use their education to "initiate the upward movement of the people" (Rutherford, p.5). Beatrice interprets Chris's final message in the novel:

*This world belongs to the people of the world not to any little caucus, no matter how talented (**AOS** 232).*

What Achebe advocates in **Anthills of the Savannah** is not democracy but perhaps an "enlightened dictatorship by the elite, and acceptable leadership style to re-establish vital inner links with the bruised heart that throbs painfully at the core of the nation's being" (**AOS** 141).

Thus, through the first four novels, Achebe clinically dissects the past of his society and traces a kind of psychic journey through the characters of Okonkwo, Ezeulu, Obi Okonkwo and Nanga, a downward path from stability to anarchy. It is a journey from the inspired and fulfilling rituals of the past to empty parodies of the present – a view which partly resembles (as Jonathan Peters tells us in **The Dance of Masks; Senghor, Achebe, Soyinka.**) "Yeats sphere with its two gyres or vortices as symbol of universal conflict" (Peters 1978:234) and partly mirrors T.S. Eliot's vision of the modern world as a moral and spiritual wasteland. It is,

... a down-to-earth exposition of the protracted fortunes of black Africa as the shape, size and focus of order have moved from clan to ethnic group and from nation to continent (Ibidem).

In his fifth novel, through Ikem, Chris and Beatrice, Achebe tries to re-establish order and stability.

In conclusion, it can be affirmed that Rand and Achebe's works are more than the works of social anthropologists. Rand explores the nature of man's mind, his ego and his reason. Rand believes that nothing existed and can exist outside the self. It is individuals who make society. To conceive of society in terms of an infinite mass of humanity, is to think of everyone in general and no one in particular. Achebe is a social anthropologist because of his interest in the socio-cultural patterns, beliefs, rituals and ceremonies of his clan. His interest stems from his study of the impact of one civilization upon another. In tracing the fall of the Ibo civilization through his fictional characters, Achebe succeeds in convincing the reader that, this which had happened to the Ibo clan in the past, is how the historical force works. Civilization is not static. It can collapse from within and be overpowered from without. The new order usually offers all that the old has overlooked, but even this new order must yield to another in course of time, for power and shift of power is an inevitable of historical determination.

The design and execution of Achebe's novels give a historical over view of the Ibo society from the pre-colonial era through the period of colonization to post-colonial Africa. Avoiding both the method of indulgence and flagellation, Achebe asserts the objective truth about the past of this tribe. He believes that nostalgia and remonstrance are both necessary, because "a people without a history is a people without a future" (Achebe, The Novelist as Teacher, 1965:2).

Achebe in his article "African Literature as Restoration of Celebration" shows how a literary artist can be nostalgic without sacrificing objectivity or realism. As a writer committed to social realism, he illustrates how disintegration of his society stems from the loss of allegiance to the religion and more of clan and ethnic group (Achebe 1990:9). He also dwells on the lessons to be learnt from the ironies of human relation and the responsibilities of an individual to ensure a valuable legacy for the progeny.

Though the tribal ethos is to a certain extent replaced by urban reality, creating a new kind of web, almost vacuous, in which individuals try to search for their own identity, they are depicted as a threat to orthodoxy and their cries turn out to be nothing more than a voice wasted in the wilderness which, in effect, suggests that the society is not yet prepared to allow space for such extreme form of individualism.

Achebe and Rand reveal a pronounced similarity of purpose in their writings; at the same time, they provide rich contrasts in their points of view, ideas, characters and representation of reality. Like most of creative writers, they too have used the fictional form with explicit social commitments, yet one perceives a striking dissimilarity in their respective efforts to endow a changing ethical mood with new values. Achebe makes use of his creative genius with great insistence on the obligations of the African writer to his people, achieving a skilful balance and synthesis of aesthetics and didacticism. Rand moves further away from the typically traditional, to explore worlds and view outside its limited confines.

Rand perhaps the more innovative of the two regarding concepts, undertakes a bold experimentation in her fiction with an uncommon earnestness and unique vision. Her intention is not just to tell one more tale, but to create through ideas, an experience, that can be shared against a reawakening tradition, and its total effect evolves out of an aesthetic merging of characters, situations and episodes.

These writers combine an insight into human predicament with a mature social vision. The major shifts in the thinking patterns of their protagonists is viewed within the structural confines of a few selected creative works. These works also mark a steady eventual progression in the image of the emerging individual. It has been fascinating to watch how from a closed, self-contained, complacent world emerges a totally transformed being, reshaped and reformed through consistent conflicts and crises. Apart from exploring deep into the intricacies of the human psyche, the effective aesthetic apprehension of a transitional phase in history, compels us to subscribe totally to and reinforce a basic sociological notion that man does not simply react to his environment, but responds.

This study brings the researcher to the fundamental problem of how to combine that degree of individual imitative which is necessary for progress, with that degree of social cohesion that is necessary for survival. Betrand Russel (in his book **Authority and the Individual**) discussing 'the role of the individual' observes that as men grow more civilized, there is an increasing differences between one man's activities and another's. a community needs, if it is to prosper, a certain number of individuals who do not wholly conform to the general type. Practically all progress, Russel observes, artistic, moral and intellectual has depended on such individuals who have been a decisive factor in the transition from barbarism to civilization (Russel 1985:48). As Hubert Bonner observes: "if a society is to progress there must be a quaint blend of the Hellenic and Hebraic view of man" (quoted by Jaideep Singh in **The Humanistic View of Man**, 1979).

The researcher realises that the need of the day is socio-cultural cohesion, that is, a successful grafting of the two best elements of the individual and the society. In other words, Rand's concept of the ideal self should be grafted with Achebe's concept of a truly meaningful communal living. In every society, there are individual creators and the society needs men of such integrity and calibre to redeem it. if Prometheus had not stolen fire from the Gods, man might have been starving today.

Rand advocates a society which she depicts in "Atlantis"- an ideal utopian society of Demi-gods – that is men created in the image and likeness of God. Rand believes that this is not beyond man's aspirations: as "Man also rises" (**TFH** i).

But Chinua Achebe in "The Nature and Fulfilment of the Individual" observes that a Westerner would be most reluctant to destroy in a page or two, her angel and paragon of perfection, the individual hero. And if he has to be destroyed, then it has got to be justified by final impressive speeches. An illustration of it is best seen in the long speeches of Howard Roark and John Galt in **The Fountainhead** and **Atlas Shrugged** respectively. But Achebe does not have these obligations, because in his scheme and hierarchy, the human hero is not even near the top. He is subordinate to his community to begin with, even when he is their leader and priest. But even more important his hero is subject to non-human forces in the universe. To powers inhabiting that order of reality, the individual counts for nothing, and if he has to fall, one is not entitled to stretch it out or give explanations. The ideal to be sought in Achebe's view is the one which combines freedom for the individual and the safety of society. A society which represses the individual spirit, will rapidly degenerate into mediocrity. But without society there can be no meaningful individuality to exercise, and no civilization. The individual needs his fellows for his survival and sanity (Achebe 1983:163). In other words, every culture that truly desires excellence will have to redress the balance between the two realities of individual freedom and social responsibility in accordance with the excesses of its own past practises. Those that have sat too heavily on the individual will have to restore liberty to him, and those that have denounced ties of social responsibility, must learn that without ties there can be no fulfilment in the complex conditions of modern life (Ibidem).

Bibliography

Writings of Ayn Rand

Primary Sources

We the Living. New York: New American Library, 1936.

The Night of January 16th. New York: New American Library, 1936.

Anthem. New York: New American Library, 1946.

The Fountainhead. New York: New American Library, 1943.

Atlas Shrugged. New York: New American Library, 1957.

The Virtue of Selfishness: A New Concept of Egoism. New York: New American Library, 1964.

Capitalism, the Unknown Ideal. New York: New American Library, 1967.

For the New Intellectual. New York: New American Library, 1961.

Introduction to Objectivist Epistemology. New York: New American Library, 1979.

Philosophy: Who needs it? New York: New American Library, 1984.

Secondary Sources

Baynes, N.H. ed. **The Speeches of Adolf Hitler**. 1922-39. Boston: Houghton Mifflin, 1943.

Bhalla, B.M. ed. **The Twentieth Century American Novel.** New Delhi: Kalyani press, 1981.

Bible, The Holy. Revised Standard Version: Catholic Edition London: Catholic Truth Society, 1952.

The Book of Job. 40:6

The Book of Ezekiel. 18:1-4

Branden, Barbara. **The Passion of Ayn Rand**. New York: Doubleday, 1986.

Branden, Nathaniel. **The Psychology of Romantic Love**. New York: Bantham Books, 1983.

---. **The Psychology of Self-Esteem**. New York: Bantham Books, 1987.

---. **The Disowned Self**, New York: Bantham Books, 1984.

---. **How to Raise Your Self Esteem**. New York: Bantham Books, 1988.

---. **Honouring the Self**. New York: Bantham Books, 1985.

Chase, Richard. **The American Novel and its Tradition**. London: Bell and Sons, 1958.

Dewey, Donald J. "Antitrust Legislation", **International Encyclopaedia of the Social Sciences.** ed. D.L.Sills, New York: Macmillan, 1968.

Eliot, T.S. **Selected Prose**. Ed. J. Hayword, Harmondsworth: Penguin Books, 1955.

---. "Journey of the Magi" 1955. **The Faber Book of Modern Verse**. London: Faber and Faber, 1965.

Ellis, Albert. **Is Objectivism a Religion?.** New York: Lyle Stuart Inc, 1968.

Ekrich, Arthur A. Jr. **The Decline of American Liberalism**. New York: Longmans Green & Co., 1969.

Progressivism in America. New York. Franklin Watts, 1974.

Fiedler, Leslie. **Love and Death in the American Novel**. New York: Criterian Books, 1960.

Fromm, Erich. **Marx's Concept of Man**. New York: Ungar, 1966.

---. **The Sane Society**. London: Routledge & Kegan Paul, 1956.

---. **Man for Himself**. Greenwich: Fawcett Pub. Znc., 1947.

Gladstein, Mimi. **The Ayn Rand Companion: An Analysis of her Fiction.** New York: New American Library, 1982.

Goldman, Eric. **Rendezvous with Destiny**. New York: Knopf, 1952.

Greensburg, Sid. **Ayn Rand and Alienation: The Platonic Idealism of the Objectivist Ethics & a Rational Alternative**. USA : San Francisco, 1987.

Hassan, Ihab. **Studies in Contemporary American Literature**. New York: Ungar Publishing, Co., 1973.

Hegel, B.W.F. **Phenomenology of the Mind**. trans. J.B. Baillic. New York: Harper & Rowe, 1967.

Horney, Karen. **Neurosis and Human Growth**. London: Routledge and New York: Kegan Paul, 1951.

Huxley, Aldous. **The Perennial Philosophy**. London: Chatto and Windus, 1946.

Josephson, Eric and Maria. **Man alone**. New York: Dell Publishing, 1963.

Kazin, Alfred. **Bright Book of life: American Novelists and Story Tellers from Hemingway to Mailer**. New Delhi: Allied Publishers, 1973.

Kenner, Hugh. **A Homemade World: The American Modernist Writers.** New Delhi: Allied Publishers, 1975.

Kermode, Frank. **Continuities.** London: Chatto and Windus, 1968.

Kinsely, Alfred, C. et. al. **Sexual Behaviour in the Human Male**. Philadelphia: 1948.

Kristol, Irving. **On the Democratic Idea in America.** New York: Sterling Press, 1972.

Lawrence, D.H. **Studies in Classic American literature**. Middlesex: Penguin Books, 1991.

Lerner, Max. **America as a Civilization**. London: Burns and Oates, 1957.

Lucas, George. **The Historical Novel**. London: Merlin Press, 1981.

May, Rollo. **Man's Search for Himself.** New York: New American Library, 1953.

Marx, Karl. "Economic and Philosophic Manuscripts, 1844" Karl Marx-**Early Writings: A Collection**. trans. Rodney Living Stone & Gregor Benton. Middlesex: Penguin & New Left Review, 1975, 323-324.

Mc. Connell, Frank D. **Four Postwar American Novelists: Bellow, Mailer, Barth and Pynchon.** Chicago The Univ. Press, 1977.

Mishra, A.K. **Loneliness in Modern American Fiction: With Special reference to Sherwood Anderson, Ernest Hemingway and Thomas Wolfe.** New Delhi: Anthers Guild Publication, 1987.

O'Neil William F. **With Charity Towards None**. New York: Philosophical Library, 1971.

Peikoff, Leonard. ed. **The Early Ayn Rand: A Selection from her Unpublished Fiction**. New York: New American Library, 1984.

---. **The Ominious Parallels**. New York: New American Library, 1982.

Rasmussen, Douglas B**. The Philosophical Thought of Ayn Rand**. Urbana; University of Illinois Press, 1984.

Riesman, David. **The Loney Crowd**. New York: Viking Press, 1968.

Rao, Ramachandra**. The American Fictional Hero**. New Delhi: Bahori Publication, 1979.

Richard, Rupp H. **Celebration in Post War American Fiction.** 1945-1967. Florida: University of Miami Press, 1970.

Robbins, John W. **Answer to Ayn Rand: A Critique of the Philosophy of Objectivism.** Washington: Mt. Vernon Pub. Co., 1974

Roth, Philip. "Writing American Fiction", Novel Today, Malcom Bradbury (ed) Glasgow: Collins, 1977.

Russel, Bertrand. **"Social Cohesion and Human Nature".** Authority and the Individual. London: Unwin Paperbacks, 1985.

Singh, Jaideep**. The Humanistic View of Man**. New Delhi: Cambridge Press, 1979.

Tibor, Machan. "Reason Individaulism and Capitalism: The Moral Vision of Ayn Rand". **The Philosophic Thought of Ayn Rand**. Urbana: University of Illinois Press, 1984.

Tindell, William York. **The Literary Symbol**. New York: Columbia Uni. Press, 1955.

Vargo, Rev. Edward P. "Struggling with a Bugaboo: The Priest Character in Achebe and Greene and Keneally". **Awakened Conscience**. ed. C.D. Narasimhaiah. New Delhi: Sterling Publication, 1978.

Vickery, Olga W. "Language as Theme and Technique". **Modern American Fiction**". ed. A. Walton Litz. New York: Oxford University Press, 1970.

Watt, Ian**. The Rise of the Novel.** London: Chatto and Windus, 1967.

Wilson, Colin. **The Outsider**. London: Pen Books Ltd., 1970.

Articles, Interviews and Speeches

Branden, Barbara. "Interview with Ayn Rand", Los Angelus, 9, Nov. 1981.Clark, Charles Worcester. "Applied Christianity: Who shall Apply it First". **Andover Review.** Jan. 1983,205.

Daniel, Aaron. "Remarks on a Bookseller: **The Fountainhead. Partisan Review.** Vol. 14. July-Aug (1947): 443.

Evans, Stanton M. "The Gospel Accoring to Ayn Rand". **The National Review.** Oct. 3, 1967, 1059-61.

Fairchild, Henry Pratt. "The Great Economic Paradox". **Harper's Magazine.** May (1932): 14.

Gladstein, Mimi. "Ayn Rand and Feminism: An unlikely Alliance". **College English.** 39 Feb. 1978, 26.

Gordon, Philip, "The Extroflective Hero: A look at Ayn Rand". **Journal of Popular Culture.** 10. Spring (1977): 701.

Harold, Strauss. "National Rights and History". **New York Times Book Review.** April 19, 1936.

Howe, Irving. "The American Voice: It Begins on a Note of Wonder". **The New York Times Book Review**. July (1976):3.

Jeff, Riggenbach. "The Disowned Children of Ayn Rand". **Reason.** Dec. 1982. p.59.

Kennedy, John. F. "Inaugural Address, Jan. 20, 1961.

Kenneth, Smith. "Ayn Rand: Objectivism or Existentialism. **Religious Humanism.** 4 (Winter 1970): 23-28.

Kobbler, John. "The Curious Cult of Ayn Rand". **Saturday Evening Post.** 11 Nov. (1961): 98-101.

Llyod, Henry Demarest. "The New Conscience". (**North American Review**, Sept. (1888):342.

O'Quinn, Kenny. "Ayn Rand's Heroism". **Starlog.** 59. June (1982):14

Pruette, Lorine, "Battle Against Evil". **New York Times Book Review.** 16th May (1943): 7-9.

Rand, Ayn. "An Open letter to Boris Spassky". **The Ayn Rand Letter**. date unavailable. 52.

---. "The Only Path to Tomorrow". **Reader's Digest.** Jan. (1944): 39. **The Objectivist**. VII.12. Dec. (1968): 1-2.

---. "The Goal of my Writing". **Objectivist Newletter**. October (1903): 37-42.

---. "Causality versus Duty". **The Objectivist**. 9 July (1970): 4.

Roosevelt, Franklin Delano. "Inaugural Address". San Francisco Speech, Sept. 1932.

Roy, Childs. A.Jr., "Ayn Rand and the Libertarian Movement". **Update.** 2 (April 1982): 4.

Smith, George. "Atheism and Objectivism". **Reason.** Nov. (1973): 18-24.

Sobran, Joseph. "Mussolini Shrugged: Ayn Rand Revived". **National Review.** Jan (1989) : 53-59.

Tibor, Machan. "Ayn Rand: A Contemporary Heretic?" **The Occasional Review.** 4 (Winter 1976): 133-50.

Uyl, Douglas Den and Rasmussen Douglas: "Nozick on the Randian Argument". **The Personalist.** April (1978): 192-94.

Writings of Chinua Achebe

Primary Sources

Things Fall Apart. New Delhi: Heinemann, 1975.

No Longer at Ease. London: Heinemann, 1960.

Arrow of God. London: Heinemann, 1977.

A Man of the People. London: Heinemann, 1966.

Anthills of the Savannah. London: Heinemann, 1987.

Girls at War and Other Stories. London: Heinemann, 1972.
Morning Yet on Creation Day. London: Heinemann, 1970.

The Trouble with Nigeria. London: Heinemann, 1987.

Secondary Sources

Bier, Ulli. ed. **Introduction to African Literature: An Anthology of Critical Writings from Black Orpheus**. London: Longmans, 1967.

Abrahams, W.E. **The Mind of Africa**. London: Weidenfield and Nicolson, 1967.

Achebe, Chinua. "The Nature and Fulfilment of the Individual **"The Colonial and Neo-Colonial Encounter in Commonwealth Literature".** ed. H.H. Anniah Gowda. University of Mysore: University of Mysore Press, 1983.

Carroll, David. **Chinua Achebe,** New York: Twayne, 1980.

Conrad, Joseph. **Heart of Darkness.** New York: W.W. Norton & Co. Inc. 1963.

Delafosse, Maurice. **The Negroes of Africa: History and Culture:** Washington: Associated Publishers, 1981.

Duerden & Pieterse. eds. **African Writers Talking: A Collection of Interviews**. London: HEB, 1978.

Emenyonu, Ernest. N. **The Rise of the Igbo Novel**. Ibadan: Oxford University Press, 1978.

Fanon, Frantz, **The Wretched of the Earth.** trans. Constance Farrington Harmondsworth: Penguin Books 1982.

Gowda, Anniah H.H. **The Colonial and Neo Colonical Encounter**. University of Mysore: University of Mysore Press, 1983.

Griffiths, Garreth. **A Double Exile: African and West Indian Writing Between Two Cultures**. London: Marion Boyars, 1978.

Groves, C.P. **The Planting of Christianity in Africa**. 4 Vols. London: Lutterworth Press, 1948.

Hastings, Adrain**. African Christianity: An Essay in Interpretation**. London: Geoffrey Chapman, 1976.

Innes, C.L. **Chinua Achebe**. Cambridge: University Press, 1990.

Innes, C.L. & Lindfors. B. Eds. **Critical Perspectives on Chinua Achebe.** London; HEB 1979.

Irele, Afiole. "The Tragic Conflict in the Novels of Chinua Achebe" **Introduction to African Literature: An Anthology of Critical Writings From Black Orpheus**. Ed. Ulli Bier. London: Longmans, 1967.

Jahn, Janhein Muntu. An Outline of the New African Culture. (Trans. Marjorie Green). New York: Grove Press Inc., 1967.

---. **A History of New African Literature.** London; Faber and Faber, 1968.

Killiam, G.D. ed. **African Writers on African Writing.** London: HEB, 1978.

---. **The Novels of Chinua Achebe**. London: HEB, 1969.

---. **Exile and Tradition: Studies in African and Caribbean Literature.** Ed. Rowland Smith. Great Britain: Longman and Dalhousie, 1976.

King, Bruce. ed**. Introduction to Nigerian Literature.** Lagos: University of Lagos, 1971.

Larson, Charles. **The Emergence of Nigerian of African Fiction.** London: The Macmillan Press Ltd., 1978.

---. **The Search for the Past: East and Central African Writing**. London: The Macmillan press, 1980.

Lindfors, Bernth. ed. **Critical Perspectives on Nigerian Literature**. London: HEB, 1979.

Mbiti, John S. **African Religions and Philosophy**. London: Heinemann, 1967.

McEwan Neil. **Africa and the Novel**. Atlantic Highlands: Humanities Press, 1983.

Narasimhaiah, C.D. ed. **Awakened Conscience; Studies in Commonwealth Literature**. New Delhi: Sterling Publishers Pvt. Ltd., 1978.

Ngara, Emmanuel. **Art and Ideology in African Novel**. London: Heinemann, 1985.

Obiechina, E. **Culture, Tradition and Society in the West African Novel.** Londong: Cambridge University Press, 1975.

---. "The Human Dimension of History in **Arrow of God", Critical**

Perspectives on Chinua Achebe. Eds. Innes and Linfors. London: HEB, 1979.

Ogungbesan, Kolawole. **New West African Literature.** London: HEB, 1979.

Palmer, Eustace. **The Growth of the African Novel: Studies** in West African Literature. London: HEB, 1979.

---. **An Introduction to the African Novel.** London: HEB, 1972.

Peters Jonathan. A. **A Dance of Masks: Senghor, Achebe, Soyinka.** Washington D.C: Three Continent Press, 1978.

Ravenscroft, Arthur. Chinua Achebe. Essex. Longmans, 1969.

Roscoe, Adrain. **Mother is Gold: A Study in West African Literature.** London: Cambridge University Press, 1971.

Soyinka, Wole. **Myth, Literature and the African World. London:** Cambridge University Press, 1976.

Taylor, John V. **The Primal Vision: Christian Presence Amid African Religion.** London: SCM Press Ltd., 1963.

Walsh, William. A Human Idiom: Literature and Humanity. London: Chatto & Windus, 1964.

---. **A Manifold Voice: Studies in Commonwealth Literature.** London: Chatto & Windus, 1970.

Wauthier, Claude: **The Literature and Thought of Modern Africa.** London: Heinemann Educational Books, 1978.

Weber, Max. **The Protestant Ethic and Spirit and Capitalism.** Tan Parson. London: Scribner, 1930.

---. Sociology of Religion. trans. ed. Fischoff. London: Methuen and Co., 1971.

Wren, Robert. **Achebe's World: The Historical and Cultural Context of the Novels of Chinua Achebe.** London: 1980.

Article and Interviews

Achebe, Chinua. "African Literature as Restoration of Celebration". **Kunapipi.** Ed. Anna Rutherford, XII, 2 1990.

---. "The Role of a Writer in a New Nation". **Nigerian Magazine,** 81 June (1964):159.

---. "Cultural Events in Africa: **New Statesman**. 29 March (1967): 11.

---. "The African Writer and the Biafran Cause". **Conch.** 1 (1969): 12.

---. "The Black Writer's Burden, "**Presence Africane.** 3159 (1956): 38.

Alexandre, Kojeve. "Hegel, Marx and Christianity". trans. Hilail Gild in. **Interpretation: A Journal of Political Philosophy.** 1. No.1 (Summer 1970): 34.

Amadiume, Ifi. **"Class Gender in Anthills of Savannah". PAL-Platform. 1.** 1 March (1989): 9.

Ascherson, Neal. "Betrayal". **New York Review.** 3 March (1988): 4.
Barbar, H. "Image of the African in Transition". African Quarterly vii.1 (April-June 1967): 29-40.

Boehner, Ellke. "Of Goddesses and a New Politics in Achebe's **Anthills of Savannah". Kunapipi.** XII, 2 (1990): 142.

Chellappan, K. "Literature Without Walls: A Search for the Still Centre". **Journal of Asian Studies.** Thiruvanmiyur: Institute of Asian studies. Sept. (1984): 41.

Colmer, Rosemary. "The Development of Moral Values in **A Man of the People". Kunapipi.** Vol. XII. 2 (1990): 201.

Duerden, Dennis. "An Interview with Achebe", **Spectrum**. Sept. (1965): 64.

Fabre, Michel. "Chinua Achebe on **Arrow of God:** Interview with Achebe". **The Literary Half Yearly.** XXI. 11 Jan. (1980): 1-10.

---. "The Colonial Encounter: Achebe's Criticism". **The Literary Half-Yearly.** XXII, 2 July (1981): 11-22.

Griffiths, Garreth. "Language and Action in the Novels of Chinua Achebe". **African Literature Today.** 5 (1971): 21.

Iyasere, Solomon Ogbede. "African Critics on African Literature: A Study in Misplaced Hospitality". **African Literature Today.** 7 (1975): 20-27.

Jones, D.A.N. "The Writings of Wole Soyinka" **New Statesman.** 28 January 1966: 132-133.

McDonald, Bruce F. "Chinua Achebe and the Structure of the Colonial Tragedy". **The Literary Half-Yearly.** XXI, 1 Jan (1980): 62.

Niekerk, Van Phillip. "Chinua Achebe breaks his Silence". **Weekly Mail.** 8 Sept. (1988): 9, 14.

Niven, Alstain. "Chinua Achebe and the Possibility of Modern Tragedy". **Kunapipi.** XII. (1990): 9, 14.

Okare, Gabriel. "Towards an Evolution of an African Language for African Literature". **Kunapipi.** XII, 21 (1990): 187.

Rutherford, Anna. "Interview with Chinua Achebe". **Kunapipi.** IX, 2. (1987): 4.

Sparrow, Fiona. "Review of **Anthills of the Savannah". World Literature Written in English.** 28, 1 (Spring 1988): 36.

Stock, A.G. "Yeats and Achebe". **Journal of Commonwealth Literature.** July (1968): 105-11.

www.ingramcontent.com/pod-product-compliance
Lightning Source LLC
Chambersburg PA
CBHW070639170726
48291CB00003B/1066

* 9 7 8 1 9 2 5 8 2 3 2 0 2 *